Silver Lemon Strainers

1686–1846

by

Michael Adams

Grosvenor House
Publishing Limited

This book is published by
Grosvenor House Publishing Ltd
Link House
140 The Broadway, Tolworth, Surrey, KT6 7HT.
www.grosvenorhousepublishing.co.uk

A CIP record for this book
is available from the British Library

ISBN 978-1-83975-394-7

CONTENTS

PREFACE

This is a monograph on an item of antique silverware which was in common usage in the British Isles and America from late in the 17th century until the early 19th century, but has rarely been collected or studied before. This is the first time that silver lemon strainers (which at the time were more often known as orange strainers or punch strainers) have had a book entirely devoted to them.

I begin with the generalities: how, where and when were they made, how they might have been used and how and where were they marked. I give the stories of some lemon strainers which have appeared several times on the market and assess the relative desirabilities – and monetary worth – of the different sorts.

Drawing on my paper database of nearly 900 lemon strainers, amassed over nine years of research, I have classified them into 27 categories, on the basis of their place of manufacture, the patterns of holes in their bowls and the shapes of their handles. Ten of these hail from London, two from other centres in England, two from Ireland, seven from Scotland and six from America. The bulk of this book gives descriptions of each of these groupings, illustrated by 220 lemon strainers and showing how their designs and shapes evolved. In doing this, I hope I have never lost sight of just how lovely and fascinating they are. One of the groups is the 'Oddities', which include strainers converted from other silver items, in other words fakes. The sections on London, Ireland, Scotland and America are each given an historical preface, to give a feel of what it was like to live there in the 18th century.

Not only do lemon strainers vie with any other branch of antique silver, such as spoons, drinking vessels, teapots, baskets, candlesticks, boxes, tea tongs or vinaigrettes, in terms of their variability, craftsmanship and sheer beauty, but they also have a tantalising mystique about them. So many of them are missing marks, either through the piercing process or over-polishing in the past, that they are not always easy to place. And, most of all, even though it is beyond doubt that they were used in the preparation of that highly popular social beverage, punch, no-one really knows exactly how. I almost didn't write this book because of the lack of pictorial or written evidence from the 18th century of their mode of use, and it didn't help that I also can't explain the extraordinary initial efflorescence of lemon-strainer design in the 1710s; but I resigned myself to the possibility that direct evidence may not exist, and I've done my best to speculate without it.

ACKNOWLEDGEMENTS
(and a bit of autobiography)

The important milestones in my life all arrived by serendipity. A spare butterfly net, made by my mother in Singapore for my father's secret mission to Borneo, set me up – aged 10 – as a lifelong biologist. A chance friendship with George Bernard (now George Gainsburgh) five years later and a common love of natural history led to joint butterflying trips in the Swiss Alps. My knowledge of butterflies and birds helped me through my Cambridge University interview and the Cambridge Exploration Society later supported our plan for the first of what turned out to be eight butterflying expeditions to the Andes, five of them with George (and six supported by the Natural History Museum in London). My years as a post-graduate zoology student gave me the time to write a series of scientific articles on the taxonomy and geography of the high-altitude brown butterflies of the Andes, which impressed my old biology schoolteacher enough to persuade me to apply for a teaching job at my old school, which kept me busily fulfilled for almost 35 years.

My wife Jennie happily put paid to my bachelor existence when she chanced upon the same school for her next teaching job. And it was Jennie who sparked my interest in antique silver by buying some as presents for ourselves and our son soon before our retirement. Then followed nearly a decade of visits to innumerable antique shops, antiques centres, fairs and museums all over England: the double appeal of the aesthetic and the academic chimed perfectly, reminding me of my butterfly research – and these lovely objects didn't fly away! We first came across a lemon strainer in 2011 and we haven't looked back. I now have six Lever-Arch files choc-a-bloc full of lemon strainer images and descriptions.

So, I dedicate this book wholeheartedly to Jennie, in gratitude for her original inspiration and later indulgence and patience. I'm also hugely grateful to George Gainsburgh for regular exchanges of ideas, particularly on the ways these strainers may have been used, for his interest and encouragement and for his helpful comments on the text of this book.

I am very grateful to the dealers who've given of their time and expertise to discuss antique silver and to allow me to handle their wares: Henry Willis, Terry and Tim Spearing (of Eastdale Antiques), Elizabeth Nicolson, Tristrem Carlyon, Maurice and Jonathan Dubiner (of Paul Bennett Antiques), Edward, John and Julia Bourdon-Smith, Peter Cameron, Duncan Campbell (of Beau Nash), Gary Bottomley (of Reign Beau and antiquesilverspoons.co.uk), Jon Shaw (of Jack Shaw Antiques), Ken Bull (of John Bull Antiques), Luke Schrager (of Schredds), Stephen Kalms, Francis Norton of S.J. Phillips, Mike Wilson of Highland Antiques, Richard & Diana Apsimon of Vine Antiques, Peter Williamson of Wingfield Antiques, Peter Szuhay, Christopher Hamlyn of Mayflower Antiques,

H. & W. Deutsch, Howards Jewellers of Stratford-on-Avon, James Baldwin, Adam Langford, Alastair Dickenson and Jeremy Astfalck (of The Old Corkscrew in Franschhoek, South Africa).

In the preparation of this book, I've been helped by several silver experts: Dr Kirstin Kennedy at the Victoria & Albert Museum; Dr David Mitchell; Edith Andrees at the National Museum of Ireland; Morna Annandale at the Aberdeen Art Gallery; Craig O'Donnell at the Birmingham Assay Office; Janine E. Skerry at Colonial Williamsburg in Virginia; Dr Peter Kaellgren, Curator Emeritus of the Royal Ontario Museum, Toronto; Ellis Finch at Bonhams; and Kathryn Jones of the Royal Collection Trust in London. Many thanks to them, to the staff at the Woolley & Wallis Salisbury Salerooms, who allowed me to take the photographs in figs 4, 9 and 10, and to Jennifer Kinnaird at the Royal Ontario Museum for going out of her way to take photographs of the maker's mark on Princess Amelia's strainer. For all the figures involving stencil images of lemon strainers, I'm indebted to the Rapid Resizer website and its excellent Free Picture Stencil Maker. Southampton University's Library kindly allowed me access to the digital Burney Collection of 17th- & 18th-century Newspapers and the University of Bath Library unearthed an important image of a lemon strainer in an old magazine and scanned it for me. I acknowledge with thanks the existence of the wikipedia.org website, which helped me put together my little historical prefaces to the chapters on London-made, Irish, Scottish and American lemon strainers. Two online auction platforms, which have search engines for past sales (and facilities for emailed alerts whenever a lemon strainer comes up for sale by auction), have been very helpful indeed: the-saleroom.com and invaluable.com.

The images in this book come from downloads from online catalogues and archives and my photographs taken directly of strainers and from books, journals and print-outs of internet catalogues. To seek permission to reproduce them, I've tried my best to contact the numerous museums, dealers, auctioneers, online auction users, authors and publishers who have – mostly unwittingly – supplied them and I apologise to the very few who failed to reply to repeated requests. Image credits appear together on pp. 171-173. Several people sent me (unsolicited) high-resolution images of the figured strainers which I then incorporated into the book; many thanks for this to Dr Janine Skerry, Marianne Martin and Erin Lopater at the Colonial Williamsburg Foundation; Nancy Stedman at Yale University Art Gallery; Dr Matthew Potter of Limerick Museum; Lynn McCarthy of Winterthur Museum, Delaware; Tricia Walker of the Royal Ontario Museum, Toronto; Miles Harrison; Cliff Nunn Antique Silver & Decorative Arts, Dravosburg, Pennsylvania; Elizabeth Rickenbacker of Ahlers & Ogeltree Auction Gallery, Atlanta, Georgia; Tim Martin and Mary Braren of S. J. Shrubsole Corp., New York; Millicent Ford Creech of M. Ford Creech Antiques, Memphis, Tennessee; William Crofton, formerly of J. & W. Duvallier, Dublin; Karen Lawson of the Royal Collection Trust, UK; Penny Wilden of The Fancy Fox, Bungay, Suffolk; and Sarah Marr of Iain Marr Antiques, Beauly, Inverness.

Chapter One
INTRODUCING LEMON STRAINERS

WHAT ARE LEMON STRAINERS?

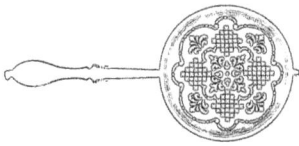

a)

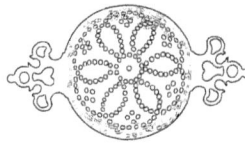

b)

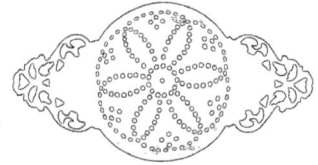

c)

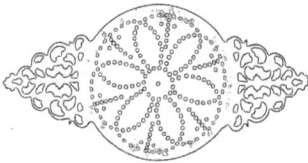

d)

e)

f)

g)

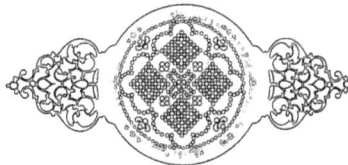

h)

i)

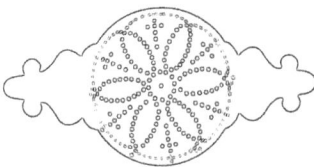

j)

k)

l)

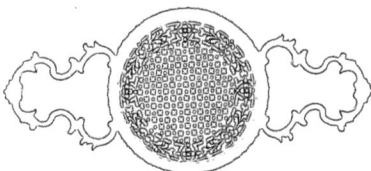

m)

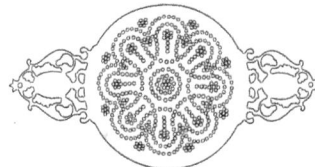

n)

o)

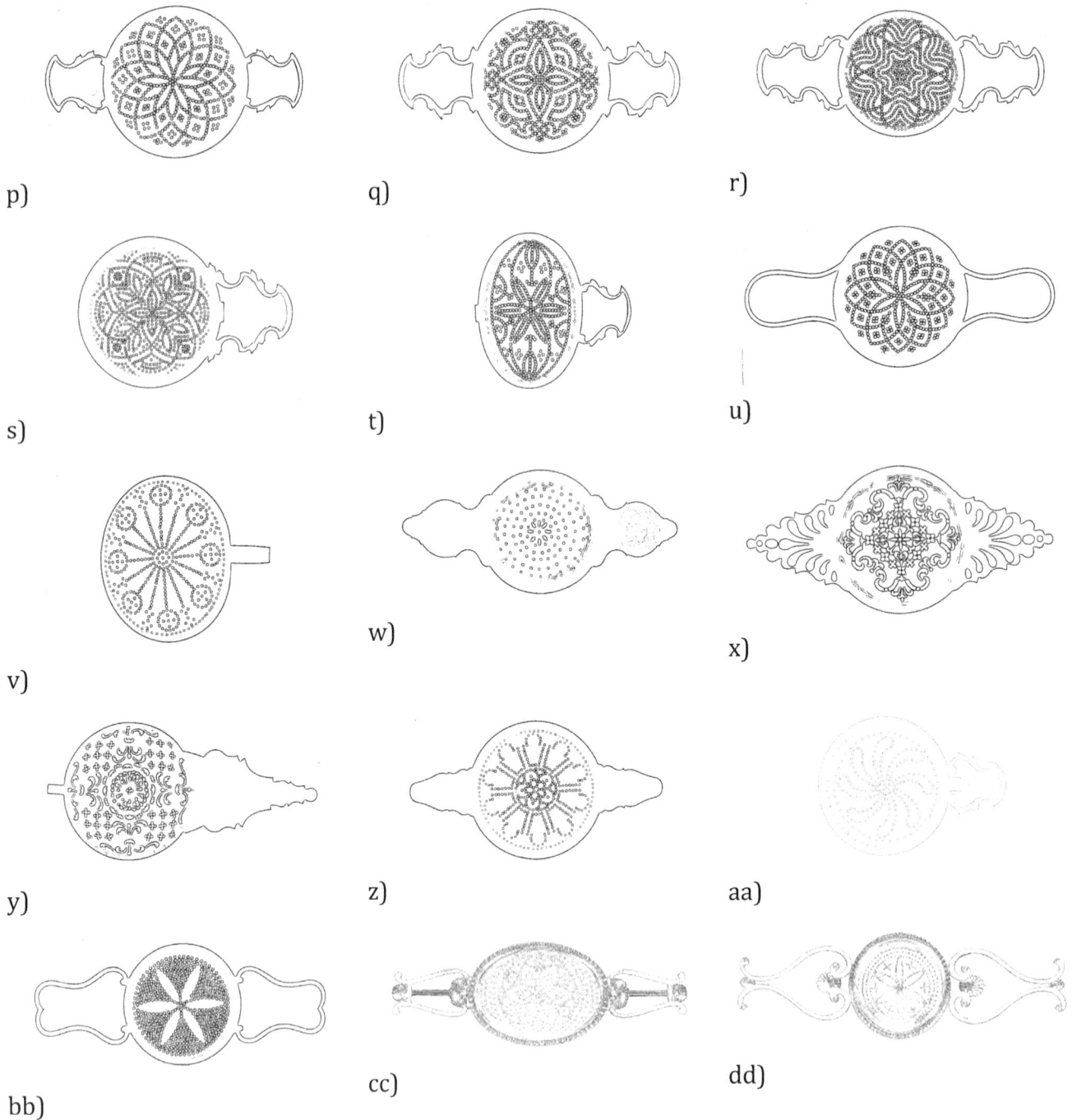

Fig.1: Lemon strainer silhouettes – London, English provincial, Irish, Scottish. a) London Group 1, 1737; b)-h) London Group 2: b) c1695, c) 1716, d) 1718, e) 1719, f) 1720, g) 1730, h) c1750; i) & j) London Group 3: i) 1719, j) 1729; k)-m) London Group 4: k) 1742, l) 1749, m) 1765; n) London Group 5: 1734; o)-p) London Group 6: o) 1734, p) 1770; q) & r) London Group 7: q) 1752, r) 1766; s) & t) London Group 8: s) 1769, t) 1779; u) London Group 9, 1785; v) English provincial: Plymouth 1736; w) & x) Dublin: w) 1732, x) c1750; y) possibly Irish, c1740; z)-dd) Scottish: z) Edinburgh 1742, aa) Glasgow c1770, bb) Edinburgh 1784, cc) Glasgow 1819, dd) Glasgow 1823.

Very few people have collected them, very few experts have written about them, most textbooks on antique silver barely mention them and in most antiques guides they don't have their own category but are consigned to the 'Miscellany' pages. It's not even certain what they were called and it's certainly not known exactly how they were used.

Yet lemon strainers (also known as punch strainers or orange strainers) must have been in many upper-class – and probably upper-middle-class – households throughout a period of well over 100 years from the late 17th century to the early 19th century in England, Ireland, Scotland and America. They were often engraved with their owner's initials or crest or coat of arms and given as wedding gifts – and they beautifully reflected the silver fashion of their times, evolving new shapes, designs and sizes during the decades of their popularity. And although (or perhaps because) they are not common in auctions and on traders' stalls, and can command quite high prices, they are definitely collectable. Varied and often very beautiful in their bowl piercings and their handle shapes, their small size makes them easy to display and as eye-catching as they must have been in the houses of the wealthy in Georgian times.

Bernard Crewdson, one of the very few people to have written articles specifically about lemon strainers (back in 1950), wrote that "There is…practically nothing to be found in contemporary literature which has much bearing on the strainers of the Seventeenth and Eighteenth Centuries." He could have added that neither do there seem to be any contemporary images, in the form of prints or paintings, which show lemon strainers. Punch drinking, both raucous and restrained, was quite a popular subject for 18th-century artists, but in not one of their pictures does a lemon strainer appear, despite the clear presence on the table of punchbowl, punch ladle and punch glasses. Yet no-one doubts that they were used almost exclusively for the straining of orange or lemon juice at some stage in the ritual of punch-making.

Some well-respected authorities on antique silver have been distinctly sniffy about them. Charles Oman, the Keeper of Metalwork at the Victoria & Albert Museum, wrote (in 1934 and again in 1959) about 'lemon-strainers' that "They show little variation…." W.A. Young, earlier in the 20th century, wrote that "These small pieces are favoured by collectors *in spite of their plainness*." Douglas Ash (1972) thought that "One rare late 17th-century type had a single handle, but others were of *much the same design whatever their period…..Decoration of any kind was uncommon* and generally confined to borders." [My italics] (see figs 1,2,3)

Others have been more appreciative of their charms. Margaret Holland (1973) wrote that "Strainers, for the orange or lemon juice used in punch, [gave] the imaginative craftsman immense scope, both in the piercing of the straining part and in the formation of the handles…". Elizabeth de Castres waxed lyrical in 1980: "Many fine examples were made, beautifully pierced and decorated…" Judith Banister (1965) thought that "Lemon (and orange) strainers…..are among the most charming of all of the silversmith's smaller wares". As for me, I would say that all silver lemon strainers, even the most humdrum and workaday, are attractive works of art and their study is an endless source of fascination.

Every decade of the 18th century had its distinctive style or styles of strainer and each of the main places where they were made – London, Plymouth, Edinburgh, Glasgow, Dublin, Limerick, Boston, Philadelphia, New York – had its own particular variations. Yet it is still possible to come up with a generic description of a lemon strainer.

A lemon strainer is made up of a bowl and one or two handles. The rim of the bowl is almost always circular (rarely oval and very rarely octagonal) and the bowl itself is a shallow inverted dome, between 8 and 12 cm across and between 19 and 38 mm deep. Most of the bowl is pierced with numerous holes, in a floral and/or geometric arrangement. The simplest patterns are circular holes in concentric rings; circular holes also occur in highly complex, radially symmetrical designs, often involving 'petals'. Perhaps the most beautiful patterns involve pierced scrolls, crosslets, fleurs-de-lis, curved dashes, splashes and rosettes.

The handles, for all their variability in size and shape, nearly always taper away from the bowl to which they are soldered and they are rarely longer than the bowl's diameter. When paired, they are fixed to the rim of the bowl diametrically opposite each other. On one-handled strainers, there is also a clip on the rim of the bowl, either under the handle or opposite it.

Including its handle or handles, a lemon strainer may be between 12.5 and 35.9 cm in length (most commonly 17-18 cm) and may weigh from 1.9 to 8oz (60-272g), most commonly 2 to 3.2oz (65-100g).

Very occasionally silver lemon strainers were given a coating of gold by gilding, which in those days involved applying an amalgam of gold and mercury and then heating off all or most of the mercury. I know of nine such silver-gilt examples, ranging in age between 1688 and 1794, seven of which were made for the British Kings, George II and III, and for George IV when he was Prince of Wales (two of these by the royal goldsmith, Thomas Heming).

THEIR BOWLS

Fig.2: Silhouette photographs of the bowls of lemon strainers from London, Plymouth, Scotland and Ireland

As photographs are usually taken of lemon strainers resting on a surface and the angle is often partially sideways on, they rarely do justice to the intricate piercing in their bowls and back-lit silhouettes are the best way of showing them off (fig.2). It is rare ever to come across two with identical patterns, even by the same maker in the same year.

However thick the bowl's silver is, it would have been made from a flat sheet of silver and 'raised' into the domed shape by repeated hammering and 'annealing' (heating to 'cherry red' and then quenching in cold water, to keep the silver malleable). The smooth finish was provided by small 'planishing' hammers, before the final polishing with jeweller's rouge. (I know of only two strainers – identical to each other – whose bowls were cast in a mould instead: see p.75.) The great majority then had their rims strengthened by the application (soldering on) of one or more strips of silver. Early London-made strainers had a 5-mm band soldered to the top, wider than the bowl but with a central channel on its outside (a 'double fillet' arrangement); this band may well have been created from three separate strips. The rims of others may appear simply to curve gracefully outwards but they too were strengthened and beautified with added rings of silver. Some rims have additional gadrooning (repeated protruding notches), beading (repeating protruding mini-hemispheres) or reeding (engraved parallel lines running lengthways) on top. The final job of piercing the holes was laboriously carried out using hand drills, chisels, minute saws and files.

The great majority of bowl piercings involve small and equal-sized circular holes. The ones in the earliest strainers comprise either concentric rings around the whole bowl or circles which overlap, usually to form a central six-petalled flower. Wider bowls enable a bewildering profusion of designs, radially symmetrical except in the rare oval examples. The most common are primarily floral and could be described, for example, as 'six overlapping circles forming an unfilled 6-petalled flower; six additional petal tips; infilled by clusters of 4', 'twelve overlapping pointed ovals forming a 6-petalled flower; infilled by ringed clusters of 7' or 'six-petalled flowers sharing one petal with each neighbour'. Some dispense with botanical allusions and are purely geometric, such as 'five overlapping multi-layered pointed ovals around a central ring; 5 mini-rings outside' or 'cross in 4-armed star, points opening into crossed diamonds; crossed diamonds and curved rectangles between the arms; zigzag lines and clusters outside'. A few combine floral with geometric, as with 'cross in 4-petalled flower with extended tips; crossed diamonds and curved rectangles outside'. I refer to some of the geometric additions to the more complex patterns as 'curlicues'. Also present in some dot-pierced bowls are triangles, 'tulip flowers', 'lollipops' (stalked rings) and arcs.

The most beautiful (and labour-intensive) patterns involve radially symmetrical groups of scrolls, fleurs-de-lis, squiggles, stalked trefoils, crosslets, dot-&-dash lines, curved dashes, crescents, commas and other not-easily-described shapes, often arranged together in rosettes and 'splashes' and always giving the feel of movement and airiness; in some, these baroque shapes are confined to the outside of the design, the centre taken up by a square panel of crosslets. Dot-holes are sometimes sparingly included, giving an austere contrast. Again, the variety of different patterns is staggering.

The shape of the bowls is an indicator of age: the shallower lemon strainer bowls tend to be later in origin, and are generally broader, flatter-bottomed and with more bellied 'sides', while the deeper, more hemispherical ones are older and smaller.

Every circular (and octagonal) strainer bowl has its piercing design arranged around a hole in the dead centre. The rare oval bowls, with their bilateral symmetry, usually also have this central hole. This would have been the guide hole for the set of dividers (or similar tool) which measured and scored the original circle (or ellipse) in the flat sheet of silver from which the bowl was raised. The only strainers that I know of which lack this central hole are the pair by William Plummer (London Group 5, p.75) whose unique bowls were cast from a mould.

THEIR HANDLES

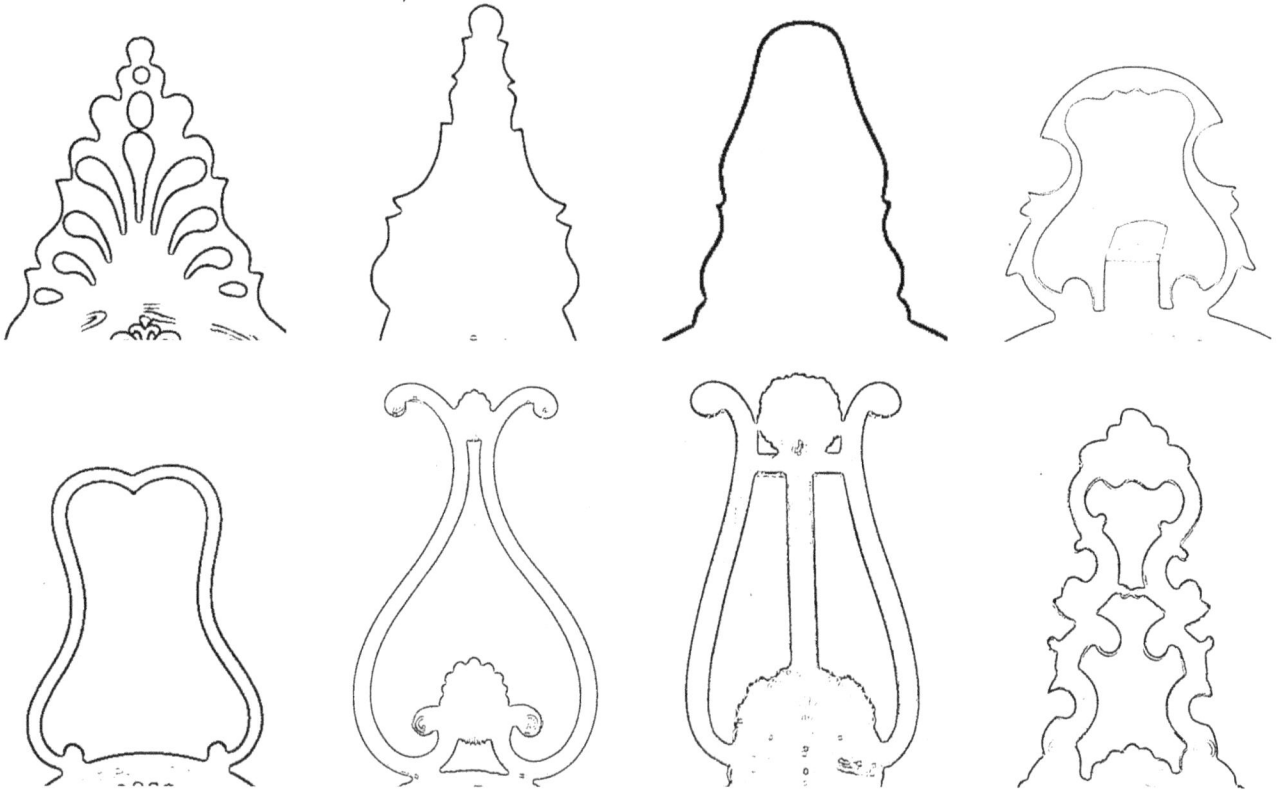

Fig.3: Stencil images of lemon strainer handles from London, Scotland and Ireland

It is as hard to generalise about lemon strainer handles (fig.3), which have a bewildering variety of shapes and sizes, as it is about their bowls. Individual lengths vary from 2.5 to 12 cm. When they occur in pairs, their shape may be flat and solid, usually with an intricately shaped edge and often 'pierced' to create scrolling patterns; or open-centred with scrolling sides and curved ends which sometimes bear shell motifs; or consisting of a simple, sometimes beaded strut which loops around and back on itself. Some open handles are shaped like lyres or bells and some flat ones are flat-chased (the design created by fine hammering on the top side only) and/or engraved (the design cut into the silver).

Unlike the bowls, most handles were cast in moulds, both the early flat, triangular ones (pierced or unpierced) and the later styles, whether openwork or flat-with-relief. Handles made from flattened sheet silver were the exception rather than the rule: examples include the early cannon-shaped handles; loops from the late 18th century; a few of the early London- and Scottish-made flat and broad ones; Plymouth-made ring handles; and Irish snub-nosed handles. Obviously, casting only required a single cut-out original, which *via* a mould could create numerous identical copies of a handle, and this would have been much less labour-intensive than individually cutting, drilling, chiselling and sawing every one. The 'missing' areas in a cast handle described as having been 'pierced' wouldn't actually have been cut away but created by raised, solid areas in the mould where molten silver couldn't reach.

The handle on *single*-handled strainers was usually of the open-centred, scroll- or loop-sided sort – except for the very early and rare types with a tubular or flat, shaped and maybe pierced handle, and those with a very small, vertical ring. Strainers with one handle always have a downward-facing clip, typically 1.5 cm wide, under or opposite the handle. Over the 50-odd years of the production of single-handled strainers after the mid-1750s, there were similar numbers of opposite clips and under-handle clips; the former outnumbered the latter in the earlier years but it was the other way around in the late 18th and early 19th century. I know of 14 *two*-handled strainers which also carry extra clips, usually under one of the handles but sometimes to one side, dating from the 1720s to the 1820s.

Very rarely, two-handled strainers, in my experience only between 1752 and 1762 in London (and in Glasgow in the 1820s and '30s), bore downward-facing pegs, spikes or shell-shaped flanges on the extreme ends of the handles. And one Irish strainer from c1740 has an applied rib along the underside of one of its handles with six notches cut into it. The function of these contraptions was presumably to prevent the strainers from sliding into wide receptacles, as described on p.17.

WHERE WERE LEMON STRAINERS MADE?

I have been collecting images and descriptions of lemon strainers since 2011, gleaned from auction catalogues, online auction sites, online dealer catalogues and museum listings, and handled at auctions, antique centres, antique shops and antiques fairs. Many of them have reappeared on the market two or more times, but I have identified a total of 893 different ones:

> 643 marked in London, in 10 categories (including 'Oddities')
> 27 in the English provinces
> 59 in Ireland (in 2 categories)
> 78 in Scotland (in 7 categories)
> 86 in America (in 6 categories)

These do *not* include the various strainers which weren't *illustrated* in catalogues or compilations and whose descriptions were so rudimentary that they can't be assigned to particular categories, never mind compared with fully-documented examples. Nor do they include any made after 1833 in the British Isles or after 1846 in America.

It is obvious from the figures above that by far the most prolific centre of strainer making was London. Most of the English provincial ones were made in Plymouth, with a small handful from Newcastle, Norwich, Birmingham, Sheffield and Liverpool. The main Scottish centres were Glasgow and Edinburgh, with two strainers known from Aberdeen, two from Dundee and one from Perth. Scotland outscored Ireland largely because it continued making strainers until the 1830s, while Ireland's last ones dated from thirty years earlier. Dublin was Ireland's main source of strainers, with a few made in Cork and even fewer in Limerick. American silversmiths, working almost entirely in the 18th century, used a greater number of manufacturing centres than anywhere else, and a variety of styles not far short of London's: the main silversmithing towns were Boston, Philadelphia and New York, but others were Providence and Newport, Rhode Island; Medford, Charlestown and

Newburyport, Massachusetts; Stratford, Connecticut; Albany, New York; Charleston, South Carolina; Baltimore, Maryland; and Mobile, Alabama.

Of all these strainer-making towns, only London, Norwich, Newcastle, Birmingham, Sheffield, Dublin, Edinburgh and Glasgow (from 1819) actually had official assay offices, subject to British laws, whose functions were to test the purity of silver wares and to punch marks on them to prove that they'd passed the test. Plymouth makers sent their wares for hallmarking to the Exeter assay office. Cork and Limerick makers could have sent theirs to Dublin, but the danger, delay and expense meant that they hardly ever did. Glasgow items before 1819 were often sent to the Edinburgh office (although Glasgow had its own unofficial town mark and many makers only bothered with their own marks), and Aberdeen, Dundee and Perth made do with their own town marks, punched by the makers themselves. In America, where there were no assay offices nor even unofficial town marks, makers simply punched their own names, either their initials or their surname in full, but there was no testing for purity.

Lemon strainers in the English provinces, Ireland, Scotland and America – nowhere near as commonly found now as London ones – had many of their own home-grown styles and provide rich pickings for the collector. Some of the most spectacular of all strainers were made in the middle of the 18th century in Dublin, Limerick and America.

It is a surprising fact that lemon strainers are almost unheard-of from the Continent of Europe – or anywhere else in the world for that matter. I know of only one Dutch lemon strainer, made by Isacq Busard and hallmarked in The Hague in 1733, with London Group-6-like handles but a unique flat-bottomed bowl beautifully pierced right up to the rim with crosslets, scrolls, dashes and splashes. The Dutch did drink punch, calling it 'pons'. And in 2001 Phillips of London sold a "large 18th century German lemon strainer with rococo handles, by Ephraim Wischke, Danzig, c1775" with short, shell-ended handles and a bowl piercing pattern of six overlapping circles of dots forming a central six-petalled flower within a larger flower with broader petals. In 1775, Danzig was in Poland (it is now the Polish Baltic city of Gdansk).

WHEN WERE LEMON STRAINERS MADE, AND IN WHAT STYLES?

LONDON

Excluding the orange strainers listed in Royal inventories in Tudor times (see p.22), which pre-dated punch drinking by a hundred years and more, and one with a single silver and wooden handle hallmarked in 1657 and believed to have been for straining communion wine, the first recorded strainer is from London in 1675 (sadly unillustrated) and a number then appeared between 1686 and 1695. Lemon strainers were made in London throughout the 18th century, in their greatest numbers in the 1760s, with a few dating from the early years of the 19th century. Victorian and 20th-century examples tended to be pastiches of Georgian styles and I have excluded these from consideration.

Fascinatingly, few lemon strainers seem to have been made between the 1690s and 1713. Although the Goldsmiths' Company Court Books list 11 of them between 1700 and 1705 which were tested by the Wardens at retailers' shops and confiscated because of suspected substandard purity, I know of only a single survivor from the first twelve years of the 18th century. This suggests that, in spite of the increasing popularity of punch drinking (and silver punchbowls being made throughout that time), the use of lemon strainers was still limited. Then, suddenly, in London in 1713/14, strainers began to appear in numbers, initially using the old 1680s and '90s handle shapes but in a handful of years exhibiting a riot of fabulous pierced handle and bowl designs. It is a mystery why lemon strainers so quickly became fashionable and their numbers increased so dramatically at this time. It coincided, more or less, with the accession in 1714 of the Hanoverian, King George I, but as strainers very rarely featured in his fatherland (what is now Germany) it's unlikely that he himself was responsible. It also coincided with the Treaty of Utrecht in 1713 which ended the 12-year-old War of Spanish Succession and it is possible that this resulted in greater – and cheaper – imports of oranges and lemons from Mediterranean countries.

Six years after the start of the lemon strainer boom, in 1719, an alternative of flat, deeply shaped and *unpierced* handles came into being, alongside the pierced ones. Then in the early 1730s, both the flat solid and flat pierced styles of handles all but disappeared, to be replaced by open scroll-sided and arc-ended ones, which continued in fashion until the late 1770s; some handles were lovely expressions of the rococo style with leafy curves and shell-ends. A handful of very opulent ones were also made between the 1730s and 1760s, which had showy, sparsely-pierced handles cast in relief in old-fashioned Baroque designs.

Only in the 1750s did the single-handled strainer come back into being (the first ones largely dating from the 17th century), alongside those with two handles. While two-handled forms evolved in the 1770s into simple looped curves of thick wire decorated with beading or reeding, single-handled strainers became the commonest strainers into the 1780s and 1790s.

The demise of lemon strainer production in London towards the end of the 18th century coincided with the appearance of the silver wine funnel, which had its own strainer built in. Wine funnels are believed to have been used for transferring and filtering wines into decanters, but there seems to be no reason why they couldn't have doubled up as strainers of lemon or orange juice for punch-making. Like one-handled strainers, they had a clip facing down from the rim, which would seem redundant for use on a decanter but which could be used for attaching the funnel to a bowl while straining juices. Punch drinking was also on the decline by the end of the century (although it continued on a lesser scale throughout the 19th century).

A timeline of the different Groups of London-made strainers is illustrated graphically in Table 1 (p.51).

ENGLISH PROVINCES

Apart from Plymouth, whose makers had a steady production line going from 1730 until about 1775 (and who had their wares assayed in Exeter), lemon strainers from other provincial towns are so rare that their timelines are highly disparate and sometimes discontinuous and uncertain. Norwich ceased to be a silversmithing centre after 1701 and the only Norwich strainers I know of date from 1690 and 1691. Newcastle and Chester continued operating throughout the 18th century, but surviving lemon strainers are extremely few and far between. One Liverpool silversmith made a strainer in about 1720 (unassayed) and another in 1780 (assayed in Chester) and Birmingham and Sheffield only featured on the lemon strainer horizon in the 1770s, '80s and '90s.

IRELAND

The first Irish strainers date from 1714 and until the 1750s their handles tended to be variations on the 'snub-nosed' theme: flat, usually solid, 'waisted triangular' in shape, getting longer and more intricate as the mid-century approached. The second half of the century saw a variety of shapes and sizes, some London-like but many quite distinctive and quirky, going on until the 1790s.

SCOTLAND

The Scottish strainer timeline is peculiarly disjointed. The earliest recorded ones are both from Aberdeen, dated circa 1685 and circa 1730. In the early 1740s, a few were made in Edinburgh with two 'snub-nosed' handles, some nicely chased, and then followed a gap until about the mid-1760s when makers in both Edinburgh and Glasgow started using standard London-style open, scroll-sided and arc-ended handles on mostly one-handled but some two-handled strainers, usually with a distinctive Scottish piercing design in the bowls. In the 1780s, simpler twin loop handles appeared and all three styles continued until the 1820s. Finally, soon after 1810 and into the 1830s, Glasgow silversmiths made a unique series of strainers with long, heavy, usually oval bowls and handles shaped like lyres.

AMERICA

In America, the large number of silversmithing centres was reflected in a large array of strainer styles, some of them distinctively American and some copied from the British (not surprisingly, as most of the silversmiths had British ancestry, were British subjects and traded with Britain). There was no hallmarking system, so dating them is not easy and relies on knowledge of when the individual makers flourished. The earliest were made in about 1730 and 1740 and include Irish-like 'snub-nosed' flat handles and London-like flat pierced handles (both twin and – unlike London – single). Boston, from the 1740s until the 1790s, had its own style of long handles, each with a knobbed, open tear-drop at its end, beyond either a bell-like loop or double-scroll struts. Many American silversmiths, between the 1740s and 1770s, made simple two-handled strainers with leafy scrolling struts and arc ends, and single-handled ones came mainly from New York and Philadelphia from the 1740s until the end of the century, with one known from Mobile, Alabama, in circa 1840, and another from Baltimore, Maryland, in 1846.

HOW MIGHT LEMON STRAINERS HAVE BEEN USED?

The things on which all writers on silver agree are that lemon strainers were used in association with punch drinking, that citrus fruit juices were squeezed into them and their perforations allowed the juice through but prevented pips and pith from doing so. I could add that the first main Groups of lemon strainers as we know them appeared, in London, soon after punch drinking was imported by English sailors back from India and became a popular pastime in the 1670s and 80s – and this is unlikely to be a coincidence.

But I believe that it is a myth that strainers were always placed on the punchbowl itself. None of the *two-handled* strainers made before the 1750s – so for three-quarters of a century after strainers were first used in the making of punch – were long enough to straddle a punchbowl. *One-handled* strainers were very uncommon in the early days and were not made at all between the 1730s and 1750s; their clips usually had too narrow an offset to allow them to fit over the thick rims of early silver or earthenware punchbowls. Only from the 1750s were there *any* two-handled strainers long enough to reach across a typical punchbowl, but they were generally made in relatively small numbers (except in Boston, Massachusetts, and in Glasgow in the first three decades of the 19th century, where they were the order of the day). At the same time in the 1750s, the reappearance of one-handled strainers coincided with the early production of English porcelain and porcelain punchbowls had rims thin enough for the strainers' clips to fit over them. So, some of the longest two-handled lemon strainers and many of the one-handled strainers *may* have been employed directly on punchbowls after the 1750s, but even then around half of the lemon strainers made would have required smaller receptacles.

For a hundred years the only material of which lemon strainers were made was silver – until the late 18th century when the first treen (wooden) ones, usually called 'negus strainers', appeared. Ceramic strainers made of earthenwares such as creamware and pearlware and usually with transfer-printed patterns, which were much smaller and with tiny handles and are believed to have been used for sieving milk, date mostly from the late 18th and early 19th centuries. A few strainers in the late 18th century, looking like contemporary silver lemon strainers, were made of Old Sheffield Plate, a silver-coated 'copper sandwich', which was less expensive than Sterling silver but indistinguishable at the time (with usage, the copper begins to show through). The Pewter Society had (in October 2013) only seen two pewter lemon strainers, one exhibited then at the Antiques for Everyone fair in the National Exhibition Centre (dated c1750-75) and the other at the Truro Museum. Brass or copper ones seem not to have existed, probably because their reactivity with citric acid would result in leached metal – and unwanted tastes – in the punch.

The very fact that they were so beautifully crafted in precious silver and that they so often bore owner's initials or ciphers, family crests and sometimes even coats of arms, strongly suggests that they were highly prized, were meant to impress guests and were used by the gentlemen (and maybe the ladies too) rather than just the kitchen staff.

The nobility and (untitled but landed) gentry were by no means the only people who bought silver lemon strainers: several thefts from their dwelling-houses were reported in London newspapers by tradesmen such as a coal merchant, an ironmonger, an upholsterer and a coffee-house owner. Drunkenness was considered to be a normal pastime and satirists like William Hogarth poked fun at the debauchery exemplified by raucous punch parties, with drinkers falling off their chairs and urinating in the room; but punch was also drunk more decorously, by the men and women of the household after dinner, very probably sometimes accompanied by cultured conversation. Maybe it was at the latter gatherings where silver lemon strainers came into their own, as objects of beauty and status, respected and enjoyed by discerning guests?

Numerous paintings and prints exist of Georgian punch drinking, featuring punchbowls and ladles and small drinking glasses, but unfortunately not one that I've seen has any sign of a lemon strainer in it. Equally sadly, not one of the books I've seen on Georgian London or on the history of punch actually mentions lemon strainers. A learned essay titled *Barbarity in a Teacup? Punch, Domesticity and Gender in the Eighteenth Century* (2008) made just one mention, in a footnote, saying that punch strainers seemed to be rare and that the author had "found just one reference to punch strainers, in the probate inventory of a brazier". But they were surely found in the homes of many, if not most, of the gentry and well-off middle classes in London for most of the 18th century and also in many homes over many decades in Dublin, Edinburgh, Glasgow, Plymouth and the American colonies, including more than thirty years into the 19th century in Glasgow.

So, if most of them were in the room where punch was drunk but *not* on the main table with the drinking glasses and the punch itself in its punchbowl, *where* were they and how were they used? My educated guess is that they must most commonly have been placed over receptacles *smaller* than punchbowls, kept perhaps on side tables or sideboards (ideally low enough to be seen – and admired – from above while they were resting horizontally). They would have strained the pips and pith from lemons or oranges and the clear juice would then have been poured from the smaller container into the punchbowl when the punch was made and/or topped up. So long as the bowl of the strainer fits into the container, any extra length of the handle or handles would be irrelevant for the strainer's job, serving only as a measure of the taste and opulence of the owner.

The likely candidates for these putative smaller receptacles varied over the more than a hundred years of strainers' use and will be described fully later on. They include stoneware and earthenware mugs and jugs, silver porringers and bowls, and porcelain slop bowls and sugar bowls.

Although virtually all authorities on antique silver have expressed the view that lemon strainers were used for making punch, G. Bernard Hughes (1968) referred to a letter from Margaret Adams in 1714 to her cousin John Verney, Lord Fermanagh, of Claydon House, Buckinghamshire ("We toasted our friends at Claydon in claret and orange") and he claimed that claret and orange juice was another fashionable drink at that time. So, lemon strainers could well also have been used for straining orange juice in the making of this beverage.

They could, of course, have also been used medicinally, for straining herbal teas and decoctions – as was probably the case with the one that belonged to King George III's daughter, Princess Amelia (p.99).

A BRIEF HISTORY OF PUNCH

Punch is thought to have originated with British sailors in India. The word 'punch' first appeared in a 1632 letter from a man-at-arms in the East India Company in India and got its first English dictionary entry in 1658, defined as a "kind of Indian drink". Ever since an English doctor wrote home in 1676 that the English on the Goa coast, using the local distilled spirit 'Arach', "make that enervating liquor called Paunch (which is Indostan for Five) from Five Ingredients", this Hindustani origin of the word 'Punch' has been the accepted wisdom. It's probably just a coincidence that there was another meaning of the word at the time (to quote Samuel Pepys): "all that is thick and short". The five ingredients of most 17th- and 18th-century punches were spirits (brandy, rum or arrack), water, citrus juice, sugar, and spices such as nutmeg.

Pretty much as soon as the Puritan Cromwellian era had ended and the monarchy was restored with King Charles II, London started entertaining again. Two years after the king's accession, the diarist John Evelyn (in 1662) reported a trip to the docks where he was given that "spirituous drink", punch. Punch was listed in a joke book in 1666, a play in 1667 and a cookbook in 1670 and a poem in praise of it was published in 1680. By the late 1680s, punch seems to have been commonly drunk at public coffee-houses and at private men's clubs. It became a 'status drink' at the turn of the 18th century, using expensive alcohol like French brandy, West Indian rum and East Indian arrack made from rice or palm, as well as oranges and lemons which were far from cheap. The ordinary folk drank gin – so much of it that, to counter the appalling infant mortality rate and adult ill-health and early death that resulted from it, Parliament imposed legal sanctions on the sale of this spirit from 1737; but it steered clear of discouraging the punch that the upper and middle classes drank!

POSSIBLE RECEPTACLES FOR LEMON STRAINERS

I have found no fewer than 24 published references (from 22 authors, many of them highly respected) in which the assertion was repeated that the lemon strainer was placed on a punchbowl, either resting across the rim or (in 14 cases) clipped to it.

Firstly let us consider the 18 references to two-handled lemon strainers *resting across a punchbowl*. Punchbowls, whether of silver or ceramic, were generally between 23 and 42 cms in diameter with a few smaller ones down to 20 cm, while the great majority of double-handled strainers were 17-18 cm in length. So, it is obvious that most strainers would simply fall in. Admittedly, there are a few strainers, notably London ones with 'triple-scroll' sides to their handles and some from America and 19th-century Glasgow, which are long enough to have fitted, but almost all of these could also fall into the punch if they were allowed to slide along their long axis.

A standard two-handled strainer can only be safely supported if its receptacle is not much larger than the strainer's bowl, or else it could slide lengthways and one handle would lose its purchase. This can be expressed mathematically: the receptacle's diameter needs to be smaller than the sum of the strainer's bowl diameter and the length of *one* of its handles. Only if it has downward-protruding pegs at the ends of its handles to prevent sliding would a strainer be safe on a container wider than that. Typical figures for this parameter (bowl + one handle) are 11.5 to 15 cm, which dictate the maximum diameter of the likely container. Allowing at least one extra centimeter for safe purchase of the strainer on the rim, that means typical container vessels would not have exceeded 10.5-14 cm across.

I know of only ten two-handled strainers, made in London between 1752 and 1762, in Glasgow between 1823 and 1833 and in Dublin in c1740, with downward-facing pegs, spikes or other protruberances below the tips of their handles (or, in the Irish case, notches all along one handle), which presumably acted as stops to prevent this side-sliding. These strainers would only need to have been slightly longer than their bowl's diameter to avoid falling in and some may therefore have been used with punchbowls, at least small ones. One of these, by the London maker Thomas Rush in 1752, has pegs 22 cm apart, a bowl 10 cm across and its handles are 7 cm long; this means that *without* the pegs, to sit safely on a bowl without sliding in, the bowl would have to have a maximum diameter of 16 cm, but the pegs would allow the bowl to be 22 cm wide, classifiable as a 'small punchbowl'.

Returning to our published references, one writer even believed that the bowl of the strainer, resting on a punchbowl, would have been *submerged* in the punch itself so that small, squeezed, unpeeled oranges could impart "a full-bodied orange flavour" to the "liquor". As strainer bowls are usually only 2 to 3.5 cm deep, this would of course require the punchbowl to have been dangerously full to the brim. And some unwelcome bitterness from the pith may also have been imparted.

The second version of strainers' usage with punchbowls refers to the *one-handled* forms, both the very early ones with a long tubular handle and the later ones (from the 1750s) with an open, scroll-sided handle. All these have a downward-facing clip soldered to the rim, either under the handle or opposite it. Fourteen of the 24 authors say that the clip (or 'lug') would have fitted over the rim of a punchbowl. As Robin Butler noted in his description (2004) of one of the strainers (in my opinion, made in about 1720) in the Albert Collection, the 'offset' of the lug is "insufficient to allow use with a pottery bowl, the sides of which would be too thick"; and Peter Kaellgren (2002), who experimented with a 1794 strainer on the "extensive English ceramics collection at the Royal Ontario Museum", found that "the only ceramic body that was fine enough to fit in the narrow fissure between the vertical tab and the bowl of the strainer was Worcester porcelain". I can vouch for this as I have successfully placed (among others) the clip of a 1781 single-handled strainer over the rim of a Worcester slop bowl from c1760, but it was a tight fit and nothing thicker would have sufficed (see fig.8). Other manufactories of porcelain in the second half of the 18th century, such as Liverpool and Bow, also made suitable bowls.

Porcelain, or bone china, had been imported in a small way from China throughout the 18th century, largely for showcase display, but only when it was finally manufactured in England in the late 1740s did it become popular, affordable and usable. Its bowls had thinner walls than the earlier earthenware products, and it is probably no coincidence that one-handled lemon strainers reappeared (in around 1756) soon after English porcelain bowls first became available. Porcelain punchbowls after this time had nearly vertical rims, 2-3 mm thick, which did fit the clips of one-handled strainers, some of which would have been able to perch horizontally on these punchbowls (fig.4), though if I were the punch provider, I might find it hard to trust my guests faced with such a scenario, for fear of the strainer being pushed down and the punchbowl's delicate rim getting damaged. And punchbowls made in England between the 1670s and the 1740s had walls which were probably too thick to fit the clips anyway.

*Fig.4: Porcelain punchbowl (Bow c1760) with single-handled lemon
strainer (London 1781) (a good fit, but a danger to the punchbowl)*

I say 'probably' because, although the clip on the c1720 strainer by Epaphroditus Fowler from the Albert Collection would not fit a contemporary pottery bowl (and nor would one other, of 1737, that I have seen with a similar single cannon handle), the very earliest (17th-century), very rarely illustrated single-handled strainers do show clips with considerably wider offsets, which *may* have permitted them to slide down over the rim of a punchbowl. The only trouble is that even the longest cannon-handled ones were less than 22 cm in length, barely long enough to stretch across a typical punchbowl, let alone to rest safely on the opposite rim; and the ones with a shaped, flat handle were shorter still. So these may not have been safe to use on ceramic punchbowls, nor on *silver* punchbowls (which did exist as a rare luxury from the late 17th century onwards), even if their clips did fit over the rim, as most of their length would be suspended in space, supported only by the clip, exerting considerable pressure on the bowl's rim. Another problem would have been that many silver punchbowls had *everted* rims, so any clipped-on strainer would have been perched at a crazy angle above the punch.

The earliest reference I have to lemon-strainer usage is by Wilfred Cripps and dates from 1886. It describes the silver punchbowl known as a 'monteith' at the turn of the 18th century, which had a detachable rim with notches designed for carrying drinking glasses. The monteith was, he said, brought into the room empty of liquid, along with "a silver ladle and lemon-strainer"; the glasses and rim were removed and the gentlemen concocted their punch, clipping an "old-fashioned" (presumably 17th-century cannon-handled) lemon strainer to the fixed rim of the bowl. But typical monteith diameters range from 28 to 40 cm, so even the longest single-handled strainer (typically 20-22 cm long) would have needed holding in one hand while the other hand squeezed the lemon or orange. At least the rim of a monteith's bowl is vertical, so the strainer would have been flat when clipped on. A footnote on the page says "The lemon-strainers with two long flat handles were no doubt also used with these bowls." No doubt the author was hedging his bets about *how* they were used, as he failed to point out that these strainers, 15-18 cm in length, could never have fitted on a monteith.

For a one-handled strainer, with a clip *opposite* the handle, to allow its handle to rest on the rim (to avoid straining both its clip and the bowl's rim), the receptacle's diameter must be at least 1 cm smaller than the sum of the strainer's bowl diameter and the length of the handle opposite. In a one-handled strainer with its clip *under* the handle, the handle itself could not rest on the receptacle at all but would stick out away from it, so theoretically the receptacle could be of any size so long as its rim is thin enough to fit the clip; but with the bowl 'dangling' unsupported over the container, there would also be a danger of damage to the container's rim or the strainer's clip.

Downward-facing clips are not only found on one-handled lemon strainers: I know of fourteen *two-handled* strainers, thirteen produced in London between 1726 and 1821 and one in Edinburgh in 1782, which have them, either under one of the handles (in eleven cases) or to the side, between the handles (in the other three). These presumably helped to steady the strainer on its container but provide no evidence that their receptacles were much wider than the strainers' bowls. In fact the rare strainers with clips to the side would not fit on large bowls as their handles would be poorly supported.

So I believe that many, if not most, lemon strainers were *not* employed directly on punchbowls and the fact that punchbowls and lemon strainers first appeared at around the same time, in the 1670s and 80s, merely reflected the new popularity of punch on the London scene. Punchbowls and lemon strainers were both concerned with punch-drinking, but their paths did not directly cross until at least the 1750s. Strainers must have been used in other ways.

I would first rule out some published suggestions by silver experts: one (2017) thought a two-handled strainer would "sit comfortably on top of a goblet"; another (2016) imagined a single-handled American one hooked on to a glass; one (2014) believed a one-handled Hester Bateman strainer to have been part of a tea service, "secured to the rim of a teacup via the side hook"; and two authors (2002 and 2013) had two-handled ones sitting on jugs. It seems to me that the openings of goblets, glasses and teacups were all too small for strainers to fit into, and that 18th-century jugs were deep items designed for ale or beer and probably unlikely candidates for pouring small quantities of citrus juice into the punchbowl. There is, however, an exhibit in the Royal Ontario Museum of a punch table with a 17th-century two-handled strainer resting in the mouth of a contemporary stoneware pint jug; and the curator, Dr Peter Kaellgren, points out that citrus juice may have been filtered into measured quantities of spirits or water in such jugs, which were often made to hold specific volumes. No-one, to my knowledge, has suggested that porcelain mugs might be suitable, but the ones – for example made by Bow or Liverpool in the 1750s and 60s – that have a wide enough diameter (10-15 cm) to fit the smallest strainers are also quite tall and therefore also over-capacious.

Three authors (Bernard Crewdson in 1950, G. Bernard Hughes in 1968 and Elizabeth de Castres in 1980) and the Art Institute of Chicago in 2017 suggested that lemon strainers were placed over *smaller bowls whose contents after straining were poured into the punchbowl*. This makes the most sense and my feeling is that, if these smaller bowls were kept 'out of the picture', as it were, on side-tables, it would explain why no strainers appear in contemporary images.

Some of these images do provide evidence that the punchbowl on the main table was topped up by the drinkers themselves: in one, a gentleman pours the contents of two bottles (probably spirits) into a punchbowl; in another, a maid squeezes a lemon directly over the bowl (using her hand); and another shows a number of empty spirit bottles in the room. Other pictures, however, show a servant bringing in a full punchbowl, so clearly punch was drunk in different ways in different places and households. I would guess that not every household, punch-house, coffee-house or drinking club had a silver lemon strainer, partly because punch ladles – usually with a silver bowl and a turned wooden stem – have survived in greater numbers than strainers, despite their more delicate nature.

Fig.5: Tin-glazed earthenware mug, Lambeth 1685-95 (blue & pink on white background)

Fig.6: Lemon strainer (London c1695) on porringer (London 1699)

What might lemon strainer receptacles have been? The candidates would have differed as the 150-odd years of lemon strainer usage went on. In the late 17th century – at least for two-handled strainers – they may have been mugs made of salt-glazed stoneware or tin-glazed earthenware in London factories such as in Southwark and Lambeth, whose openings typically had diameters of 7-9 cm (fig.5), or the small silver two-handled cups called 'porringers' or 'caudle cups', commonly produced in the late 17th and early 18th centuries (the porringer in fig.6 has a diameter of 10 cm and the strainer's bowl is 8 cm across). Salt-glazed stoneware jugs could also have been used, if they already contained other punch ingredients ready for the punchbowl.

Fig.7: Sugar bowl with its upside-down lid acting as a saucer for a lemon strainer (both London 1734)

As there are no known specific lemon-strainer *stands* in existence, a strainer may have been left on its receptacle throughout the evening (or whenever punch was being drunk), except briefly when the strained juice was periodically emptied into the punchbowl. As acidic juices do not damage silver in the short term, pith and pips could be left in the strainer bowl with impunity, even for hours at a time, before being washed out later by the servants.

But there is one candidate for a strainer stand, unfortunately only made from the 1720s to the 1740s, and that is the silver, lidded 'sugar bowl' (normally about 11.5 cm across) whose cover, when turned upside-down, becomes a saucer on a central foot. It is usually assumed that the inverted cover was to hold a pair of tea tongs (aka sugar nips) for transferring sugar lumps from the bowl to the tea-cup, but there seems no reason why the bowl and cover couldn't have doubled up as lemon-strainer container and strainer stand (fig.7).

Fig.8: Lemon juice straining through strainer (London 1726)
into small silver bowl (London 1738)

In the first half of the 18th century, other – usually weightier – small silver bowls were made which probably never had covers and whose functions are unknown. Typically 11-12 cm in diameter, they are now rare (more so than lemon strainers) and they command very high prices. These too could have been strainer receptacles. Fig.8 shows one of these, including the pips and pith of a squeezed lemon in the strainer resting on it.

Fig.9: Lemon strainer (London 1781)
on blue-&-white slop bowl (Worcester c1760)

Fig.10: Lemon strainer (London 1763) on
blue-&-white slop bowl (Lowestoft c1760-65)

From about 1750, when English porcelain became commonly available, the most likely receptacles may have been 'slop bowls' (generally between 12 and 15 cm across) or 'sugar bowls' (typically about 10 cm across) made in finely decorated porcelain in manufactories such as Worcester, Liverpool, Lowestoft, Bow and Vauxhall. These would have been as redolent of high taste and deep pockets as the strainers themselves. The slop bowls in figs. 9 and 10 are of similar sizes, but the one-handled strainer in fig.9 is only 12.5 cm long while the two-handled one in fig.10 is 30.5 cm in length and would have been a much more impressive sight.

It is also possible, of course, that punch may have been drunk by solitary individuals, directly from the small bowl that was used as the lemon-strainer receptacle. Samuel Johnson's Dictionary, first published in 1755, explains that a small bowl of punch is known "in several places" as a "sneaker".

WHAT WERE THEY CALLED: LEMON, ORANGE OR PUNCH STRAINERS?

Finding out what these strainers were called at the time they were made is not easy. Very few inventories have survived and the only other sources are Old Bailey trial proceedings, reports from contemporary newspapers (most of them notices of thefts) and mentions by assay offices and the London Goldsmiths' Company.

The earliest references to silver strainers are in 16th-century Royal inventories. Elizabeth I's 1574 inventory of jewels and plate lists eight, six of which are described as "Strainers for Orainges", all of them gilt or parcel (partially) gilded and two of them with crystals and/or blue enamel set into their handles. Four of them had also been included in the Royal inventory of 1550 (during Edward VI's reign) and one may have been the same as "a stryner gilte...for oringis of Siluer" in the 1521 inventory (Henry VIII). Their weights are given, but not their dimensions. Given that the great majority of Georgian lemon strainers weigh less than 100 g (about 3 troy ounces), most of these Elizabethan ones, five of them weighing between 8 and 18 ounces, would seem to have been enormous, maybe more like colanders. The heaviest 18th-century strainer I know of is 8oz 10dwt (274g). Punch as a drink didn't hit the London scene until the 1660s, so the Elizabethan ones must have filtered orange juice for a different purpose, perhaps on to fish at the dinner table?

The "little cullender for oranges" in the inventory of plate (= silverware) at the magnificent stately home, Knole in Kent, dated 1665/66, may well have been among the first to have been used in the making of punch, but we will never know what it looked like nor how big it was.

The Goldsmiths' Company Court Books report two fines for "orange strainers" which failed to reach Sterling standard, in 1678 and 1697; the first weighed a hefty 4oz 3dwt. Searches of the Burney Collection of 17th & 18th-Century Newspapers and Old Bailey Online – and published references to a probate inventory of a brazier in Marlborough, the Jewel House list of silver for Lord Chesterfield as Ambassador and a Goldsmiths' Hall notice of theft – show that until 1731, almost all the strainers (12 of 14) were referred to as *orange strainers*, the two exceptions being 'punch strainers' in 1710 and 1724.

The term 'orange strainer' was still in use between 1757 (as supplied to the 5th Duke of Bolton according to Parker & Wakelin's Gentlemen's Ledger) and 1775 (including the Earl of Leicester's 1760 inventory of Thanet House in London). The online dealership, silfren.com, believed that while the Birmingham assay office called them lemon strainers when it first opened in 1773, by 1777 they were exclusively listed as orange strainers.

Between 1731 and 1753, even though strainers were being made in substantial numbers, the only mentions of strainers that I have found appear in George Wickes's ledger with reference to the mighty Leinster dinner service, which included a "Fine Pierced Orange Strainer" (1747) and a record of another "orange strainer" being mended (1748).

It's worth noting that even an assiduous reader of Elaine Barr's 1980 book on the Wickes ledgers may well not be aware of this strainer supplied by the Wickes silver workshop to the Duke of Leinster. The photograph of the relevant pages in the ledger requires a magnifying glass to read the entries and no mention is made of the strainer in the text. She points out that much of the original service remained intact (with some 170 pieces in a private collection); she specifies the differences between what remains and what was supplied (except the flatware) but omits the strainer. Nor did it appear among the 184 items from the service sold as one lot by Christie's London in July 2012 (which realised £1,721,250). It's as if the "fine pierced orange strainer" had never existed. I wonder where it is now? (The only George Wickes strainer I know of sold at auction at Woolley & Wallis in Salisbury in 2004, dated 1739, eight years earlier than the Leinster strainer.)

After 1753, in addition to 'orange strainer', the terms *lemon strainer* and *punch strainer* were both used, 'punch strainer' being the commonest of them all: I know of 33 references to 'punch strainer', 9 to 'lemon strainer' and 4 to 'orange strainer' from this second half of the century. American silversmiths employed all three terms: Joseph Richardson of Philadelphia ordered "24 Silver Lemon Strainers" from London in 1760, Samuel Edwards had four silver "punch Strainers" in his 1762 Boston inventory and Edward Milne of Philadelphia received "orange strainers" from England in 1763.

Some dealers and auctioneers (and Elizabeth de Castres, 1980) call those with the longest handles 'punch strainers', maybe because they are the only ones which could possibly fit across a (small) punchbowl. Nowadays, however, almost all of them, whatever their size or design or origin and despite the fact that it was the least-used of all the descriptive terms when they were made, receive the epithet 'lemon strainer', maybe through the influence of Sir Charles Jackson (whose 'bible' for students of antique silver was first published in 1905 – see p.28) who also called them all 'lemon strainers'. I propose to do likewise.

So, to summarise, what today are usually called 'lemon strainers' in Britain (and 'punch strainers' in the USA) were almost always known as 'orange strainers' until the 1750s, after which all three names were used with 'punch strainer' predominating.

MARKS ON LEMON STRAINERS

'Hallmarks' are the marks stamped on to silverwares, after they have been tested for their purity, by Assay Offices (such as the one at Goldsmiths' Hall, London), and they generally include a purity mark, a town mark, a date letter and (when relevant) a duty mark to show that duty has been paid. Saying that a lemon strainer is 'marked', however, doesn't necessarily mean it is 'hallmarked', as silversmiths often stamped their punch on their wares and sold them to their customers without sending them to an assay office at all. This was forced on silversmiths in America, where no assayers existed, and was common practice in provincial towns in the British Isles which also had no assay office of their own, such as Liverpool, Glasgow (before 1819), Aberdeen, Perth, Dundee, Cork and Limerick, even though travel to the nearest office was officially required. In London, failure to have a lemon strainer hallmarked was against the law and was especially common during the periods when a silver tax was payable (hence the term 'duty dodging' – see p.31).

Unhallmarked – and, worse still, completely unmarked – silver wares provide a nuisance factor to auctioneers, museum curators and collectors, who have to make stylistic comparisons with known pieces and to establish the dates between which the makers practised their trade.

Testing the purity of a piece of silverware at the assay office was done by 'cupellation', involving taking a scrape from the surface of the piece, weighing it precisely, heating it in a furnace (in a bone-ash cup called a cupel) and reweighing it after the base metals had been oxidised and absorbed into the cupel. The Goldsmiths' Hall also sent out wardens to silversmiths' premises and retail outlets in London for random purity tests, for which they generally used a 'touchstone': the silver item in question was rubbed on to the stone to give a narrow streak, whose colour could be directly compared with a streak produced by the 'touch-needle' of known silver purity.

For most of the period of time that lemon strainers were produced, each mark was separately punched, firstly the maker's mark back at the workshop and then, at the assay office, the town, purity, date and – when needed – duty marks and this was true even when the marks appeared in a line near the rim on the outside of a lemon strainer's bowl. After 1784, however, in England, Scotland and Ireland, the assay offices usually set all their marks into one long punch so that silver objects could be marked in one single operation: this resulted in a neat straight line of hallmarks. On strainers, this was true when the marks were applied under the rim, but not always when punched into the bowl: in the 1790s, the London office sometimes split its marks into two groups, town and purity marks in one punch and date and duty marks in another or continued to use individual punches on some strainers in a ring around the central hole. The Glasgow Assay Office used individual punches on lemon strainers between 1819 and the 1830s.

HALLMARKS – THE CITY OR TOWN

Only when a strainer has been assayed officially, found to have the minimum required percentage of silver in its silver-copper mix and stamped with proper hallmarks can we be certain of where and when it was assayed and if duty had been paid. The 'where' – in other words which assay office did the hallmarking – was shown in the following ways:

London: a crowned leopard's head (or lion's head erased for Britannia standard pieces).

Dublin: a crowned harp.

Edinburgh and Exeter: a three-turreted castle.

Newcastle: three separate castles.

Birmingham: an anchor.

Glasgow: a tree with a bird, a bell and a fish.

Norwich (before its assay office folded in 1701): a castle above a lion passant *and* either a crown or a Tudor rose.

Sheffield: a crown within the date-letter punch.

HALLMARKS – THE YEAR

The 'when' is given by a punched letter: in London, 20 of the 26 letters were used (omitting 'j', 'v', 'w', 'x', 'y' and 'z') and therefore repeated every 20 years; but a different style was used for each series, such as upper case, lower case or Gothic. The letter was changed annually on May 30th, so the date of production of a lemon strainer (and any other silver piece) should strictly be given as two consecutive years, e.g. '1725/26' to denote the period from one May to the next: a strainer dated '1725' may have been assayed up to five months into 1726. Exeter, Edinburgh and Dublin left out 'j' and 'v' during the 18th century but used 'w', 'x', 'y' and 'z', so their cycles were longer than London's and out of sync with them. After Glasgow started its own hallmarking system (in 1819), it used all 26 letters of the alphabet.

In cases where the date letter is rubbed or pierced through, some idea of the date of the piece may be gleaned from the shape of the hallmarked punch. The London date letters, for example, in the 1716-1735 series had triangular bases to their rectangular punches and so did the crowned leopard's heads from 1729 until 1739. From 1740 until 1755, the date letters' punches had a very distinctive wavy outline and the lions passant had double protrusions or indentations, compared with their ogee bases from 1756 onwards.

HALLMARKS – THE PURITY: STERLING TO BRITANNIA – AND BACK AGAIN

Hallmarks in London were very different between 1697 and 1720 from how they were before and after these 23 years, which comprised what is now known as the 'Britannia Period'. Prior to 1697 there was a severe shortage of silver for making items of silverware. The coins of the time were of the same 'Sterling' purity as silverware (92.5%, the remaining 7.5% being mostly copper, that is 11oz 2dwt of silver in every pound Troy), so they were often illegally 'clipped' to provide more raw material without destroying the money. This clipping became so widespread (despite the fact that the maximum penalty for the offence was death) that King William III enacted a law in 1697 whereby all silver goods must be made using a purer form of silver than Sterling (11oz 10dwt of fine silver in every pound Troy, or 95.8%). At the time this was simply called the 'new standard'.

The London assay office (and, a little later, the Exeter and other provincial offices) showed that a piece met the required new standard of purity by replacing the old Lion Passant with the seated figure of Britannia (the origin of the name now used for the new standard, 'Britannia Standard'). The London town mark was also changed, from a 'crowned leopard's head' to a 'lion's head erased'. A new series of date letters was instigated in London as well, using the (hard-to-decipher) court alphabet. Last but not least, all silversmiths were required to reinvent their maker's mark, as the first two letters of their surname rather than the initials of their first name and surname – and they had to register it at the Goldsmiths' Hall. The fact that silversmiths have had to register their marks from then on has been of great benefit to students of old silver. Maker's marks from before 1697 *were* recorded, it seems, at least in some cases, by the Goldsmiths' Company and these records still existed in 1675 (so had survived the Great Fire of London); but they were all lost – perhaps in the fire of 1681 which badly damaged the Goldsmiths' Hall – with the result that few of the names represented by the makers' initials have been identified with certainty, despite much scholarly work by historians.

After complaints from many of London's silversmiths about the more expensive and softer Britannia-standard silver, the law was changed again in 1720 to reintroduce the Sterling standard for silver goods; but Britannia standard was not abolished and many craftsmen continued to use it for some of their pieces. Once again, Sterling silver was given lion passant and crowned leopard's head punches by the assay office and the silversmiths now had to register new maker's marks (their initials) for putting on their Sterling wares. So it was that lemon strainer makers changed their marks: John Albright from AL to IA (the letter 'I' being used for 'J' until late on in the century), James Goodwin from Go in a figure-of-eight punch to IG in script, and Francis Turner from Tu to FT. William Fleming, it seems, carried on using Britannia standard (including lemon strainers) for at least five years after the new law; he never registered a Sterling mark but an (unregistered) 'WF' mark on what is believed to be a 1727 strainer has been attributed to him and he may have retired very soon afterwards.

A hiccup, however, in the continuity of silversmiths' marks occurred decades later, when two of the registers (of smallworkers from 1739 to 1758 and of largeworkers from 1758 to 1773) were sent in 1773 to the House of Commons for an enquiry by a parliamentary committee and never returned, and then presumably destroyed when the old Houses of Parliament burned down in 1834. As lemon strainers were mostly made by largeworkers, this means that many strainer makers who registered their only marks between 1758 and 1773 may never be identified. This probably includes 'IS and AN' and 'IW over TB', two silversmithing duos who made at least one strainer each in 1765 and c1770, as well as the 'TT' maker of one dating probably from 1764 (p.93, fig.117).

HALLMARKS – THE DUTY ('INCUSE HEAD' & 'DUTY DRAWBACK')

Although duty had been payable to the London assay office (at sixpence per Troy ounce) between 1720 and 1758, it wasn't until the next imposition of a tax on each item in 1784 that a punch was first used there to verify the payment. This was the head, in profile, of King George III. In the years 1784/85 and 1785/86 the head was 'incuse' or intaglio, impressed deeper than the punch; from then on it was in relief, like the other marks. These same 'duty marks' were also used simultaneously in Edinburgh and the English provincial assay offices such as Chester, Exeter and Newcastle. In Dublin, a sixpenny tax had been imposed back in 1730 and a new duty mark introduced then, of a seated Hibernia with a harp of her own, which accompanied the crowned harp town mark for the rest of the century.

Wares destined for export were exempt from the silver tax and for a very short time (between December 1784 and July 1785), the London assay office punched not only the incuse monarch's head but also a 'duty drawback' mark (of a standing Britannia) – a very rare and sought-after mark which I've seen on only one lemon strainer which returned to England some time after its original exportation (see pp.101-102).

HALLMARKS - THE FRENCH SWAN MARK

I know of one lemon strainer, fully hallmarked for London 1719 (Britannia standard) and with the maker's mark of John Albright (fig.38), which is also stamped with the French swan mark (in three places, on the outside of the bowl under the rim and under both handles). This tiny mark in its deep oval punch is shrouded in some mystery: it guaranteed a minimum silver purity of 80% between 1893 and 1970 and most authorities associate it only with silver watch casings imported into France, but it seems that it was also used – between those years – on larger (and usually important) foreign articles of silver before they could legally be sold at auction in France. The mark is so small that it is easily missed – and Sotheby's in New York made no mention of it in their description of this strainer when it sold there in 2018.

MAKERS' MARKS

Silversmiths were free to create their own punches and the sizes, shapes and styles of lettering were very varied, in addition to the shapes of the punches themselves. Especially before 1739, when all silversmiths had to register new Sterling-standard marks, there was quite a profusion of pellets, mullets, crowns, fleurs-de-lis, crosses, rebuses and other devices inside the punch along with the letters; and the punches were far from always oblong, with many circles, hearts, shields, figures-of-eight and much more elaborate shapes. There were rules and restrictions, however. We've already seen that initials of forename and surname were required by the English assay offices before 1697 and – on Sterling pieces – after 1720, while during the Britannia period between those dates (and on

Britannia-standard items after 1720) using the first two letters of the surname was mandated. From 1739 onwards, originality in punch shapes diminished markedly.

A widow who wished to continue her late husband's firm was expected to employ a diamond-shaped cartouche for her initials, as was the case with the women lemon strainer-makers Anne Tanqueray, Dinah Gamon and Elizabeth Aldridge (but not Hester Bateman who, although widowed, started a new business of her own). Makers in dual partnership either grouped their initials above each other or as a cross, one reading across and the other downwards.

Many silversmiths registered more than one mark during their working lives and not just because of rule changes like those in 1697 and 1720. Some, such as Edward Aldridge I, also used different marks which they never registered. Letters in script or Gothic styles are often the most difficult to decipher, but confusion also arises when two contemporary makers had the same Roman capital letters in similar rectangular punches.

On silverwares made in places where there was no assay office, such as Liverpool, Cork, Limerick, the Scottish provinces and America, the maker's punch was often the only mark; and the same is true of 'duty-dodgers', pieces whose makers never submitted for assay even though there was a local office (see p.31).

Three good websites exist for identifying British makers' marks (*silvermakersmarks.co.uk*, *925-100. com* and *silvercollection.it),* but for a silver collector there is no substitute for the two 'bibles' in book form. Arthur Grimwade's (1976) *London Goldsmiths 1697-1837* (with addenda in later editions) is excellent for London makers' marks and *Jackson's Silver & Gold Marks of England, Scotland & Ireland* (edited by Ian Pickford in 2009) is a must-have for all British hallmarks and the English provincial, Scottish and Irish makers' marks that are absent in Grimwade. For town marks and date letters when I'm out and about, I love the tiny-format *Bradbury's Book of Hallmarks* (regularly updated but not always easy to find), and there is also a 'Pocket Edition' of *Jackson's Hallmarks* (for much bigger pockets, literally). For identifying American makers' marks, Ensko's (1948) *American Silversmiths and Their Marks* – although not including the results of more recent research – is as good as any.

IMPERFECT MARKS ON LEMON STRAINERS

Lemon strainers were sent to the assay offices *before* the silversmiths did the piercing in the bowl (except in 19th-century Glasgow), so the later creation of the holes often obliterated portions of the crucial hallmarks and maker's punches. This is why 22% of the London strainers in my database have unidentified makers, and another sizeable proportion have been attributed to particular makers on the basis of damaged maker's punches which are only partly visible. By the same token, many of the date letters have been partially pierced, so there may be disagreement over the attribution of the year of manufacture. Dealers and auctioneers are forced by uncertainty to hedge their bets and to use the ubiquitous 'circa' prefix, in front of a year that their prior experience helps them to estimate. 'Circa', of course, is the Latin for 'around', used here to mean 'approximately'.

The strainers would have been sent with the identifying maker's mark already punched into the bowl, whose position may have indicated to the assayers where to put the hallmarks, with the result that they usually end up grouped together. In the 17th century, the marks (maker's and assay) were stamped on the outside of the bowl under the rim (where there was no danger of being pierced through) – as was the case at that time with 'bleeding bowls' (known in the USA as porringers). After the 'lemon strainer boom' in the mid-1710s, they had their marks put on the inside of the bowls. Where they were concentrated around – and close to – the central hole, these marks often avoided being cut into; but they were just as likely to be placed further away from the centre and, especially when the piercing involved scrolls, crosslets, curved bars, fleurs-de-lis and splashes rather than just dots, they were subject to wholesale cropping. (Every rule has an exception: Paul de Lamerie, arguably the greatest of the 18th-century silversmiths, had at least one of his lemon strainers marked in 17th-century style, under the rim on the outside, well out of the way of the pierced dots; so too did William Bond in 1756.)

I have never found any specific reference in the literature to the practice of sending unfinished, unpierced strainers to the assay offices, which seems to have happened consistently throughout the 18th century. The rationale for doing it may have been that piercing weakens the bowl and subsequent punching of the hallmarks could cause damage. But apart from the damage to the marks themselves done by the piercing (and silversmiths, as well as their clients, usually had less respect for the marks than we do today), there would have been a major downside: when duty was paid by the silversmith at so much per ounce, there would have been over-payment of duty on a not-yet-pierced strainer that became appreciably less heavy when completed and ready for sale. According to my (laborious) measurements, the loss of area from the base of a typical, early dot-holed strainer bowl such as James Slater's of 1729 (fig.50) would have been about 4%, and a very substantial 16% from a flamboyantly pierced one such as John Albright's of 1720 (upper left image in fig.40). Duty on silver items was levied by the London Assay Office from 1720 to 1758 and again from 1784 (until 1890). I wonder – but I have no evidence – if there was ever an arrangement for a certain percentage to be subtracted from the actual weight of lemon strainers, so that duty was charged for the expected weight after piercing? Or did the silversmiths compensate for their loss by charging their clients more than usual for 'fashioning' their strainers? George Wickes levied a labour charge of 8 guineas (8 pounds and 8 shillings) for a 'fine pierced orange strainer' for the Duke of Leinster in 1747, on top of the 2 pounds, 9 shillings and threepence for its silver content of 8oz 4dwt, but we'll never know if this took account of over-payment of duty.

Every rule about lemon strainers, of course, has its exceptions and it looks very much as if the Glasgow Assay Office from its inauguration in 1819 allowed strainers – at least the large-handled ones – to come in for assay *pre-pierced*. This is the only way to explain how the individual hallmarks were no neatly impressed *between* the holes; and in the last piece I know of, one of D.C. Rait's from 1833, the four hallmarks were punched precisely in the centres of the four 'tear-drop' rosettes in its oval bowl.

Pierced holes through maker's marks and hallmarks aren't the only reason why the age and maker of many surviving lemon strainers are uncertain. The expression 'marks rubbed' commonly accompanies sale descriptions of strainers and it means that they have been 'pre-loved', used over and over again for years and polished regularly with the abrasive pastes which were the norm in

Georgian times. Maker's marks tend to lose their definition before the hallmarks, presumably because they were often punched with less force in the first place.

HANDLE MARKING

Some of the authors who have advised on silver collecting, noting that some lemon strainers have additional assay marks on the underside of their handle or handles, recommended frowning on any strainer which lacks these, on the grounds that unmarked handles may have been added later, casting doubt on its genuineness. Most auctioneers and dealers – and even museums – fail to state in their descriptions whether or not the handles are marked, and photographs don't often help; but in my experience handle-marking varied greatly with the age and style of manufacture and *large numbers of strainers were never handle-marked*.

It seems that, even though most of the late 17th-century ones had not been given assay marks, all handles made in the Britannia period *were* hallmarked, with the lion's head erased (the London town mark). The practice continued with the flat, shaped handles made in Sterling silver after 1720 (now given the lion passant or, occasionally, the crowned leopard's head).

From the start of the fashion for openwork, scroll-sided handles in the 1730s, however, and for the whole of the rest of the 18th century, handle-marking at the London assay office was inconsistent, to say the least. There are five London Groups whose handles fit the description of 'open and scroll-sided or loop' (4,6,7,8 and 9), comprising 404 lemon strainers in my databases. Of these, a total of 61 are definitely hallmarked on at least one handle, while 53 are definitely not. The latter figure does not include those strainers which weren't hallmarked at all. The remaining 290 were not well enough illustrated or described for me to assess their handle marks.

The open-handled Group with the best record of handle marking is the earliest one (Group 6), in which the twin handles have single-scroll sides and arc ends, helped by the fact that in its first three years (from 1730) none seemed to have escaped the hallmarker's punch. The Groups with the worst record are the one-handled Group 8 (with 20 marked and 21 unmarked), the shell-ended Group 4 (only 7 marked but 10 unmarked) and the late-century Group 9 with two loop-shaped handles (none marked and 3 unmarked). As for chronology, the decades with the lowest proportions of handle marking were the 1740s and 1750s and then the 1780s and 1790s; in the 1760s, 24 in my databases were hallmarked on their handle(s), compared to only 10 which weren't, by far the best record of all, followed by the 1770s. This means that in Group 8, the one-handled strainers which were only produced from the 1750s, the majority of the ones with an unhallmarked handle date from the late 1770s.

The main strainer makers, such as Edward Aldridge I, Samuel Herbert & Company and William Plummer, came up with both hallmarked and unhallmarked handles, in all the Groups. Among the openwork, two-handled lemon strainers known to have hallmarks on at least one handle, the commonest markings are the lion passant hallmark and the maker's mark on *both* handles, followed in frequency by a lion passant only, either on one handle or – slightly more likely – on both. Very few have the lion passant and maker's mark on just one handle and only one that I know of has a lion passant on one handle and a maker's mark on the other. Note that it is almost unheard of for a strainer to have a maker's mark on a handle *without* a hallmark as well: I know of only one example.

All but one of the marked handles have their punch or punches on the underside; the solitary statistical outlier with the lion passant on *top* of its two handles was made in 1766 by an unidentified 'I*B'.

Normally, secondary marking like this on silverwares was reserved for detachable parts, like teapot and tankard lids and sugar-bowl and caster covers. It is very unlikely, I think, that lemon strainer bowls and handles would have been sent separately to the assay office, so an explanation is needed for their separate assays. While strainer bowls were raised from sheets of silver, the flat handles from the 1710s to the 1730s (pierced or not) were almost always cast from shallow, open-topped moulds and it is likely that different craftsmen were involved in their manufacture. Wickes's ledgers show how commonplace it was for silversmithing firms to outsource and subcontract, so it is possible that separate firms may have made strainers' bowls and handles. A 1725 strainer marked in the bowl by William Fleming has handles with a different maker's mark stamped on each (Joseph Steward I); the bowl and both handles bear the lion's head erased, the London town mark from the assay office. This is the only example I know of where bowl and handles have different, but contemporary, maker's marks; however, this does not mean that it wasn't common practice for handles and bowls to come from different sources. Some specialist handle makers, for example, may have been journeymen, free of apprenticeship but not registered as silversmiths and, as such, would not have been entitled to strike their own maker's marks. And if the assay office was aware of this, it would make sense for it to test the different parts of each strainer, in case the two employees or outsourced firms used silver of different levels of purity.

With this is mind, what is harder to explain is why the open, scroll-sided handles, which were also cast, were so often *unmarked* by the assay office, right from the 1730s soon after they first appeared (and indeed why so many handles of all persuasions were unhallmarked after the 1730s). They certainly can't all be explained away as later additions as they form such a high proportion of strainers legitimately marked in their bowls. It can't have been entirely because the narrower strut-like handles had less room for the lion passant punch, as the unmarked shell-end and relief-cast handles did have plenty of room. Maybe it was a labour-saving concession on the part of the assay office, indicating in just one set of hallmarks that both bowl and handles had been separately and successfully assayed? But why the Assay Office was so inconsistent in this matter remains a mystery.

UNASSAYED LEMON STRAINERS AND 'DUTY-DODGING'

Not every lemon strainer was sent to the Goldsmiths' Hall (or any of the equivalent assay offices outside London). Most of the strainers known from the 17th century only bear the maker's mark, sometimes punched three times to look (a bit) like a set of hallmarks. At that time there was no duty payable to the assay offices, so the failure to get silverwares hallmarked would have merely been for the sake of convenience (ignoring the small matter of it being against the law): the pieces could then be sold more quickly to the clients.

One aspect of the silver trade in the 18ᵗʰ century, though, was deliberate 'duty-dodging' by silversmiths. The more serious offence, of cutting out the hallmarked section of a smaller, or damaged, older item and 'letting it into' a newly-made piece (such as a false base in a coffee-pot) and not sending the piece for assaying, didn't apply to lemon strainers as the soldered-in section would have been much too obvious. Instead, to avoid paying the tax on silver between 1720 and 1758 and again after 1784, strainers were sometimes treated in the same way as the 17ᵗʰ-century ones, stamped with the maker's mark (usually just once but sometimes – more disingenuously – several times) and sold directly to clients, bypassing the trip to the assay office. A lovely lemon strainer pierced with fountain-like scrolls and a panel of crosslets, with two open, single-scroll, arc-ended handles, was punched four times by Ralph Maidman with his mark in about 1735; and two similar ones at around the same date were given exactly the same treatment, by IL – probably John Luff. Two of the best-known makers, Edward Aldridge I and William Plummer, struck their initials four times on unassayed lemon strainers with double-scroll, open handles in the late 1750s (presumably before duty was discontinued in 1758). With their four marks, these may look to an untutored eye as if they've been hallmarked. Louis Dupont struck his mark only twice on a duty-dodging strainer with similar handles but simple dot piercing in concentric rings in its bowl, in about 1745. Only one of William Solomon's known lemon strainers, from between 1747 and 1761, was hallmarked and that was after 1758; I believe that each of the others bears just one punch with his own mark.

WHEN IS A LEMON STRAINER *NOT* A LEMON STRAINER?

Most of the lemon strainers in my London 'Oddities' (Group 10, p.104) are alterations: strainers that began life with different handles or have been converted from something else altogether. They were all on sale (or are in a museum collection) labelled as 'lemon strainers' but basically they are fakes.

Fashions changed and some strainers, from the 1730s onwards, would have been returned to silversmiths to have their handles replaced with the latest models. But, as the designs of both bowls and handles evolved through the 18ᵗʰ century, incongruous marriages between older bowls and newer, more fashionable pairs of handles stand out, for example loop handles (having replaced the original scroll-sided handles after the 1770s) on a bowl with a piercing design from the 1750s.

Sometimes, one-handled strainers with no clip come up for sale, both with the flat handles of the 1710s to the 1730s and with the later open, scroll-sided and arc-ended handles. Yet the former were always made with *two* handles and the latter always had a supporting clip. These have all had one handle removed. None of them would fit on any receptacle without instantly falling in and they can't really be glorified with the name 'lemon strainer' at all.

The most serious alterations are conversions of circular 'cauldron' salt-cellars and wine funnels (and one case described later of a de Lamerie bowl). Salt-cellars need to have their legs removed, their bowls pierced with holes and new handles added. They end up too small, their bowls are too hemispherical, their hallmarks are in the 'wrong' place, their makers may be specialist salt makers and the designs of their handles were unknown at the time. The give-away signs of a converted wine funnel are a bowl too deep and with a circular foot, and perforations confined to a small central area, combined with having its hallmarks on the outside under the rim.

Silver tea strainers could possibly be confused with lemon strainers, but there was no overlap in their manufacture, so age would be diagnostic. Contemporary sources in Georgian times did refer to 'tea strainers', but these were what we now know of as mote spoons, probably used for removing from the tea in a teacup any leaves that slipped through the sieve at the base of the teapot's spout. What we think of now as tea strainers – whether with one or two handles – are much smaller than any lemon strainers and were first made in the late 19th century. Some were designed to look like miniature versions of Georgian lemon strainers and could be confused with 20th-century copies of full-sized lemon strainers, of which there are a few on the market, which were perhaps aimed at tea straining on the top of mugs.

WHO HAS COLLECTED OR WRITTEN ABOUT LEMON STRAINERS?

While lemon strainers occur as incidental items in numerous general collections of antique silver (eleven of them from the Arthur Holder Collection, for example, were auctioned by Woolley & Wallis in 2016 and 2017), I know of only one specific collection of silver lemon strainers, the John A. Hyman Collection of 'punch strainers'. Voted the 1998 Collector of the Year by the Collectors Circle of the Virginia Museum of Fine Arts, John A. Hyman was a New Yorker who retired as a furniture businessman and began collecting early English, Irish, Scottish and American silver; he settled in Williamsburg, Virginia, in 1988 and lent his sizeable collection of lemon strainers in that year to the Colonial Williamsburg Art Museums in the city. He carried on collecting and lodging his pieces at Colonial Williamsburg until at least 2007 and died in 2008, aged 86. In the August 1991 edition of *Antiques* magazine, the curator of metalwork at Colonial Williamsburg, John D. Davis, wrote an illustrated account of this collection, which magnificently represented the strainers made in all four countries with an eye-catchingly beautiful group of high-quality and varied items. In 1991, the collection numbered 42, of which Davis illustrated 28, and Hyman carried on purchasing strainers over the next 16 years, bringing his tally of silver ones to 55. Sadly, the collection was broken up and sold off after his death, mostly to collectors as very few have reappeared on the market since then.

The only other articles, besides John Davis's, exclusively on silver lemon strainers were two by Bernard Crewdson. The first, published in the magazine *The Connoisseur* in May 1950, was titled *Silver strainers: a little-known field for a collector*. After considering Greek and Roman strainers, he gave a brief overview of London strainers up until the 1720s, illustrating 14 of them as well as a Glasgow lyre-handled example from 1827. "In the world of silver to-day," he wrote, "there are so few things about which someone does not know a great deal. Candlesticks, tankards, cups, spoons, all have their obvious uses. Strainers are more or less a closed book. No one seems to know much about them." He added, "It is a very great interest in life to collect something, it hardly matters what. The most satisfactory thing, of course, is to collect that which other people do not, and about which there is still something fresh to be known. That is why I have found strainers so fascinating." He noted that the "sunflower" petal patterns of bowl piercing harked back to some of the Etruscan and Roman bronze strainers (which apparently were used for wine mixtures) and was bemused by the absence of any strainers known between about 400 AD and Stuart times after 1660 (he cannot have been aware of Elizabeth I's inventories). He believed that late 17th- and early 18th-century strainer bowls were made by the process of casting (in other words, by pouring molten silver into a mould), whereas I don't believe that this was the case (with very rare exceptions): they were raised by hammering from a flat sheet of prepared silver. He was right to assign a 'Thomas Allen' strainer to John Albright and a 'Robert Kempton' one to Thomas Kedden, but the strainer in his figure No. XIV is credited to Robert Williams, but I know the piece and the maker was Samuel Welder, a recognised producer of strainers (and casters, whose covers require similar piercing techniques); his mark also appears on another strainer with the same, unusual, piercing pattern in the bowl.

Crewdson's second article occupied one page of *Country Life* in November 1951, noting that around half of the good George I strainers at auction in London in the previous ten years were made by John Albright and identifying and illustrating this prolific maker's two marks.

G. Bernard Hughes's article, *Evolution of the Orange Strainer*, appeared in *Country Life* in May 1968 and covered both lemon strainers (which he called 'orange strainers') and wine funnels, illustrating only Old Sheffield Plate strainers and making some suspect generalisations, such as the size of the handles of two-handled strainers being "about 4 in. long and 1 ¼ in. broad except where they were expanded to join the strainer rim." Although it was Hughes who made the improbable suggestion that small, whole lemons were left in the (later, longer) strainers, somehow immersed in the punch in the punchbowl, he did also write that "The juices were squeezed from the fruit through a strainer, but not directly into the liquor. Instead, a small vessel was used..." and this idea ties in well with my own view on the usage of most lemon strainers.

FOLLOWING THE PROVENANCE OF (SOME) LEMON STRAINERS

Most of the lemon strainers in my databases were found online, relying on museum collection search facilities, auction house archives, *the-saleroom.com* and *invaluable.com* price guides and alerts, dealers' websites and online auction sites. The majority of these online strainers have appeared on the market only once in the recent internet age and any earlier appearances are hard to find, as early online catalogues tend to drop their illustrations and most lemon strainers in pre-digital catalogues were never illustrated in the first place; and finding relevant mentions by trawling through them is a pot-luck process.

I have, however, stumbled across some illustrated strainers in early catalogues whose present whereabouts *are* known. And some strainers have been up for sale a number of times in recent years. Following these has yielded some interesting 'stories', some made more spicy by variations in auctioneers' descriptions of the same items and the mysterious movements of lemon strainers between auction houses.

The wonderful 1769 strainer by William Plummer – 28.5 cm in length – on display at the Victoria & Albert Museum in London was formerly in the Makower Collection, along with another one of the same size and design assayed two years earlier (fig.68), and both were sold together in one lot at Sotheby's London in 1961; they came up for sale again in 1963 at Sotheby's, being bought by a 'Mr Hyam' (possibly the reclusive property tycoon, Harry Hyams, then aged about 35) for a hammer price of £650. In 1993, the 1769 strainer became the property of the V&A. I don't know who owned the two between 1963 and 1993, nor what became of the 1767 strainer of the pair; and no others like them are known to me.

The extremely valuable 1751 lemon strainer by Paul Crespin (fig.67), on sale at least until 2021 by S.J. Shrubsole, the New York dealership, for US$27,500, had been in the Rothman Collection before it was sold at Christie's in London in 1995, with a realised price of £4,370 (that is the hammer price plus the buyer's premium). At that time it was believed to be dated 1742, no doubt as the letter 'g' for 1742 is confusable with the letter 'q' for 1751: it is unclear which is correct because the date letter was badly overstruck or double-struck. Its price doubled in two years, as it sold at Christie's in New York in 1997 for the dollar equivalent of £8,800. At some stage it was in the hands of the English dealer Alastair Dickenson and the American collector Benjamin F. Edwards III. In 2010, it was on the market at Christie's in New York again, when its realised price was the equivalent of £9,400.

Paul Crespin is widely considered to have been among the best British silversmiths of all time. A Dublin maker in the early 18th century with a similar current reputation is Thomas Bolton. A lemon strainer (fig.192), not hallmarked but with his maker's mark punched three times (on each handle and in the bowl), was the property of Lord Harlech, who sold off the contents of his late father's house, Glyn Cywarch, through Bonhams in London in 2017. The auction description of the strainer was spot on: Dublin circa 1725, maker Thomas Bolton. It did, however, have a couple of bad cracks in the bowl and the handles had come adrift in the past and been reattached quite crudely. It fetched £812. A year later, the auction house Toovey's in Washington, West Sussex, put it up for sale; they described it as "18th century Irish", maker "TB" or "JB", and put an estimate on it of £1000-1500; it failed to meet the reserve. Four months after that, it reappeared at Bamfords in Derby, described this time as "18th century, probably Irish provincial. FB, circa 1775" with an estimate of £700-900, and its successful hammer price was £900. So, whoever the dealer was, he or she did make a small profit, despite the variability in the descriptions.

In the 1960s, only the most important lots at the big London auction houses were illustrated in their catalogues, so it was a rare honour for lemon strainers that Christie, Manson & Woods, Ltd. chose to include photographs of two of them for their sale on 4th July 1962. One of these (see p.58) was a very early (c1690) example with two flat, shaped handles pierced only with a tear-drop; unhallmarked, it had an unidentified maker's mark ('IC pellet below in heart') struck four times. Other London-style strainers with similar maker's marks are known from the late 17th century. This one had also been illustrated in Bernard Crewdson's article in *The Connoisseur* in May 1950, where it was described as "probably Charles II" on the grounds that its marks resembled ones given in Jackson (1921) for the years 1659 and 1668 (although both of those have a star-shaped mullet rather than a round pellet below the 'IC'). It was purchased at the Christie's auction by How of Edinburgh. Mrs Jane How ('Ben' to her friends) had helped to curate and had accompanied an important exhibition of English domestic silver at the Royal Ontario Museum in Toronto, Canada, in 1958, where she had met and enthused several Canadian collectors, including Norman S. and Marian A. Robertson, who joined her list of trusty clients. The Robertsons either commissioned Mrs How to bid for the strainer at Christie's or they purchased it from her later, but it found its way to Toronto. After Norman's death in 1988, Marian gifted over 300 pieces from their antique silver collections to the Royal Ontario Museum, whose curator of European Decorative Arts, Dr Peter Kaellgren, spent many hours at her home selecting them before subsequently researching and cataloguing them. The 'IC' strainer became accession number 933.53.15 at the Museum in 1993 (Princess Amelia's strainer of 1794 – see p.99 – was also chosen).

As an aficionado of antique silver, I love poring over rubbed marks with an eyeglass, hoping to identify makers and dates, but I'm very aware that many auctioneers have better things to do. A one-handled strainer with gadrooned rim and maker's mark 'EA' went to auction at Christie's in South Kensington in 2001; as its only other mark is a lion passant (the Sterling purity mark) and both the London mark (leopard's head crowned) and date letter are missing, it was described as "mid 18th century"; the maker's mark was not registered with the Goldsmiths' Hall but it has been identified as one of the unregistered marks of Edward Aldridge I, used in 1763 and 1764, so Christie's correctly described its maker as Edward Aldridge. It realised £294. The same strainer emerged again in January 2017 with Bamfords of Derby, with the description "early George III…, Edward Aldridge I, London c.1760" and the hammer price was £200 (£250 including premium). Two months later, there it was again, this time with Toovey's of Washington, West Sussex, with a "circa 1770" date; it failed to sell. Edward Aldridge I died, by the way, in 1766. Thirteen months after that, in 2018, it resurfaced at Bamfords, now dated "George II, c.1750"; hammer price was down, at £150. It then reached Whittons, the auction house in Honiton, Devon, in 2019, who misread the 'EA' as 'SA' and merely described it as "Georgian". This time it sold for £320 (£389 all in), to someone who may also not have minded who the maker had been, but who apparently didn't want to hold on to it, as it reappeared at Whittons at an online-only auction during the first 2020 coronavirus lockdown. This time it bore the correct maker's attribution but was given a confident "1760" date despite its lack of a date letter and sold for only £240. Even if dealers get concessions from auction houses on buyer's and vendor's commissions, no-one except the auction houses wins when pieces of silver like this are bought and sold so often with any profits being overturned at the next sale.

A similar lemon strainer (with a smooth applied rim and a different piercing design in the bowl, but stylistically 1750s or 1760s) bears the tantalising maker's mark of 'TT' (fig.117). Because the only registered 'TT' (with no pellet – or dot – between the two letters) is for a Thomas Tombs, Neales auctioneers in Nottingham (in 2001) ascribed the strainer to this silversmith. The date letter stamped in the bowl looks like a capital 'L' and the only one of those in the 18th century was in 1726, so Neales gave it that date. The only problems are that one-handled strainers with clips didn't appear until the 1750s *and* that Thomas Tombs first entered his mark in 1738. Dreweatts of Newbury, in 2008, realised the Thomas Tombs error, describing the maker's mark as "'TT' (not traced)", but they kept the 1726 date and sold it for £400. In 2012, the strainer was billed as having been sold on the antiquesilverspoons.co.uk website, still listed as 1726 but now credited to "Thomas Tearle (probably)", whose only mark (entered in 1720) had a very large 'topknot' containing a flowerhead and a crown above the letters, which do not appear in this strainer's mark. The date letter is, in my opinion, a Gothic 'I' (upper-case 'i'), looking like an upside-down Roman 'L', making the strainer a 1764 production. It's possible that a 'TT' mark was registered at Goldsmiths' Hall, but the silversmith's identity was forever lost when the 1758-1773 register of largeworkers' marks was lost after being lent to Parliament and not returned, probably in the Great Fire of the Houses of Parliament in 1834.

Mellors & Kirk in Nottingham tried in September 2019 to auction a heavy lemon strainer (fig.160) with two peculiar, very long handles and a bowl with a delightfully complex geometric piercing design. It was by "William Justis, London 1744 [with its] marks well spaced and reasonably clear". The estimate was £1000-1500 and it did not sell. Five months earlier, Golding Young & Mawer (in Bourne, Lincolnshire) had auctioned it successfully; they obviously liked the piece and not only published a good photograph of the marks but also included it in a pre-auction publicity article in the *Antiques Trade Gazette* titled *Five Highlights from Golding Young & Mawer's sale of Stamford dealers' St George's Collection later this month*. But the hammer price of £400 was exactly the same as it had been at Mellors & Kirk a year before when they had given an estimate of £300-500 and downplayed its attributes with a "marks rubbed" description. On all three occasions there was agreement that the date letter ('i') was for 1744 (although the *Gazette* misprinted it as 1742); its published weight, however, inexplicably went from 10oz 4dwt to 10oz 3dwt and then down to 9oz.

A quite attractive, well-marked and accurately described lemon strainer with two open, single-scroll, arc-ended handles (1756, by William Bond) remained for a while in 2018 on a US online auction site; its estimate was $700-800 (around £550-600) and later $600 (£460) would have been accepted. Its seller was in the UK and in July 2019 consigned it for auction at Elmwood's in London with a much lower estimate (£200-300), which still failed to attract a buyer. So why did it reappear three months later at C & T Auctioneers and Valuers Ltd in Kent, with a £300-500 estimate? The result ('passed' or unsold) was – not surprisingly – the same again.

My last 'story' follows a simple one-handled Scottish lemon strainer with an Edinburgh thistle (the purity mark), a duty mark (George III's head) in a punch with a 'triple cusp' and very rubbed Edinburgh castle and maker's marks. The three inward points in the duty mark punch signified that the extra duty had been paid: the increase (a doubling from sixpence to one shilling) was imposed in 1797 and no duty mark ever had these cusps before that date. In 2017, Hampstead Auctions listed it as "George III Scottish, maker's mark indistinct, Edinburgh, circa 1795"; with an estimate of £200-220; it did not sell. In 2018, it popped up in Honiton, where Whittons described it as "Georgian Scottish, circa 1760" and upped its estimate to £250-350. It failed to sell again. Whittons tried twice more, in 2019, with £150-200 estimates and their (dateless) descriptions were "Scottish Georgian" and then "early Scottish". It finally went for a £140 hammer price.

The moral of these stories is, of course, that many dealers – and many of the auctioneers who help to sell their wares – have neither the time nor the inclination to get the details complete or correct on antique silver lemon strainers; and many of the people who purchase them are not that fussed either.

WHAT ARE LEMON STRAINERS WORTH?

Lemon strainers don't really have any use nowadays: they are too big for teacups or even mugs to act as tea strainers and the tea leaves would have to be very roughly cut not to slip through the holes; and

– to be honest – collecting them is an esoteric pastime and never has been particularly fashionable. But, all the same, they do 'punch above their weight' and command quite high prices.

Generally speaking and referring to those from London, the earlier the date, the more expensive they are. Seventeenth-century strainers – which are small, have simple piercing designs and are only rarely hallmarked – are pricey because of their rarity. Early eighteenth-century ones with shaped, flat handles, especially those with elaborate piercing in the bowl, are very desirable. Most auctioneers don't specify whether a strainer is of Britannia standard, so the purer standard *per se* doesn't seem to command a premium, even though the great majority of strainers bearing the lion's head erased and Britannia marks came from the years 1697 to 1720. Admittedly some strainers from the 1720s were still made in Britannia-standard silver, as silversmiths after 1720 were allowed the choice between it and Sterling standard.

Octagonal silver objects from the Britannia period are generally particularly collectable, and George Gillingham's strainers from 1718 and 1719 are the only ones that fit the bill. I know of only three of them.

As with other items of Georgian silverware, strainers made by the most prestigious makers attract higher prices: for a Paul de Lamerie one would expect to pay four or five times the going rate for a similar example from a lesser silversmith; but, of course, it may be hard to find a similar example, as his work was of such heavy gauge and good quality. Edward Aldridge I, however, who was a prolific maker of lemon strainers perfectly happy to make workaday examples for ordinary middle-class clients, also made some very classy ones with designs similar to the best of de Lamerie and Paul Crespin, which might have been as well-made and weighty – and may therefore be bargains if they came on to the market.

Strainers with open, scroll-sided, arc-ended handles (including one-handled ones) are the most inexpensive, those with single scrolls being valued less highly than those with double or triple scrolls. Shell motifs in the handles' terminals improve their desirability.

To my knowledge, the lemon strainer that has sold at auction for the greatest sum is quite a modest one, 18.7 cm in length and 4oz 6dwt (134g) in weight, by Paul de Lamerie (fig.64) which belonged to the Bolivian collector, Jaime Ortiz-Patiño, and sold in 1998 at Sotheby's in New York for $48,875 (the equivalent then of about £29,250). Its bowl has a geometric arrangement of crosslets, curved dashes, splashes, crescents and teardrops and its flat, shaped handles are engraved all over with scrolls, stylised foliage and brickwork and each has a medallion bearing the crest of Sir Charles Kerneys, Baronet. A longer, heavier and more flamboyantly rococo creation by Paul Crespin in 1751 (fig.67) was the second most expensive London-made strainer: its handles are flat and heavily chased, deeply shaped and shell-ended, and its bowl is pierced with crosslets and scrolling patterns. It measures 30.5 cm across the handles and weighs 8oz 10dwt (273g) and it sold in 1997 for US $14,950 (then approximately £8,800). I would imagine that William Plummer's 1767 lemon strainer (fig.68), even more ornate, which last appeared on the market in 1963, might well fetch more than that if it came up for sale now. To see what the Plummer strainer looks like, visit the Victoria &

Albert Museum and see its double (marked two years later, in 1769) on public display in the Whiteley Galleries.

The largest sums paid for British lemon strainers made outside London were for two wonderful ones by the silversmith Joseph Johns in Limerick, Ireland, in about 1750: one fetched US $32,900 in 2001 (equivalent to £21,100) and another £17,696 in 2015 (fig.200). These are of similar size to the Crespin and Plummer examples (although lighter), but with flat, shaped handles chased with scrolls, flowers and baskets (and each pierced with a heart), and the wide and deep bowl pierced with dots, squiggles, scrolls, commas, crosses and rosettes, whose broad rim is chased with foliage. Not only are they beautiful in their own right, but anything made in Limerick is extremely rare and is nearly always a spoon. Examples from Cork are less rare, but the very early (c1725) strainer by William Newenham, with its deep bowl and flat handles each pierced with a diamond and two kidney shapes (fig.193), went for the equivalent of nearly £9000 at Sotheby's, New York, in 2010.

Rarity value and distinctive styles make all lemon strainers from Ireland more valuable than their London counterparts of the same age, as well as any from Scotland before the middle of the 18th century. Glasgow-made 19th-century strainers with oval bowls and lyre-shaped handles are desirable too. American lemon strainers very rarely come up for sale, as most of them are secure in museums in the USA; when they do, they regularly make several thousands of dollars. One made by Joseph Edwards II with the classic Bostonian 'bell, loop and knob' handles (fig.250, p.159) fetched the equivalent of £15,600 at Sotheby's in New York in 2004 and a small strainer by the New Yorker Myer Myers (fig.258, p.162) went for the equivalent of £11,900 at Christie's in New York in 2011.

CONDITION

All the above, of course, is strongly affected by condition. Lemon strainers are quite delicate and don't take kindly to being dropped. Their bowls may have dents and dings and their rims may be bent out of shape, and cracks may appear between the piercings or on the rims. And, as their handles were soldered on to the bowls, usually with a small zone of contact, they have commonly broken away and have often been re-attached by crude re-soldering. The handles themselves, especially the longer double- and triple-scroll varieties, get bent into asymmetrical contortions and some have been broken along their length and poorly mended. Some have cracks which may have appeared during the original casting, but are more likely to be 'stress fractures'.

Good patina is a strong selling point, but hard to define. When a lemon strainer was first made, it would have had a perfect blemish-free, mirror-like surface, but during the following 200-300-plus years – even if immaculately maintained – two changes occur. Firstly, the surface silver becomes oxidised. This is not the same as the tarnishing that is caused by sulphur compounds in the air and which yellows and then blackens the surface and it is an immensely slower process. The effect of oxygen is a very slow change of surface colour to a mellow greyness (which John Luddington likened to "heavily frosted hedgerows glowing in the waning winter sunshine"). At the same time, usage and regular household polishing bring about the second change, in the form of numerous little surface scratches and nicks, which help the 'antique look', adding to the effect of the long and slow oxidation. Good patina on a lemon strainer means it takes longer to tarnish than more recently made pieces of silverware because the presence of silver oxide seems to protect against the formation of silver sulphide. All this means, of course, that over-polishing is the bane of collectors: using a buffing wheel, either to polish a blackened piece or to smooth out scratches (or – perish the thought – to erase a previous owner's initials), is anathema as it removes the patina and destroys half the beauty of the silver.

As just hinted at, it is not unusual for the owner of a lemon strainer (or even a dealer) to have wanted to remove a previous personalised engraving such as initials or an heraldic device, but this sort of erasure removes the patina in that area and often results in differential tarnishing rates, so the erased area stands out all too clearly. The value of such a piece is reduced.

A good crisp set of marks raises the price, especially if they are clearly visible and legible (in other words, not pierced through). Those that have no hallmarks are generally less collectable, unless the maker or age or place of creation gives the strainer special value (like Joseph Johns of Limerick or William Solomon of London, anything by a Boston, Massachusetts, maker or anything from the 17th century).

ENGRAVED IDENTIFICATION

It says a lot for how important lemon strainers were in the 18th century that so many of them were engraved with owner's initials, married couple's initials, ciphers, family crests and (very rarely) coats of arms, all of which – in increasing order – generally add monetary value today. This is especially true if the heraldry can be attributed to a single family or even to a single person – or a married couple – in that family.

Ciphers are letters combined artistically but, even if the letters are hard to decode, they remain separate; in the case shown in fig.12c two normal 'S's are repeated backwards. They are sometimes, but wrongly, called 'monograms', in which the letters are actually joined so that one forms part of the next. A family crest is an heraldic device on a horizontal two-toned wreath, which belongs on the top of the coat of arms and so by itself is an abbreviated version of the family logo. A coat of arms (sometimes complete with its crest, helmet, supporters and/or motto) is set inside a shield and is a fuller representation of an ancestor's 'achievement', passed down to his descendants; it sometimes includes both husband and wife's arms.

The positioning of these additions varies: the place most visible to admiring onlookers would have been on top of a handle, but only some handle designs provided the space, meaning that many were 'relegated' to the side of the bowl under the rim or (in one-handled strainers) to the clip.

Initials

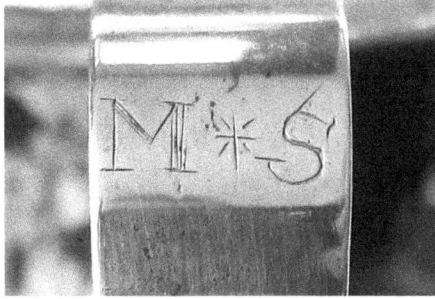

Plymouth 1736, Symons

London 1716, Kedden

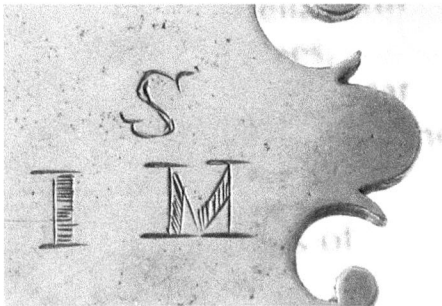

London 1719, Albright

London 1752, Rush

Fig.11: Initials on lemon strainers (on the Plymouth
strainer's clip, the others on top of a handle)

In the case of separated initials – the least expensive method of identification (and also, by the way, as a deterrence against theft) – the owner may have simply used his own name (as in the 'M*S' on the Plymouth strainer by Pentecost Symons in 1736 and the 'RD' on the London one by Thomas Kedden in 1716) or, to commemorate a marriage, three letters were used on two levels, the upper letter, on its own, being the common surname initial and the others representing the husband and wife's first names. So, on the examples pictured here (fig.11), John Albright's 1719 lemon strainer was owned by a Mr J. S. and Mrs M. S. and Thomas Rush's 1752 example by a Mr R. D. and Mrs M. D. The Americans are particularly good at identifying the original possessors of such wedding initials, because of their passion for ancestry, but it is usually impossible to do so with any certainty. One can sometimes determine if initials were added later than the production date of the strainer if the lettering style is not contemporary. I suspect that the Gothic letters 'RD' on Kedden's strainer come from a date considerably later than 1716, maybe engraved by a descendant of the first owner. For some purists, this would reduce the appeal of the piece.

Ciphers and crests

a)

b)

c)

d)

e)

f)

g)

h)

i)

Fig.12: Crests (and a cipher, c)) on lemon strainers

It was much more costly than simple letters to have crests (and ciphers) engraved at a silversmith's shop, but lemon strainers were clearly owned by the wealthy, judged by the number of these adornments which have survived. Researching crests using *Fairbairn's Book of Crests* is an additional pleasure for collectors of lemon strainers. Here (fig.12) are examples that I know of (in the 'blazons' or descriptions, I have omitted the 'tinctures' or colours, as these – even when 'translated' into their corresponding hatching or stippling patterns – are rarely visible on lemon strainers' crests):

a) A strainer by George Greenhill Jones (1730, fig.30)) bears the crest of *'a savage's head affrontée couped at the shoulders, round the temples a wreath, issuing therefrom a plume of three ostrich-feathers'*, uniquely fitting that of the Earnley family.

b) One by William Plummer (1755, fig.88) has *'a horse's head between two wings pelletée'* under a viscount's coronet, almost certainly representing Lionel Tollemache, eldest son of the 4th Earl of Dysart, who inherited the earldom in 1770.

c) Another one with a viscount's coronet (by Meschach Godwin in 1725, fig.20) has a cipher spelling 'SS' forwards and backwards, which may well have been the property of Laurence Fiennes (c1690-1742), who from 1709 or 1710 was the 5th Viscount Saye & Sele of Broughton Castle, Oxfordshire.

d) *'A stork resting the dexter claw on a bezant'* on a William Solomon masterpiece from about 1750 (fig.41) fits only the Pitt family of Cricket Malherby in Somerset. (A bezant is a gold disc, the name deriving from the Latin name for a gold coin from the Byzantine Empire.)

e) Edward Aldridge's 1734 strainer (fig.63) sports *'a sun in his splendour between two branches in orle'*, representing a Jackson family. 'Orle' is an heraldic term meaning an almost complete circle.

f) The Edinburgh family, Pentland, owned a William Plummer strainer made in 1769 (fig.126) and gave it their crest of *'a lion's head erased, gorged with a collar, charged with three crescents'*. 'Erased' in heraldry means 'torn off at the neck'.

g) The *'goat passant'* (in its intricate Baroque cartouche) on Matthew Alanson's 1732 Dublin-made strainer (fig.196) may have represented the 4th Duke of Bedford, who inherited the dukedom in that year and went on to become the Lord Lieutenant (Viceroy) of Ireland.

h) Patrick Robertson's Edinburgh-made strainer (1784, fig.232) is the only one here with a motto, *Spare Nought*, over a *'goat's head erased'* crest; this may well have been the property of George Hay, who three years later became the 7th Marquess of Tweeddale.

i) My favourite, however, is the simple *'wolf rampant, collared'* on a Dublin lemon strainer by Thomas Bolton (circa 1725, fig.192), which was sold by Bonhams from the collection of Francis Ormsby Gore, the 6th Baron Harlech, and which corresponds to his ancestral family, Gore, whose main representative – and possible owner of the piece – in 1725 was Sir Ralph Gore, Speaker of the Irish House of Commons and Chancellor of the Irish Exchequer.

Coats of arms

London 1726, Samuel Welder   *London 1719, John Albright*

Fig.13: Coats of arms on lemon strainers (both on the top of a handle)

While crests are very often non-specific as many of them were shared by several different families, coats of arms are more likely to be unique identifiers of just one surname. Despite this, it is sometimes hard to identify the bearer, even if you can describe it and fathom the complexities of the heraldic dictionaries such as Papworth's *British Armorials* or Burke's *General Armoury*. The coats of arms on the two lemon strainers pictured above (fig.13) – each of which pertains to the owner and not to his wife – are, I'm afraid, unidentified.

Engraved weights & dealers' codes

Also engraved on a few strainers is what's called the 'scratch weight', because it was engraved by amateurish scratching rather than by professional calligraphy: it was a record, usually made by the maker's firm, of the weight at the time of sale, in ounces and pennyweights, for example '2.15' on a James Slater 1729 example (fig.50) which now weighs 2oz 13dwt, having lost about 2 pennyweights during its 300-year existence. As adding a scratch weight was a common practice in Georgian times, especially on larger items of silverware, it has little if any effect on desirability. The same holds true for other barely-visible scratchings, such as shopkeepers' and pawnbrokers' stock codes (fig.14).

Fig.14: Scratched code (dealer's?) on a 1742 lemon strainer
by Paul de Lamerie (see fig.54)

RARITY

Rarity always bestows a premium on monetary value, so provincial pieces – strainers, for example, from Cork or Limerick, Plymouth, Dundee or Perth – command good prices. But to advertise on eBay a lemon strainer purporting to come from Chester (where I know of only one strainer to have been hallmarked and that one made in Liverpool) was a classic example of misrepresentation: the blurb (in 2018) said "Very rare Chester antique Georgian solid silver lemon strainer, marked underneath, maker's mark very clear, other marks could be struck a little better, Robert Green c1795". But the strainer in question was a typical Glasgow piece by Robert Gray, assayed in Edinburgh in about 1800, and the Edinburgh thistle is just about decipherable. I suppose the seller looked up 'RG' in Jackson's classic book of silver and gold marks and plumped for Robert Green of Chester without any evidence from the other marks.

DEALERS' MARK-UPS

Another thing that ups prices is being on the stock list of top dealers, in London, Dublin or New York, who have high overheads, excellent reputations and wealthy clients who trust them to sell only the best-quality pieces. These dealers tend to buy their pieces at rates similar to what anyone else could get; but their clients prefer to buy from them rather than risk purchasing unvetted items by bidding at auctions or patronising 'lesser' dealers. In doing so, they accept the mark-up, which is commonly at least two or three times the dealer's purchase price.

The biggest mark-up I have seen was on an Exeter-marked 1733 strainer with a typical oval bowl by the Plymouth maker Pentecost Symons but with an uncharacteristic handle (fig.184). It had been at auction in Nottingham in 2002 and reappeared at Thomas Watson Auctioneers in Darlington in 2014, this time described as 'London 1784', where it sold for £240 (including premium). In 2015 it was on the website of a specialist West-Country silver dealer for £2,800. Close behind was a 1762 strainer by Samuel Herbert & Co. which had a hammer price of £260 in 2016 at Gorringes in Lewes and a ticket price at a top London dealership of £2,200 in 2017 and £2,450 in 2018. (Admittedly, this one had sold for £956 at Christie's in London back in 2004.)

Other examples of big mark-ups follow. A strainer with shell-ended handles similar to the Samuel Herbert one, but from 1755 and by Edward Aldridge I, went for $650 in 2012 at Hudson Valley Auctioneers in New York and, later that year, appeared on American eBay at a 'Buy It Now' price of £1,895. A lovely strainer with solid, flat, shaped handles and two crests, by Gurney & Cooke (1731), realised £420 in 2013 at Tennants in Leyburn, North Yorkshire, and had been sold by a top (north-country) dealer by early 2014 with a ticket price of £1,495. Someone had a bargain at Mealy's in Ireland in 2012, securing a 1716 (Britannia standard) lemon strainer by Thomas Kedden for £644; not surprisingly, one of the best London dealers, the following year, wanted £2,750 for it. A similar one by Francis Turner (1721) went for £1,264 at Woolley & Wallis in Salisbury in 2011 and a different prestigious London dealer put £2,400 on it. That same dealer wanted £1,850 for a 1729 strainer by George Greenhill Jones, which Woolley & Wallis had sold in 2018 for £695; and £2,100 for a 1738 Gurney & Cooke auctioned for £875 by S.J. Phillips in London in 2017. Finally, a strainer with beaded rim and long, reeded loop handles, from 1786 but with its maker's mark indistinct, which failed to sell twice at Canterbury Auction Galleries (and whose estimate came down from £400-600 to £175-250 as a result) and finally went in 2018 for a hammer price of £150, ended up for sale at a top London dealer's for £975. I think, by the way, from the photographs, that its maker was Robert Hennell I.

PRICE VARIATIONS AT AUCTIONS

Dealers are quite often obliged to consign antique silver items to auction, maybe if they have failed to sell over a period of time in their shop or at fairs, and they then may have to cut their losses. A Colchester seller, after having a 1719 John Albright strainer on eBay at £1,800, put it in for auction with Reeman Dansie in Colchester in 2017, where the hammer price was £720 (and he or she may have had to pay the official vendor's premium of 16% plus a £3 fee). It then reappeared on eBay with a different dealer asking for £1,845; two years later, that dealer was willing to settle for £1,585. A strainer with a single reeded loop handle by Peter & Ann Bateman (1792) had a ticket price of £1,100 in 2013 at one of the best London dealerships; but when it appeared at Lawrence's in Crewkerne in 2015, it didn't sell, despite an estimate of £250-300, and it went at their next sale for £230. The auctioneer and prospective clients had no doubt noted that the piece was not perfect: excess solder at both of its handle joins showed that the handle had been reattached after breakage. The vendor was possibly also aware of that.

Sometimes, lemon strainers have gone back into auction after selling (or being highly valued) at a previous auction and sold for less than before. I don't know why the Pentecost Symons strainer (made in Plymouth and hallmarked in Exeter in 1736; fig.185), which sold for a £480 hammer price at Toovey's in West Sussex in May 2012, was consigned to Woolley & Wallis for its October sale the same year, where its hammer was only £300. It might have got more being sold directly to the West-Country silver dealer mentioned three paragraphs back! Toovey's thought that a mid-18th-century un-hallmarked strainer (fig.79), struck twice with an 'LD' punch, was worth £600-900 and its reserve was not met; but nine months later, in 2019, and despite its fanciful (and more appealing) description as "18th century American", Whittons gave it an estimate of only £250-350 and the hammer went down successfully on it at £260. Actually, the 'LD' was for Louis Dupont, a mid-18th-century London maker whose only known strainer this is and both its bowl design and handle shape are distinctive.

It was perhaps surprising that Christie's, who specialise in high-end pieces, offered for sale in 2005 a lemon strainer with "maker's mark indistinct"; to give it credit, it does have a date mark (1745) and beautiful bowl piercing with crosslets, dashes, and scrolls in 'splash' patterns. It realised £600, yet Duke's of Dorchester in 2019 put a low valuation on it of £200-300 and its hammer price was only £200. What the vendor in 2019 wasn't aware of, I suppose, was the spin that Christie's had given it 14 years earlier: "The crests are those of Byng, for John, 1st Earl of Strafford G.C.B. (1772-1860). Presumably supplied to Admiral John Byng (1704-1757) and then by descent."

Occasionally, the same strainer re-sells at a later auction and commands a higher price (encouraging for collectors who might worry that past purchases were not good investments). A Paul de Lamerie strainer from 1742 realised £2,990 in 1995 and £4,750 in 2011, both at Christie's in London (this outstripped the inflation rate). Christie's sold a 17th-century strainer with a single, hollow 'cannon' handle by 'IC, pellet below in a heart-shaped shield' for £45 in 1962; when it resurfaced at Woolley & Wallis in 2010, its hammer price was £2,400 (much more than the £750 the original £45 would have been worth).

DEALERS' 'FOOD CHAINS'

For collectors who know their stuff and are prepared to take risks, the 'food chain' of dealers is a study in itself. Car-boot sales, flea markets and some of the less salubrious antiques fairs attract sellers at the 'bottom end' of the food chain, who might have to set up stall outdoors with merely a rickety table to display their wares. Sometimes they have an overblown view of the commercial value of hallmarked silver, so charge more than dealers with well-lit, indoor glass cabinets, but they do sometimes overlook valuable pieces, especially if they are unmarked or bear only a maker's mark. This is rare in the case of lemon strainers, sadly, but one lucky fellow posted photographs on an American 'silver salon forum' in 2005 of a late-17th-century, unmarked, two-handled strainer from London that had "turned up at an antique show this weekend", which he thought might have been 18th-century American.

It seems to me that most interactions within the dealers' 'food chain' are between nearby 'links'. Dealers in the upper echelons don't go to ordinary bric-à-brac and antiques fairs and the dealers at the latter don't offer their wares directly to the top dealers. 'Small' dealers may buy at auctions and sell on, with very small profits, to middle-ranking dealers who may, in turn, pass some pieces to the top-ranking ones. Some collectors are faithful clients of the top sellers (and may even commission them to buy for them at auction and pay for the privilege), but most are free and happy to dip their hands in at every level, searching both for desirable pieces and for bargains. One of the joys of being a collector of antique silver is one day hobnobbing with the best traders in the world who have fabulous de Lameries and Storrs at a posh antiques fair, letting common interests do the talking, and then scouring a flea market the next day to find an unexpected gem at an excellent price.

A final word about the value of lemon strainers: I am forever impressed by the numbers of 17th- and 18th-century lemon strainers that have survived to this day, even though they have had no obvious use for 200 years; this is especially true for the earliest examples, many of which would have been superseded almost 300 years ago when fashions changed. Original owners must have valued these beautiful creations and the descendants who inherited them must have continued to appreciate them, even after antique silver began to have commercial value. Thank goodness so many escaped the melting pot, either for refashioning in Georgian times or more recently for the scrap value of their silver content!

Chapter Two
LONDON LEMON STRAINERS

Reconstruction after the Great Fire of 1666 has transformed the City of London, which in the late 17th century is a throbbing centre of ship-building and international trade, as well as the world centre of insurance and banking. Outside the City walls, the West End with its public parks and royal palaces (including the Palace of Westminster where Parliament met) is developing desirable residences for the gentry, including grand Palladian squares such as Hanover, Cavendish and Berkeley. Wren's new Baroque St Paul's Cathedral is built followed by a series of new Palladian churches such as St Martin-in-the-Fields. The 'Glorious Revolution' of 1688 marks the overthrow of King James II by the Protestant William of Orange and, even though there are almost non-stop wars with France from that year until 1714, London continues to grow and flourish.

Early in the 18th century, London overtakes Paris as the world's biggest city and with the accession of King George I after Queen Anne's death in 1714 there is a 40-year-long period of peace and prosperity in which the ruling classes (the nobility and gentry) encourage the arts, music and theatre and set the fashions for periwigs and head-dresses, knee breeches and hoop petticoats. The well-to-do travel in horse-drawn carriages and keep out of the mud in the unpaved streets whose open drains encourage the personal use of vinaigrettes to mask the smells. A rich merchant bourgeoisie forms a class below the gentry and below them are the 'middling classes' of lawyers, clergymen, scientists, artists, writers, shopkeepers, teachers, innkeepers – and master silversmiths and other professional craftsmen.

Life expectancy is low and infant mortality high, particularly among the poor, exacerbated by cheap gin. The first big hospitals are built, such as St Bartholomew's, St Thomas's and Guy's, but the links between poor hygiene, contaminated piped water and diseases like cholera, typhus and smallpox are unknown. Fourteen-hour working days are normal and wages meagre, but at least there is little inflation of the prices of food, drink and rent. Cock-fighting and bear-baiting are popular pastimes; gentlemen take mistresses (copying their kings George I and II) and fight duels, prostitutes openly advertise their wares, drunkenness is considered normal and 'hanging days' are declared holidays so that the public can witness the executions. London has hundreds of inns and taverns and thousands of beerhouses and brandy shops; hundreds of coffee-houses have become venues for news and gossip, intellectual discussions and gentlemen's clubs.

The honorary Londoner George Handel writes Zadoc the Priest *as the anthem for George II's coronation in 1727, Daniel Defoe publishes* Robinson Crusoe *and Jonathan Swift writes* Gulliver's Travels. *David Garrick gives his first theatrical performances and William Hogarth paints* Marriage à la Mode *in the 1740s. William Kent inaugurates the concept of the English landscape garden and Thomas Chippendale revolutionises furniture design with his* The Gentleman & Cabinet-Maker's Director. *The great silversmith, Paul de Lamerie, whose early work was in the plain 'Queen Anne' style, leads the new 'Rococo' movement with its elegantly curvaceous, often asymmetrical ornamentation.*

It is important for the rich to be seen to have an array of worldly possessions, including fine clothes and jewellery, paintings, furniture, silver, china and a coach drawn by six horses; in the hierarchy of these goods, silver wares apparently come top.

The second half of the 18th century sees a blossoming as the Age of Enlightenment brings improvements in the appreciation and understanding of science and medicine, a proliferation of the arts and a refinement of manners among the upper classes. Streets in the capital are paved with stones from the 1760s and street lighting has improved. The Gin Laws make cheap spirits less accessible to the poor. London – with a population of 675,000 in 1750 – continues to expand beyond the City and the West End into Knightsbridge, Chelsea, Hammersmith, Marylebone, Tottenham Court, Hoxton and Mile End; Westminster and Blackfriars Bridges are opened and new residential squares are created, such as Bedford, Manchester and Portman. George III begins his long reign in 1760. There is still, however, no sign of a proper sewerage system.

The Rococo gives way to the Neoclassical in interior design and decorative arts, led by the Scottish architect/designer Robert Adam. 'Capability' Brown continues the great tradition of English landscape gardening on a grander scale than Kent had done and some of England's greatest portrait painters work in London, including Joshua Reynolds (the Royal Academy's first president) and Thomas Gainsborough. In the City of London, the Court of Common Council representing the freemen of the Livery Companies – such as the Worshipful Company of Goldsmiths which includes silversmiths – is the first example in the world of a citizen's democracy, often at odds with Parliament in Westminster; but the great majority of the populace have no parliamentary voting rights throughout the century, and they have to make do with political satire – for instance by caricaturists like James Gillray – and rioting, against inflation in the cost of grain, against foreign competition in the silk trade and against the granting of new rights to the Catholics.

The century ends with war against France and some draconian measures from Parliament to prevent any London equivalent of the French Revolution.

I have records of 643 different lemon strainers – almost all illustrated – from pre-Victorian London, which I have separated on the basis of handle design into nine categories, along with a section titled 'Oddities'.

The Groups, with their dates of production and the numbers of examples known to me, are as follows:

1. Early single handle (cannon or flat, shaped, pierced) (1657) 1686-1737   19

2. Two shaped, 'pierced' handles 1685-1750   108

3. Two shaped, solid handles 1719-1734   47

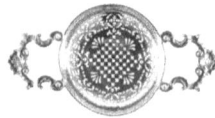

4. Two open, shell-ended handles 1733-1777   56

5. Two shaped, engraved or relief-cast handles 1731-1769   11

6. Two open, single-scroll-sided, arc-ended handles 1730-1793   110
(+ 1 from 1822)

7. Two open, double/triple-scroll-sided, arc-ended handles 1749-1783   62

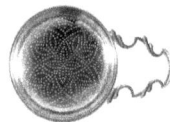

8. Open, scroll-sided (or loop) single handle 1756-1813   152

London lemon strainers: years of production

	1680	1700	1720	1740	1760	1780	1800	1820

Group 1

Group 2

Group 3

Group 4

Group 5

Group 6

Group 7

Group 8

Group 9

Table 1: Timeline of the 9 main Groups of London lemon strainers

Except for the 1657 example in Group 1, the earliest strainers (then called 'orange strainers') coincided with the new popularity of punch drinking in London in the 1680s when three styles were produced: the single cannon-handled and the single, shaped flat-handled (both in Group 1) as well as those with two shaped and pierced handles (in Group 2).

Cannon-handled strainers appeared in very small numbers into the 18th century, while after 1713 the double-handled Group-2 strainers became by far the most popular and were made in numbers massively greater than at any time previously. The sudden 'explosion' of new designs, both in handle shape and in the piercings of handle and bowl, in the second half of the 1710s, and the creative experimentation that lay behind it, reminds me of the evolutionary changes that take place in an animal species when it experiences particularly benign conditions, such as an absence of predators or a surfeit of food: the conservative forces of natural selection are lessened and natural variation is allowed to express itself, as if nature is experimenting. This is often how new species of animals and plants arise.

Before the 1710s were up, a new handle style emerged, with shaped edges but no piercing (Group 3). This was the most short-lived of all the designs: after only 15 years it was superseded by strainers with open handles made of 'leafy' scrolling side-struts and curving 'arc' ends (Group 6). At first, in the early 1730s, these all had 'single-scroll' sides to their handles. Some were given extra decoration in the form of a stylised shell in the middle of their terminal arc (Group 4). Bowl piercing designs continued to diversify into a bewildering variety, helped by larger bowl sizes and by smaller and more densely packed holes. The rims of the bowls stopped having the 'double-fillet' strengthening on the outside that had been a feature since the 17th century.

A rare new style also emerged in the 1730s, again with great variety but having in common a solid (or sparsely pierced) pair of handles with bold relief designs of leafy scrolls, shells and medallions (Group 5). These eye-catching creations must have been the most expensive strainers, made only for the most prestigious clients and often probably 'one-offs' from silversmiths happy to show off their creativity.

In around 1750, without supplanting the popular strainers with single-scroll handles, longer-handled strainers came into production with the sides of their handles comprising two, or even three, leafy scrolls in series (Group 7).

It wasn't until the mid-1750s that single-handled lemon strainers reappeared (Group 8). These were not at all like their 17th- and early 18th-century predecessors – except in their possession of a supporting clip in lieu of a second handle – but resembled the contemporary two-handled types in having open, leafy-scroll sides and arc ends. They also mimicked the other styles of their times, some having shells on their arc-ends and some extending to double-scroll sides; the vast majority, though, had single-scroll sides to their handle. These single-handled strainers are the most commonly encountered today, so were presumably the most popular at the time. The clip was either under the handle or opposite it. After 1760, some in this Group sported a 'loop' handle made from a simple strip of silver, usually embellished with reeding, beading or gadrooning. This type of loop handle, on *two*-handled lemon strainers, made up Group 9, arriving in 1760, ten years after the previous two-handled innovation.

The two-loop-handled type, along with the ubiquitous single-handled ones, were the only lemon strainers to have continued their production into the 19th century, finally petering out in the 1810s and 20s. Strainers made in Victorian times and in the 20th century were pastiches, based on much earlier designs.

It is sometimes said by dealers that one-handled lemon strainers are the 'norm' and that two-handled ones are more unusual. Although single handles are more commonly found than twin handles from the last three decades of the 18th century (81 compared with 49 in my databases, excluding 'oddities'), surviving *two-handled strainers make up 70% of the overall London total*, thanks to their huge preponderance between the 1710s and the 1750s, inclusive (289 compared with only 14), In the intervening decade, the 1760s, the two types existed in very similar numbers. (Outside London, two-handled lemon strainers were much commoner than single-handled ones, representing 98% of the total in Ireland, 61% in Scotland and 69% in America; only in the English provinces (thanks to Plymouth where they were all one-handled) did one-handled strainers outnumber two-handled ones, making up 83%.)

The greatest *choice* of lemon strainer styles in London was available in the early 1760s: no fewer than six were made then (Groups 4 to 9, inclusive) out of the nine that London ever produced. The years 1763 to 1765 share the distinction of having the largest number of strainers (18, 25 and 20, respectively) in my databases (followed by the 17 from three Groups in both 1718 and 1719, during the first main surge of strainer popularity; the 21 strainers from '1750'are discounted here because most of them derive from 'circa 1750' attributions).

The tops of the rims of the bowls were embellished in three ways from the 1750s onwards. *Reeding* (parallel lines scored around the whole circumference of the rim) was the least used. *Gadrooning* (repeated oblique raised strips, varying in width from delicate to bold) flourished between around 1760 and 1775; and *beading* (repeated small raised domes) was the commonest style from around 1760, especially on loop-handled strainers from the mid-70s until around 1790. In addition, a very small number of strainers (in Group 4) had the rims of their bowls extended outwards with complex piercings and applied, cast scrolls and shells creating a rococo pattern in relief.

The 643 London-made lemon strainers in my databases were made by 127 different silversmiths (not including four more whose productions were subsequently converted into specious 'lemon strainers'). Jackson refers to 8 others. Of 'my' 127, no fewer than 75 makers are represented only by a single strainer and another 9 have only two each in my lists. A sobering general statistic is that 22.0% (almost a quarter) of the 643 strainers have their maker's marks so badly rubbed as to make them indecipherable.

The London silversmiths who produced the largest numbers of lemon strainers are listed below, with their numbers and date ranges in my databases:

Edward Aldridge I	45	1734-1766
William Plummer	45	1755-1788
John Albright	36	1718-1724
Samuel Herbert & Co.	26	1750-1768
James Goodwin	16	1713-1729
Charles Aldridge & Henry Green	14	1767-1785
Thomas Kedden	13	c1695-1719
John Gamon	12	1729-1738
Richard Meach	11	1771-1776
George Greenhill Jones	10	1724-1740
Hester Bateman	9	1767-1789
John Luff	9	1730-1742
Thomas Daniell	8	c1775-1779
Paul de Lamerie	8	1731-1742
Francis Turner	8	1721-1726

Of the most prolific makers, Edward Aldridge I, William Plummer and Samuel Herbert & Co. tended to specialise in pierced silverware including baskets for cakes, fruit and sweetmeats, sugar baskets, cream pails, mustard pots, fish slices and serving trowels. John Albright, James Goodwin and Thomas Kedden, whose large strainer outputs were earlier in the 18th century, were more generalist but did include pepper and sugar casters (which have pierced covers). A few of the best-known generalist Georgian silversmiths, such as Paul de Lamerie, Hester Bateman and Paul Crespin, produced reasonable numbers of lemon strainers.

LONDON GROUP 1: EARLY SINGLE HANDLE

There are two sorts of strainers in this Group. Both have a single handle, but in different styles: either a hollow, tapering, tubular 'cannon' handle, narrowest near the bowl, or a much shorter, flat and shaped handle pierced with a heart. Their bowls have dot holes, either in concentric rings or in a simple floral pattern around a central ring.

Fig.15: London 1657, GB, flower below (George Bullen?)

The earliest extant strainer I know of (fig.15) was probably used for straining *not* citrus juices but wine, but this type of wine strainer may have doubled up 30 years later as true lemon (or orange) strainers. It is fully hallmarked – on the outside of the bowl under the rim – as London 1657 by 'GB, flower below' (with a possible attribution by Dr David Mitchell to George Bullen). The dot holes in its bowl have a floral pattern made up of separate 'petals'. The bowl's rim is strengthened by an applied 'double fillet' of two rings with a channel between them, a style used on all London lemon strainers until the 1730s. The single handle has a hollow silver 'cannon' portion, 9 cm long (with faint signs of its own hallmarks and maker's mark), and a turned wooden outer portion, 11 cm long; the wood is unlikely to be the original, but its size and shape may have been based on what was originally there. Opposite the handle is a downward-facing clip. The whole piece is 28 cm in length. As it was made when Oliver Cromwell was in charge of a puritan Commonwealth before punch drinking came to England, it must have had a function different from punch preparation and the dealer who had it for sale believed it was a communion wine strainer. I imagine, if this was the case, it would have been held over the communion cup and that a piece of cloth must have been inserted into the bowl to catch the sediment in the wine. It may be fanciful to suggest a deliberate connection with the Church, but between some of the 'petals' in the bowl's piercing are four 'Christian crosses' each made of 7 holes. (Its piercing pattern was copied faithfully by John Albright in at least two of his Group-2 lemon strainers in 1719, including the crosses, but this doesn't detract from the idea of a possible Christian origin.)

It's quite probable that this type of one-handled strainer with its tubular, 'cannon' handle (with or without the turned wooden extension) had been used for straining wine for years before punch arrived on the London scene and maybe not just in church but also in the home. My reference on p.18, to the

1886 description (by Wilfred Cripps) of a 'monteith' punchbowl in around 1700 being brought into the room with a lemon strainer, also included the following sentence: "The pierced bowl of the old-fashioned wine-strainers (in general use when gentlemen decanted their own port wine in the parlour) served as a lemon-strainer, there being generally a small flat hook at the side of it, by which it was appended to the side of the bowl." He clearly believed that old cannon-handled wine strainers later doubled up as lemon strainers. Whether or not the other two sorts of 17th-century lemon strainer also pre-dated punch drinking, we won't know until one turns up that has a pre-1680 date mark.

The next similar strainer known to me was illustrated in Bernard Crewdson's 1950 article on *Silver Strainers*. This was silver-gilt and was part of the Royal Hospital Communion Plate, so may also have been used for communion wine. Its bowl design is similar to the 1657 example but its cannon handle lacks the turned wood, having instead a flat, circular end with a ring attached. Any clip is not visible in the photograph, its dimensions are not given and its marks are rubbed: the maker is unknown but the date mark is "probably 1688", during the reign of James II.

Fig.16: London c1688, EH in plain shield

Fig.17: London c1690, IC, pellet below in heart-shaped shield (possibly John Cooke or John Cawardine)

Fig.18: London 1715, Thomas Kedden

This last strainer set the trend, as it were, for the other, very similar, late 17th-century cannon-handled lemon strainers, whose lengths (presumably including the protruding clip) range from 16 to 18.5 cm and whose weights (based on only two of them) range from 2oz to 2oz 8dwts (62-75g). None of the others were hallmarked, except for a miniature, only 10.1 cm long, which was hallmarked for London 1691 and made by George Manjoy. This and the "probably 1688" provide evidence that, although a few (longer and mostly fully marked) cannon-handled strainers were produced in the 18th century, these 'maker's mark only' strainers were 17th century. Michael Clayton, in his *Collector's Dictionary* concurred with Christie's in London, that the one they sold in 1962 (fig.17) whose maker's mark was 'IC, pellet below in heart-shaped shield' dated from "c.1690", during William and Mary's monarchy.

Because during the Britannia period between 1697 and 1720 silversmiths had to use new, registered punches showing the first two letters of their surname, one can tell from the letters of the maker's mark if it is *unlikely* to hail from that period. After 1720, when Sterling silver was again permitted, most silversmiths registered new Sterling marks, reverting to using their initials. A maker's mark, therefore, which was neither registered after 1720 nor makes sense as a Britannia mark, would have been stamped before 1697 and there would probably be no sure identification of the maker because of the loss of the pre-1697 registers. In 1985, New York Christie's sold a cannon-handled strainer, by (the same or another) 'IC', and gave the date as "c1700", but these letters are unlikely to form the first two of a surname. Another whose maker was 'EH in plain shield' (fig.16; offered for sale by Woolley & Wallis three times and sold in January 2008) is in the same boat, a surname beginning with 'EH' being highly unlikely. Auctioneers have sometimes resorted to finding registered post-1720 marks with the same letters and ascribing dubious maker's names to these strainers. Thus the 'IC' has been attributed to Joseph Clare and the 'EH' to Edward Hall, both of whom entered their marks in 1720. Dr David Mitchell has found records from the Goldsmiths' Company's 17th-century books of two contenders for 'IC', John Cooke and John Cawardine, who were both working in the 1680s and 90s. The identity of 'EH in plain shield', however, remains a mystery.

All of these 17th-century strainers with a single silver cannon handle and no turned wood seem to have been marked twice by the maker, in some cases once on the handle and once on the bowl or, in others, twice on the handle. The bowl piercing design is either widely-spaced 'flower petals' as in the 1657 communion strainer or concentric rings as in both of those by 'IC'. There is always a 'double fillet' at the handle's terminal as well as a suspensory ring. The last strainers which fit this description, to my knowledge, are from 1715 by Thomas Kedden (fig.18) and (in silver-gilt) from 1718 by John Albright; both have longer handles (20 and 21.6 cm, respectively) but keep the 'flower petals' motif.

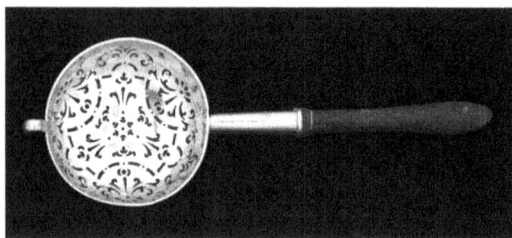

Fig.19: London 1719, William Fleming   *Fig.20: London 1725, Meschach Godwin*

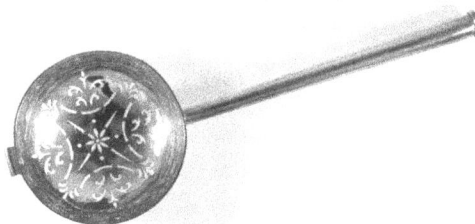

From 1719 onwards (at the start of the period of greatest experimentation by strainer-makers), tubular-handled strainers were still produced, in very small numbers and with a variety of designs. Five of the six that I know of have beautiful bowl piercings comprising scrolls, rosettes, dashes and 'splashes' (e.g. fig.19). Some of their handles have more wood than silver; one has a silver handle shaped to mimic turned wood; and one (fig.20) has a long tubular handle, entirely made of silver, with a monogram under a viscount's coronet engraved (probably for Viscount Saye and Sele) on its circular terminal. All are fully marked by the London assay office, the youngest one (by William Justis) in 1737.

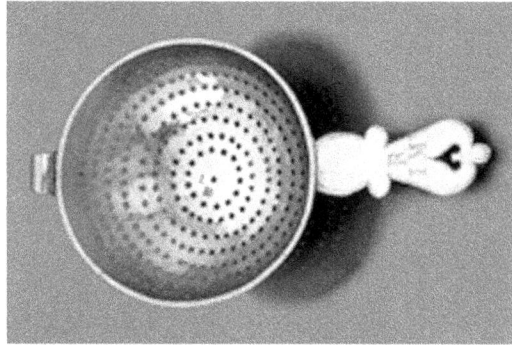

Fig.21: London c1690, EH, mullet below in shield

The second style of 17th-century one-handled strainers has a bowl similar to those with a cannon handle, but always (in my experience) pierced with concentric rings of dots, and a similar clip on the opposite rim of the bowl. But its handle is very different: rather than being circular in section, it is thin and flat and with a highly distinctive shape, never to my knowledge used in the 18th century. Rounded and broader at each end, it has a narrower central section. At the tip of the terminal is a small rounded projection and, in three examples, there is a pair of similar projections from the central portion (figs 21). The broad terminal end has a single pierced hole in the shape of a heart.

I know of only four of these, three by the same maker, 'RB'. David Mitchell has kindly given me the possible attribution of Robert Butterfield, who was active as a silversmith between 1668 and at least 1697, the approximate year, Mitchell believes, of his first registered (Britannia, 'BV') mark. The fourth is by 'EH, mullet below in shield' (fig.21), possibly the same unidentified maker represented in fig.16. They weigh between 1oz 13dwt and 2oz (51 and 62g) and the three with dimensions given have lengths between 6 and 7.5 in (15.3 and 19 cm). One has RB's maker's mark only, struck in three places, and one only has EH's mark, but the other two are fully hallmarked, London 1686 or 1688 (the letters 'i' and 'l' being hard to distinguish) and 1689.

LONDON GROUP 2: TWO FLAT, SHAPED, 'PIERCED' HANDLES

The adjective 'pierced' suggests that the holes in the handles of these lemon strainers have been cut out, but – as I explain later on (p.63) – the handles were cast in moulds, apertures and all.

Although this Group dates from 1686 to c1750, production was not uniform through this period. There was an early style until 1715, of which only a trickle survives, followed by a sudden explosion of production in a new style with numerous variations until about 1740; then around 1750 one maker reprised the theme in spectacular fashion. The most productive years were 1718 and 1719, as judged by the numbers of survivors. In total, I know of 108 lemon strainers from this Group (as in Group 1, they were probably almost always called 'orange strainers' in their day), making it the third-largest of the nine London Groups and the second-commonest of all the two-handled categories. The changes after 1715 involved not only the handle shapes and piercing patterns but also the bowl piercings, with plain dots transforming into a riot of beautiful perforations.

Fig.22: London c1695, Thomas Kedden

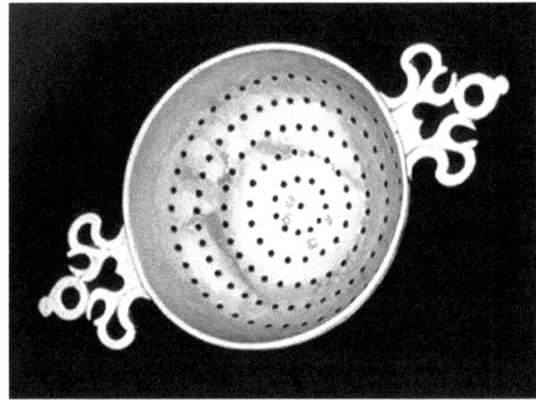

Fig.23: London 1714, James Goodwin

Certainty that the early style was in production in 1686 comes from two fully hallmarked strainers from that date, one by 'RB' and the other with a rubbed maker's mark that Sotheby's in 2007 thought was possibly by the same silversmith. This was presumably the same 'RB', attributable to Robert Butterfield, who made one-handled strainers at the same time. A very similar one is marked three times by 'TK', probably Thomas Kedden (or Kiddon), but has no hallmarks (fig.22); and a fourth unmarked one was bought by a lucky collector at an antiques fair in 2005. The only one of these with the 'flower petals' bowl design was Kedden's (note that the 'petals' represent the overlaps between six adjacent circles of dot-holes); the others have simple concentric rings.

The three whose dimensions were given range from 13.7 to 15.2 cm across the handles and their weights from 1oz 3dwt to 2oz (36-62g); the unmarked one has an engraved scratch weight of 1oz 18dwt (59g).

'RB' made another lemon strainer with concentric rings of holes in its bowl, but with unique handles, flat with a shaped outline but much less indented than the others and pierced with a heart, a stalked trefoil, two 'beans' and two dots. And 'IC, pellet below in heart' (possibly John Cooke or John Cawardine) made another with handles of similar shape but with only one pierced hole, shaped like a teardrop. Neither of these are hallmarked and they probably date from the mid- to late 1680s.

Until very recently, I was not aware of *any* lemon strainers from the years between c1695 and 1713: I hadn't found any in museum listings, auction house sales, dealers' stock lists or books on antique silver, until one with shaped, 'waisted' handles, each pierced with a heart and a circle and fully hallmarked for 1706 (made by the candlestick specialist, Joseph Bird) came up for auction in January 2021 (Fig.24).

James Goodwin, who entered his first mark in 1710, had a flurry of strainer making in 1713 and 1714 (at least six of them survive) and they are all very similar to the 'early style' of the 1680s with their deeply indented handles pierced with a heart, two teardrops and a circle; all have the simple concentric circles in their bowls (fig.23). William Looker, another newcomer (his first mark was entered in 1713) made one like them in 1715, but with the 'flower petals' motif in the bowl. Little seemed to have changed in lemon strainer design for nearly 25 years.

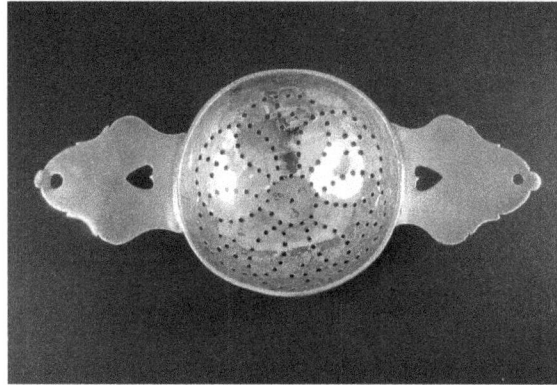

Fig.24: London 1706, Joseph Bird

But other lemon strainers *were* being made in the earliest years of the 18th century, during this long 'gap': David Mitchell provided me with records of no fewer than eleven in the Goldsmiths' Company Court Book 10, which had been sent for assay (between 1700 and 1705) but had fallen short of the required standard (Britannia standard at that time). The weights of four of them were given in the Court Book, ranging from 1oz 4.5dwt to 1oz 12.5dwt, which make them more likely to be the two-handled than the generally heavier single-handled strainers.

Fig.25: London 1716, Thomas Kedden

Fig,26: Thomas Kedden's pre-Britannia mark

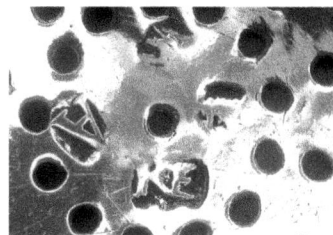

Fig.27: Thomas Kedden's Britannia mark

A new style of two-handled lemon strainer appeared in 1715, monopolised – it seems – by Thomas Kedden until it died out in 1717 (fig.25). Kedden's Britannia mark, 'KE', is quite distinctive (fig.27) and was attributed to him by Grimwade; but Grimwade, noting that he was apprenticed – back in 1682 – to a bookbinder, believed him to have been a specialist "in silver mounts for prayer-books etc." His predilection for making lemon strainers (including the 1715 cannon-handled one mentioned above) suggests otherwise – and that the 'TK' marks on the 17th-century two-handled one may be his too (fig.26). As he was free to set up shop as a silversmith in 1692, this early strainer could have dated from between that year and 1696. A similar 'TK' mark appears on tubular nutmeg graters and counter boxes, also believed to be from the 1690s.

Apart from being much sturdier, weighing about 2oz 10dwt (77g) and extending 16.5 cm across the handles, these strainers had a new-fangled handle design and their bowl piercing reverted to the 'six-petal' motif of many of the 17th-century one-handled types. The cast handles are wider and longer with a solid triangular base (ideal for engraving owners' initials or crests) surrounded by attractive perforations (with a stylised heart at the terminal). All of these Kedden strainers are fully hallmarked, inside the centre circle of the bowl's upper surface, and both handles have an additional hallmarked 'lion's head erased' London town mark on their lower surfaces.

A strainer with identical handles, in the collection of the Victoria & Albert Museum, with the date mark for 1716 visible on the bowl, is the earliest I know of with circular holes replaced by numerous ornate scrolls, curves and rosettes to give an overall floral effect. Unfortunately the piercer went so wild that he completely obliterated the maker's mark. Unusually, its marks are on the *underside* of the bowl and the assay office added a second Britannia mark for good measure (further out from the centre).

Thomas Kedden's last known strainer, of 1718, was in a different style that began in that year, so having been the creator of a new fashion three years earlier, his final action may have been to start another one, taken up by John Albright. It was in 1718 that Albright entered his first mark (fig.28) and he dived straight into lemon strainer making on a major scale until 1724. He was the third most prolific lemon strainer maker of all time (eclipsed only by Edward Aldridge I from the 1730s and William Plummer from the 1750s) and he was at the forefront of the 'explosion' of variations on the flat, pierced handle theme that continued into the 1720s and 30s.

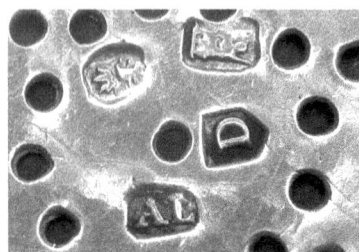

Fig.28: John Albright's 'AL' mark (on lemon strainer of 1719)

From 1718 onwards, the number of handle designs mushroomed and bowl piercings were among the most beautiful – and varied – ever produced.

Fig.29: London 1718, John Albright

Fig.30: London 1730, George Greenhill Jones

Fig.31: London 1720, John Albright

The 'classic' handle was the long, pointed triangle with narrow, curved and scrolling struts surrounding numerous gaps (figs 29,30). The furthest, pointed third of the handle was occasionally missing (fig.31), but often enough to rule out later tampering: this seems to have been just another design available to the clients of the time.

Fig.32: London 1719, William Fleming

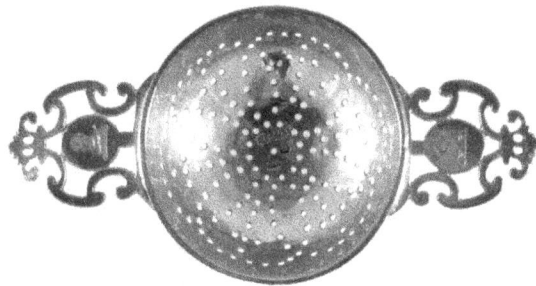

Fig.33: London 1719, John Albright

Fig.34: London 1719, John Albright

Fig.35: London ?1720, probably John Albright

Fig.36: London 1721, Francis Turner
(mark pierced through)

Fig.37: London 1725, William Fleming
(handles Joseph Steward I)

In others (figs 33,34,36,37), there was a solid central area, round or oval, large or small, commonly used for owners' initials or crests. In some cases the central motif was an open oval (fig.35). One style with a central oval medallion had a very open arrangement of leafy scrolls, (as in a Gurney & Cooke example of 1738, very similar to fig.63, p.73, but without the relief), representing a 'marriage' between Group 2 and the open, scroll-sided and arc-ended handles of Group 6 strainers which were beginning to come into fashion in the 1730s.

Fig.38: London 1719, John Albright

Fig.39: London 1719, George Gillingham

A triangular shape with a narrower base and two deep and curvy indentations on either side was briefly popular in 1718 and 1719. Bernard Crewdson (1950) illustrated two round-bowled strainers with this sort of handles, almost identical but by different makers (John Albright and William Looker), leading him to suggest that there may have been specialist handle makers who received commissions from strainer makers. This particular handle design (figs 38,39) was also used by George Gillingham, who specialised in making the only known strainers with octagonal bowls (fig.39), so it may well have been that one of the makers had an in-house handle maker, who produced extras for sale to other goldsmiths. One of Gillingham's octagonal strainers was in the 'Domcha' collection, catalogued in Christopher Hartop's 2008 book and put up for sale through S.J. Phillips in London (presumably at the request of the eponymous Dominic and Charlotte, who I believe are the collector's son and daughter).

All the Group-2 handles, even though they were thin enough to have been hammered flat and then pierced with tiny chisels and saws, were cast in pre-formed moulds. This is clear from their casting defects, both the tiny holes covering the surfaces and – in some cases – the partial 'filling-in' of small 'empty' areas where molten silver would have spilled. Presumably the moulds themselves had to be cut to shape, with their 'pierced' areas sticking out in relief, but a single mould could then be used for producing numerous handles, all of them identical. Because of the imperfect symmetry of the hand-made moulds, and because the handles always have to be cast the same way up, another line of evidence that they were cast rather than hand-hammered and sawn is that they appear as perfect mirror images on either side of their strainers (see fig.161 for a classic example of this).

All the handles were separately assayed at Goldsmiths' Hall and given the London mark of the lion's head erased (or, on Sterling pieces after 1720, the lion passant purity mark), indicating that the assay office knew that handles and bowls had different origins, the bowls fashioned from sheets of silver by hammermen and the handles cast by foundrymen. The only strainer I know of whose bowl and handles were all assayed and also have *different* makers' marks (by William Fleming and Joseph Steward I in 1725) belongs to this Group (fig.37).

Fig.40: Backlit bowl piercings of four Group-2 London lemon strainers

As for the bowls' holes, the old-style concentric rings and 'overlapping petal' pattern of round holes continued to be used, in addition to new dot designs which were more geometric than floral. Some had holes that were mostly dots but with a sprinkling of comma-shaped scrolls. The most spectacular patterns were indescribably picturesque, usually with a central rosette and a radially symmetrical riot of splashing scrolls and sometimes intersected by a progression of dots and curved dashes (fig.40). This type of beautiful, delicately baroque patterning mimicked – and expanded upon – the designs pierced into the covers of London-made casters from at least as early as the 1680s, no two of which were ever exactly alike. It is a supreme representation of the art and craft (and labour-intensiveness) of piercing using only hand-drills, saws, files and chisels, which was in use between 1716 and the early 1740s, by which time it chimed well with the new taste for rococo, but after which it perhaps became too expensive to execute.

Fig.41: London c1750, William Solomon

Fig.42: William Solomon's mark

Fig.43: Stencil of William Solomon's c1750 strainer

By the early 1730s, these lemon strainers with 'pierced' handles were already beginning to die out, but William Solomon, who entered his first two marks in 1747 and re-entered one of them in 1751, then resurrected the style in his own original way (figs 41,43), which could be described as 'Group 2 on steroids'. His bowls were larger and his handles were longer, wider, more elaborately shaped and pierced with as many separate perforations (29, for example, in each handle) as the best of Albright's. His bowl patterns were unique too, with tightly geometric groups of dots – of different sizes – interspersed with crescents and small scrolls. His strainers were typically 24.2 cm across the handles. In addition to their larger size, his bowls differed from all the strainers covered so far in not having the 'double fillet' rim strengthening; instead, their rim has a quite broad, applied 'single fillet', making it look as if the rim is slightly everted.

William Solomon very rarely sent his lemon strainers for assay and dating them is therefore insecure, but both of the marks he used are instantly recognisable as his, because of the unique shape of their cartouche (e.g. fig.42, which shows the fleur-de-lis above the W.S). And his distinctive style means that even the strainer in the Addison Gallery of American Art in Andover, Massachusetts, which is undated and by an "anonymous British" maker, is unmistakeably a Solomon creation from c1750.

Other makers of Group 2 strainers besides those mentioned above were George Beale (in 1718), Francis Turner (1721 and '22), John Fawdery (1721), Jonah Clifton (1722), Meschach Godwin (1724), Thomas Farren (1727 or '28), George Greenhill Jones (1729 and '30), Nicholas Clausen (1729), Richard Gurney & Thomas Cooke (1730s) and George Wickes (1739). James Goodwin, who spearheaded the rash of two-handled strainers back in 1713, was still producing them – in the new styles – in the mid-1720s.

LONDON GROUP 3: TWO FLAT, SHAPED, SOLID HANDLES

Lemon strainers in Group 3 have two solid flat handles, usually cast but in some cases cut from hammered sheet silver. The most common shape features three projections on each side and one at the terminal, each with its own smaller projections and with deep and curvaceous indentations between them. The first ones appeared in 1719 and the last in 1734, so they coincided with Group-2 pierced handles but had a shorter life span; in fact this was the shortest-lived of all the strainer styles.

Fig.44: London 1719, John Albright

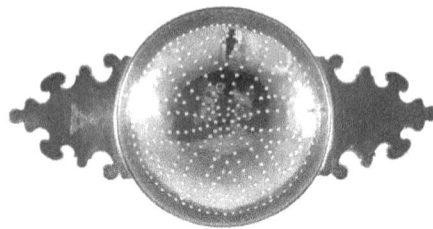

Fig.45: London 1726, Francis Turner

Fig.46: London 1719, John Albright

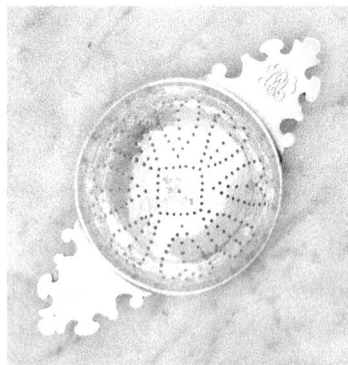

Fig.47: London 1724, probably
George Greenhill Jones

Fig.48: London 1725, probably Francis Turner

66

Most of the silversmiths, such as John Albright, Francis Turner, William Fleming, George Greenhill Jones, Meschach Godwin and Gurney & Cooke, who provided pierced-handled strainers also made these ones with unpierced handles. But their overall handle shapes are quite different from each other: what the Group-2 pierced handles gained with their intricate perforations, the Group-3 unpierced ones gained instead with their swirling indentations (figs 44-48).

Being unpierced left plenty of room for relatively large crests and initials on top of the handles, whereas most of those with pierced handles were forced to squeeze smaller ones on the outside of the bowl between rim and piercings.

While a variety of dot-piercing bowl patterns were employed, this Group of strainers had a good proportion of bowls with elaborate, radiating patterns of scrolls and flowerheads, often in two alternating designs (figs 44,48).

Fig.49: London 1726, Samuel Welder

From 1726, the 'classic' handle shape lost its coherence and evolved into a range of new designs. The strangest of these was a 'Pinocchio's nose' by Samuel Welder in 1726 (fig.49), but both handles have genuine lion passant punches and one has an engraved coat-of-arms. This strainer was illustrated by Crewdson in 1950, but he mistook the 'S' of the 'SW' mark for an 'R' and attributed it to a Robert Williams, who was not, to my knowledge, a strainer maker.

In the same year, Welder made a more typical strainer which, interestingly, has a clip facing downwards from the rim halfway between the handles. This is by far the earliest example of a two-handled strainer with such a clip, but it may of course have been added later. James Goodwin, also in 1726, experimented with a design having a trio of protrusions (and sub-protrusions) at the terminal end but only a small notch near the base. Similar handles, but with an extra protruding swirl near the base, were made by Meschach Godwin in 1725 and the unidentified 'TT' in 1729.

Fig.50: London 1729, James Slater   *Fig.51: London c1729, Anne Tanqueray*

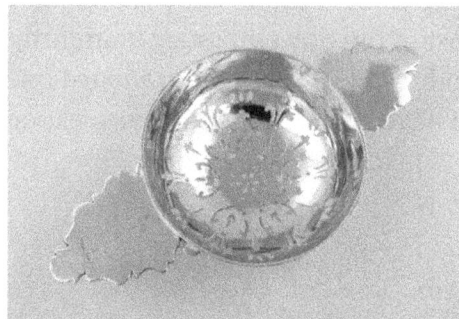

The year 1727 saw the first of numerous lemon strainers from James Slater's workshop, made until at least 1729 (fig.50), which had thinner handles (cut out from flat sheets rather than cast) with much more simplistic designs, all variations on two themes: either a broad, pointed triangle with multiple-ogee sides or something akin to a child's cut-out of a lady in a skirt.

The first of these themes was taken up by Anne Tanqueray (c1729; fig.51) and by Thomas England (1730), in both cases their only surviving strainers that I know of. I've referred before (p.63) to Crewdson's understandable belief that handles were sub-contracted by bowl makers to handle-making specialists and I'm happy that this may well have been the case – but only sometimes. It is notable that most of the numerous silversmiths whose lemon strainer production was very sparse – and no fewer than 74 (59%) of the 126 London strainer makers in my databases are represented by one solitary surviving strainer – used handles which, although fitting in with the prevailing 'zeitgeist', were distinctive and often unique. This suggests that, even if the major strainer makers did share handle patterns because they had suppliers in common, these one-off makers often made their own.

A case in point is John White's strainer, hallmarked in 1730, whose handles have another variation on the 'child's cut-out' theme, but the 'lady' has a top-knot and a broad ruff around her neck.

Beware, however, of oddly unique strainer handles, especially if they're unmarked and unengraved: sometimes they mean that the 'strainer' is in fact a fraud, a conversion for example from a salt cellar. For more on this, look at London Group 10, the 'Oddities'.

LONDON GROUP 4: TWO OPEN SHELL-ENDED HANDLES

Three Groups of lemon strainers arrived on the London scene at around the same time at the beginning of the 1730s, destined to supersede all three of the previous styles. Two of these were the first strainers with openwork handles, made of a single cast piece of silver comprising two scroll-shaped side-struts and an end-strut connecting them. The struts were solid (they were too narrow to be cast with perforations within them), but – in addition to their three-dimensional scrolling shapes – decoration took the form of stylised foliage and, in this Group 4, a shell motif in the middle of the end-strut.

The shell-ended strainers tended to be a cut above the others with open, scroll-sided handles (in Groups 6 and 7): they were usually heavier, both the bowls and the handles being of thicker-gauge silver, and the shell itself was part of a greater overall handle complexity and beauty. A fair proportion of them, right into the 1770s, had bowls pierced with crosslets and scroll shapes rather than just dot holes, while most of the contemporary, standard, scroll-sided strainers had only dot-hole decoration. Fewer were produced (56) than the standard ones (110 in Group 6 and 62 in Group 7, totalling 172) and they would have been among the more expensive strainers on sale at the time.

Fig.52: London 1749, Benjamin West

The earliest shell-end-handled strainers I know of date from 1733, one by Richard Gosling with a central panel in the bowl of dots and crosslets surrounded by splash patterns and smaller floral scrolls; each handle has, both at its base and on either side of its shell, pairs of stylised foliate 'flourishes'. A similar handle design, but with the shell reduced to a round-ended strut, graces another with a worn maker's mark and a very attractive bowl design with rosettes and 'upside-down' splashes surrounded by 'cartouches' of dots; this strainer was billed by an auctioneer in 2006 as from '1793', but I suspect that its date-letter 'S' pertained to 60 years earlier. The Metropolitan Museum in New York has one from 1737 with handles close to Gosling's, "possibly by John Albright"; but there's no evidence of any Albright strainers after 1724, so this is an unlikely attribution; the rubbed mark may be for John Gamon who was active at the time and whose bowls in some of his Group-5 strainers have similar geometric dot-hole designs. Then in 1749, Benjamin West made one with crosslets, splashes and scrolls in the bowl and with virtually identical handles (fig.52): a throw-back which seems perfectly genuine. And a rare strainer by Samuel Courtauld, from 1755, also used similar handles with their foliate 'side-shoots', both at the base and on either side of the shell terminal.

Fig.53: London c1749, probably Edward Aldridge I   *Fig.54: London 1742, Paul de Lamerie*

From 1739 until the 1760s, the general fashion for rococo in silver found its expression in shell-ended strainer handles: the side-strut scrolls ended in relief swirls and had leaf-capped edges; and areas of 'matt' chasing sometimes added to the 3-D effects. The shell itself, of course, is a classic rococo motif, the word 'rococo' stemming from the French 'rocaille' meaning rocky ground, typically graced with sea-shells, pebbles and plants. A few of these came from the workshops of George Greenhill Jones, Francis Crump (fig.55) and Edward Aldridge I (fig.53), but this was a style particularly popular with the great Paul de Lamerie, whose best silverware is so magnificent and of such excellent quality of artistry and execution that he is widely regarded as the best silversmith of all time and even his more modest productions command very high prices, lemon strainers included. (I may rate strainers as 'modest', but much more humdrum items by de Lamerie create flurries of excitement on the market, even simple spoons.) His strainer bowls are heavy and he went in for small, densely-packed dot-holes in subtle floral designs (fig.54). His handles had single- or double-scroll sides and, in one of 1739, the basal scrolls have transmogrified into lion's-head pedestals.

Fig.55: London 1742, Francis Crump

Fig.56: Bowl piercing in Crump 1742

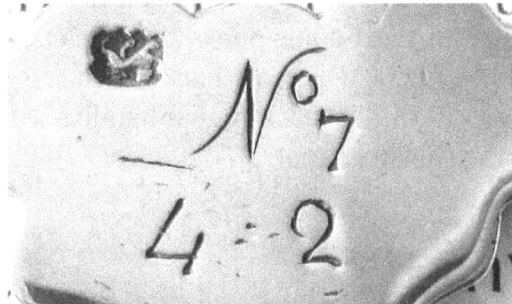

Fig.57: Lion passant, scratch weight & 'No 7' under the
shell of one of Crump's 1742 strainer handles

Francis Crump's solitary strainer, of 1742, is one of the most beautiful of all, with compact single-scroll sides to the ornate handles and a spectacular bowl piercing design with crosslets and splashes and an outer band of dots and dashes, C-scrolls and stylised flower motifs (figs 55,56). Mysteriously, along with its scratch weight (4oz 2dwt) it has 'No 7' engraved under one of the shells (fig.57); this would normally suggest that it was one of a set of seven or more, but this seems unlikely as there's no evidence that Georgian households possessed more than one lemon strainer at a time. It could be that a set of identical *handles* was cast for or by Francis Crump and soldered to different strainer bowls for different clients, in the manner of a 'limited edition'. I know of only one other 'numbered' lemon strainer, which is in the London Group 7, made by John Harvey I in c1760 and with an "engraved number 1" on it.

Fig.58: London 1742, Paul de Lamerie

Another sub-set of this shell-ended Group, in the 1740s and 50s, involved the soldered application of an extra cast rim which is broad, flat, pierced with scrolls and trefoils and edged with shells and scrolls in relief. Paul de Lamerie made at least one of these as well (fig.58) and all have handles as ornately rococo as those with standard bowl rims. Other makers of this type of strainer were Edward Aldridge I, on his own and in partnership with John Stamper, and Samuel Herbert and Co. Not all had the short, stumpy handles of the de Lamerie example above: some were twice as long.

The undersides of these elaborate handles were quite flat and smooth, showing that they were made by pouring molten Sterling silver into open, one-sided moulds. This was probably the case with *all* lemon strainer handles (except for the Plymouth ones made from sheet silver curved into ring shapes, the London cannon-handles and a few of the London Group-3 flat, solid ones), even back in the 17th century: the backs are always smooth, in contrast to any three-dimensional effects on their upper surfaces.

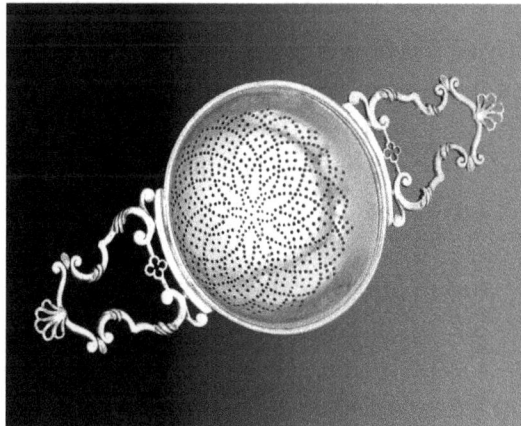

Fig.59: London c1755, William Solomon

William Solomon, best known for his oversized pierced handles and distinctive, geometric bowl piercings, made one unique strainer with a dense floral bowl design and handles with openwork shell ends and a basal cross-strut carrying a quatrefoil (fig.59).

71

Fig.60: London 1758, David Hennell I

In the late 1750s and early 1760s, some strainers had handles with much more restrained designs, resembling the standard single-scroll, arc-ended type (Group 6), differing only in retaining the terminal shell motif (fig.60).

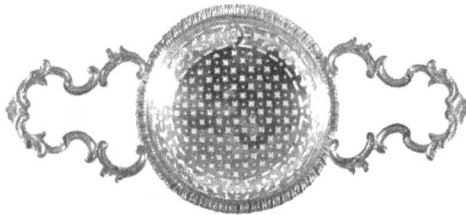

Fig.61: London 1765, Samuel Herbert & Co.   *Fig.62: London 1771, Charles Aldridge & Henry Green*

Then, led by Samuel Herbert & Co. in the 1760s, there was a final burst of handle flamboyance, along with enhancement by gadrooning of the bowls' rims (fig.61). As Neoclassicism became the fashion in the early 1770s, the scrolls on the handles were beaded and more restrained in their shapeliness (fig.62); bowls were often beaded as well (or reeded). The final 18th-century style, mirroring the strainers of Group 9 in the late 1770s, employed simple 'loop' handles made from shaped wire, on which the shells at the ends look a little incongruous.

There was a reprise of the shell-ended lemon strainer in the Regency period: one example survives from 1821, made by John Reily in heavy-gauge silver with Rococo Revival handles and bold gadrooning on the rim and handles, with the added flourish of a shell-shaped side-clip, and I know of a less substantial strainer in this group from c1830.

LONDON GROUP 5: TWO SHAPED, ENGRAVED OR RELIEF-CAST HANDLES

The lemon strainers in this Group have only two criteria in common: firstly, they don't readily fit into any of the other categories and, secondly, they have solid (or sparsely pierced) and shaped handles with a strong three-dimensional surface effect, created either by deep engraving or by casting a relief pattern (or both). Most of them count among the most opulent and valuable lemon strainers made by

London silversmiths, produced in very small numbers between the 1730s and the 1760s, and each one an expression of creativity unfettered by financial concerns. I imagine that they were commissioned by wealthy, probably aristocratic, clients as one-off status symbols to be shown off during the lavish entertainment of important members of society.

Fig.63: London 1734, Edward Aldridge I   Fig.64: London 1731, Paul de Lamerie

The first example, by Edward Aldridge I in 1734 (fig.63), would belong in Group 2 if it weren't for the engraved upper surface, as its shaped, triangular handles are pierced. The perforations highlight the curvaceous scrolling edges and the stylised foliage and shell motif facing inwards from them. All of the solid parts, including the central oval medallion, are incised with deep channels, giving added definition to the design. The scrolling sides have more in common with Group-6 cast, openwork handles, which were just coming into fashion at the time. Interestingly, Gurney & Cooke, in 1738, used a handle design of the same shape but entirely lacking the engraving; so that one belongs in Group 2.

The second strainer in this Group, by Paul de Lamerie in 1731 (fig.64), has solid, flat handles with a complex outline created by deeply engraved scrolls at the edges and a terminal shell; the central medallion is also deeply incised around its perimeter and the 'infill' between medallion and scroll-and-shell has an engraved 'brickwork' pattern. The crest – on both handles – is for Sir Charles Kerneys, Baronet, who died in 1735 and the strainer passed to his nephew and remained in the family of the Barons Wharton until being sold by Christie's, London in 1970, for £1250, the equivalent of over £20,000 in 2020. It was up for sale again at Sotheby's in 1981, featured in the 1990 exhibition of de Lamerie's silver at Goldsmiths' Hall in the City of London and was one of 32 lots of de Lamerie silverware owned by the eminent Bolivian collector Jaime Ortiz-Patiño on sale by Sotheby's, New York in 1998. It fetched the colossal sum of $48,875, worth over £29,000 at the time and making it the most valuable lemon strainer ever sold.

Fig.65: London c1740, Edward Aldridge I   Fig.66: London c1740, Paul Crespin

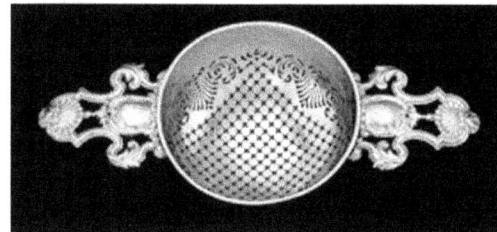

Fig,67: London 1751, Paul Crespin

Another collector, John A. Hyman in Virginia, USA (see p.33), had two strainers from this Group in his possession which he loaned to the Colonial Williamsburg museum from 1989 and 1990. Both are large (about 23 cm across the handles), neither is hallmarked and they have different makers: Edward Aldridge I (fig.65) and Paul Crespin (fig.66). Like the rest of the strainers in this opulent Group, their handles were cast (by pouring molten silver into a mould), so that their surface patterns stand out in bold relief. Crespin's handles had their 'infill' areas cut out, but their overall shape and the design of their leafy scrolls, shell and medallion were otherwise identical; both had intricate – but different – bowl piercing patterns. The same handles (as Aldridge's) reoccurred on another large Crespin strainer hallmarked in 1741, which has a splendidly ornate bowl pattern and formed part of the Albert Collection in the late 20th century. Crespin's later (1751) example (fig.67) is one of the crowning glories of this Group of lemon strainers, over 30 cm long and weighing 8oz 10dwt (272g). It boasts a glorious bowl design of panels of crosslets contrasting with sinuous scrolls and has very long handles edged with leafy scrolls and a large shell, the infill areas appearing to have been carved with their own scrolls and shell. The handle shape is similar to the previous Crespin (and Aldridge) examples with two 'wings' near the base and a narrow 'waist' between it and the shell end. This is the strainer that was sold from the Rothman Collection by Christie's in London in 1995, fetched US$14,950 in 1997 at Christie's in New York and is currently for sale by a prestigious New York silver dealer with a ticket price of $27,500.

Fig.68: London 1767, William Plummer

The final pieces in this Group are an identical pair by William Plummer, hallmarked in 1767 and 1769, very nearly as big as Crespin's masterpiece (28.6 cm in length and weighing about 8oz – 250g – each) and absolutely unique, in both bowls and handles (fig.68). In each of the strainers, the bowl – very unusually – is cast rather than raised, shaped in eight segments reminiscent of a sliced orange or lemon; its piercing pattern is a highly intricate concentration of innumerable short swirls and curved dashes, some radiating out into complex 'splashes'; its rim is not only delicately gadrooned but is also sinuous, both up and down and in and out. The cast handles hark back in outline to the Crespin ones with their scroll sides, shell end and central medallion, but their infill areas are partly cut out and partly occupied by sculptural and asymmetrical bunches of grapes, larger fruits and leaves. The earlier one bears a crest and the later one a cipher (probably 'MJS'), in each case doubled-up on both handle medallions.

The two were sold together from the Makower Collection in one Sotheby's lot in 1961 (for the equivalent in 2020 terms of over £11,000) and again at the same auction house two years later (for the equivalent of £13,650). Between those dates, it seems, they had been exhibited at the Victoria & Albert Museum – which is where the 1769 strainer ended up in 1993 and can now be viewed by the public in the Whiteley Galleries. The two were split in 1966, when this later one was sold by Christie's in St James's at the bargain price of the equivalent of £4,750.

Paul de Lamerie and Paul Crespin were general silversmiths of the very top calibre, famous for their fabulous interpretations of the rococo fashion and overall excellent quality of workmanship. So it is no surprise that some of the few lemon strainers made in their workshops rank amongst London's finest. Edward Aldridge I and William Plummer, however, were much more specialised and prolific strainer makers (and makers of other pierced items, including baskets and serving trowels) and they presumably catered successfully for the noblemen, gentry and merchants who couldn't afford to patronise de Lamerie and Crespin. But, as we saw with Aldridge's Group-4 strainers with pierced and shell-and-scroll applied rims, Aldridge and Plummer were just as capable as de Lamerie and Crespin of making top-quality lemon strainers. We don't know who first created these magnificent new handles, but their designs (and possibly their casting moulds) must have been shared between the most prestigious silversmiths and their 'lesser' colleagues in the trade.

LONDON GROUP 6: TWO OPEN, SINGLE-SCROLL-SIDED, ARC-ENDED HANDLES

In 1730, as Group-2 strainers with their broad, flat, pierced handles were dwindling in popularity and Group-3 strainers with their broad, flat, solid handles only had about four years left in production, a radical new handle style appeared. Rather than comprising a thin slab of silver, it had an open construction of narrow – but thicker – struts. For the rest of the century (and beyond), the basic design of these struts barely altered: each of the two side-struts is in the shape of an 'S' scroll with an incurving base and stylised leafage on the outside edge, attached to an end-strut shaped as a simple arc, usually with simple channel moulding along its outer edge. Each handle would have been cast as a whole, in an open, one-sided mould (their lower surfaces – the upper, open surfaces when in the mould – are always flat and smooth) and would have required very little more than smoothing off after casting. Variations on the theme were limited to the relative length of the arc, the length and sinuosity of the scrolls and the size and definition of the 'foliage'. The centre of the arc is typically 33-42 mm out from the rim of the bowl. The earliest examples can normally be recognised by their more rounded or bevelled upper edges.

The bowls remained unchanged, to begin with, from standard Group-2 and Group-3 strainers, typically barely more than 80 mm in diameter and with their 'double-fillet' rim-strengthening. Piercing patterns varied enormously, from dot-holes in floral and geometric designs to elaborate patterns of scrolls, curved dashes and crosslet panels (and combinations of the two). Although two lemon strainers with this handle style are very rarely exactly alike in their bowl piercings, some of their makers did have their own recognisable peculiarities. The elaborate, chiselled and sawn patterns died out in about 1745 and not long afterwards bowls became wider, providing a bigger area for more complex dot-hole designs. They also became flatter-bottomed and with slightly protruding, bellied 'sides'.

The rims of the bowls changed as well, quite quickly losing their applied double fillet (two close-set ridges with a channel between), so that by about 1740 they had developed a wider rim soldered to a broad outward-curving ring, which was itself soldered to the raised bowl. This meant that each bowl comprised three separate pieces before soldering: a flat circular ring on top, a moulded circular band below it and the belly-sided base. As always in London, the piercing was carried out after the strainer had been returned from the assay office.

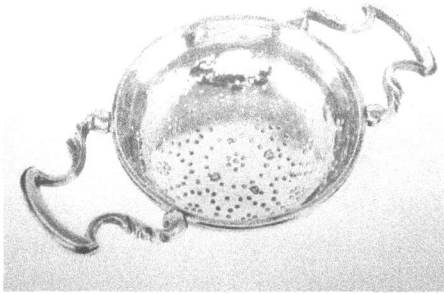

Fig.69: London 1730, John Luff

Fig.70: London 1731, Samuel Welder

Fig.71: London ?1734, John Luff

Fig.72: London 1740, John Luff

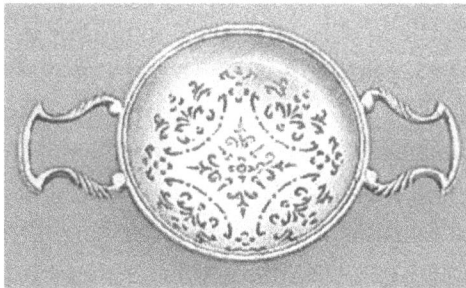

Fig.73: London 1739, David Hennell I

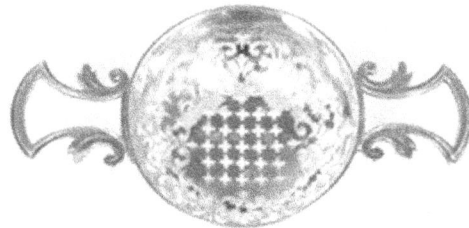

Fig.74: London ?1739, maker's mark indistinct

The earliest makers in this style included silversmiths adept at the previous ones, such as Samuel Welder (fig.70), John Gamon and George Greenhill Jones, but a new name is synonymous with the start of the new fashion: John Luff. His lemon strainers are known from between 1730 and 1742 (figs 69,71,72), but because of his relative obscurity as a silversmith, auctioneers have ascribed his 'I.L' initials (either Roman letters over a stalked trefoil or – after 1739 – in script under a trefoil) to other makers like James Langlois and John Lampfert; and rubbed marks showing '?L' are rarely recognised as Luff's. The unregistered and unidentified mark (Grimwade's No. 3650) of 'I.L, mullet above' was almost certainly his too, as I know of two unhallmarked strainers, stamped four times with this mark, which are very much in his style. He had a wide range of piercing designs at his disposal, many strikingly beautiful, all interesting and none of them – it seems – copied by or from any other silversmiths.

Most auctioneers do not supply underside photographs of lemon strainers, nor do they mention extra marks in their descriptions, so it is not easy to know how regularly these new handles were separately assayed at Goldsmiths' Hall and hallmarked with the lion passant. Of the 110 strainers in my database which belong to this Group, 20 are definitely handle-hallmarked and 12 (which are marked in the bowl) are definitely not; 10 of the marked ones have both lion passant and maker's mark, in all but one case on the undersides of *both* handles; the remaining 10 hallmarked handles bear the lion passant only, half involving just one handle. I've been unable to establish why the London Assay Office was so inconsistent, given that all the handles in this Group were cast and soldered on to raised, hammered bowls, so that there was always the chance that bowl and handles came from different sources of silver alloy; I imagine (without evidence) that Goldsmiths' Hall *did* assay both bowl and handles but did not always find it necessary to indicate that the handles' silver purity had been found satisfactory (see also pp. 30-31).

Fig.75: London 1733, probably James Stone

One that has one handle stamped with the lion passant is a lovely early example of 1733, by 'IS' (probably James Stone; fig.75), which did the rounds of auction houses and then came into the hands of an online dealer who supplies excellent photographs (and who made the attribution to James Stone on the basis of a fault in the punch below the letter 'S', identical to his known mark on a salt cellar on which the distinctive cinquefoil above his 'IS' had not been pierced through). Stephen Helliwell, in his *Collecting Small Silverware*, illustrated an identical-looking 'fruit strainer' from 1739 with maker's mark not specified, which could also have been a Stone production. Not dissimilar is a 1735 strainer by 'WG' (probably William Garrard) which came up for auction in late 2020 and another probably from the same year, maker unknown, which belonged to the first signatory of the American Declaration of Independence and Massachusetts' first Governor, John Hancock.

Fig.76: London 1734, John Gamon

Fig.77: London 1737, John Gamon

John Gamon (figs 76,77) had his fair share of misattributions too, thanks no doubt to the perennial problem with strainers: piercing carried out after the punching of all the marks and with a greater desire for correct design than caution over the partial disappearance of the marks. One quite prestigious auction house thought that one of his was by John Clare I, who had been dead for eight years before its hallmarked date of 1736. A nice strainer with crosslet, splash and scroll piercing in the bowl came up for sale at auction in 2020 with the maker's mark of Dinah Gamon (set in a diamond punch meaning that she had been widowed), hallmarked for 1740; John had died some time after his last known strainer's assay (1738) and she presumably registered her own mark to continue – or wind up – the business.

Of the 110 lemon strainers belonging to this Group in my databases, no fewer than 26 – a quarter of them – have a maker's mark so rubbed or pierced (or not found or non-existent) that it cannot be surely identified.

Fig.78: London 1731, Paul Crespin

Interpreting auctioneers' photographs can be frustrating, especially historic ones for which condition reports and supplementary images can't be requested (never mind the possibility of handling the piece in person). An intriguing Group-6 lemon strainer by Paul Crespin (1731) came up for sale in Essex in 2018 with a highly original piercing design in the bowl (fig.78) and a lion passant under one handle, making it likely that the handles were *bona fide* and fitted in Crespin's workshop; yet a close-up of one of them showed that it had long rectangular supporting brackets soldered under the rim of the bowl, as if they'd been reattached later. It's possible, of course, that this was Crespin's way, in 1731, of ensuring stronger contact with the bowl than is normally afforded by soldering the small rounded base of each handle.

Even when a strainer can be handled and examined personally, if it isn't purchased it can leave unanswered questions. This was true of a Paul de Lamerie strainer at an antiques fair, fully hallmarked in the bowl for 1734 (among the crosslets and scroll perforations) but with peculiar handles with *outward-curving* bases, very pronounced foliage protruding from the side-struts and (as I remember) thread-moulding decoration throughout. These handles were not marked. Sadly I wasn't permitted to take photographs of the strainer as it didn't belong to the dealer who had it for sale (for almost £7,850). Earlier that year, a Colchester auction house had offered a similar strainer, with very similar handles and a closely-related bowl pattern, with hallmarks and maker's mark indistinct and a "possibly 1779" date attribution (fig.74). Although the punch shapes are different, the 'd' date letters for 1739 and 1779 are the same, so I suspect that this strainer hailed from 1739. An unsolved conundrum!

Fig.79: London c1740-45, Louis Dupont

After the Luff era ended in 1742 and before the prolific strainer-makers Edward Aldridge I, Samuel Herbert & Company and William Plummer cornered the market from the late 1740s, there were a number of strainers in this Group by 'one-off' makers and sometimes in eccentric styles. Louis Dupont's foreshortened handles and old-fashioned concentric rings of bowl dots (with a central rosette) is a case in point (fig.79): it is struck twice with Dupont's distinctive mark, was unattributed and failed to sell at one auction house in 2018 but managed to reach its reserve at another in 2019, when it was described as "18th century American". One with similar concentric rings but more standard handles, from 1746, was the work of Peter Taylor and sold in North Carolina in 2008. Another from that year whose central bowl panel of pierced crosslets appeared to be unfinished was offered in 2003 and attributed to Robert Innes, who Grimwade believed to have specialised in inkstands. These makers – as well as Fuller White, who produced a strainer in 1751 with an unusual four-pointed star, delineated by triangles, and a central four-armed 'squiggle' in its bowl – had unmistakeable marks, so there is no reason to doubt the auctioneers' attributions. Phillips Garden, some of whose work bore such strong similarities to de Lamerie's that there was an unsubstantiated suggestion he had bought de Lamerie's posthumous tools and casting moulds at a 1752 auction, also made a Group-6 lemon strainer in 1743, surprisingly lightweight in construction but not unique in design: its piercing pattern was used by David Hennell 14 years later in a Group-7 strainer. Finally, among the eccentric Group-6 strainers from the 1740s, one from 1748 was sold in Canada in 2015 with a unique bowl pattern of seven circles, each composed of three concentric rings of dots; unfortunately, its maker was not given by the auction house.

Fig.80: London 1748, Edward Aldridge I

Fig.81: London c1750, Edward Aldridge I

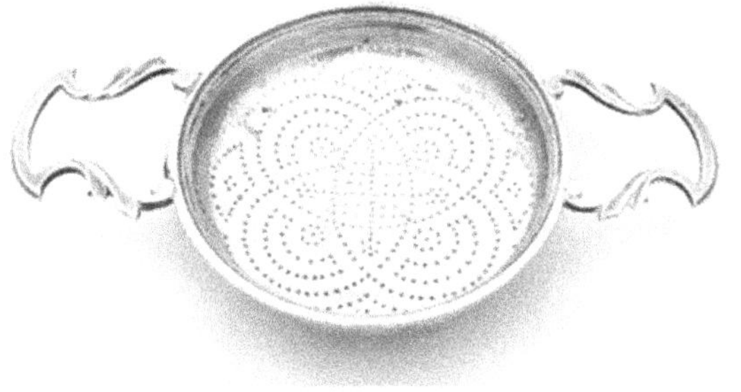

Fig.82: London 1751, Edward Aldridge I

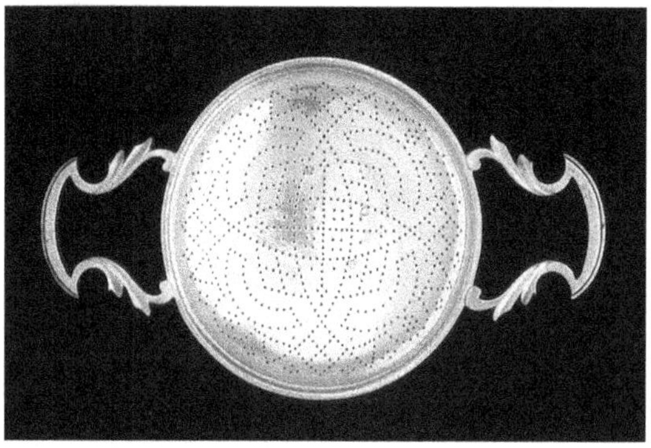

Fig.83: London 1755, probably Edward Aldridge I

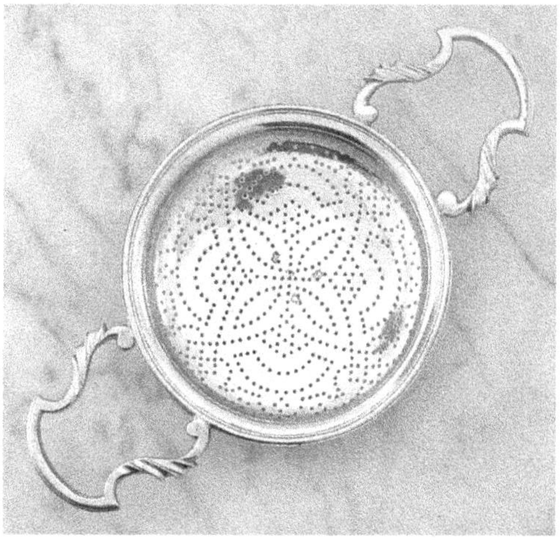

Fig.84: London 1754, maker's mark pierced through

Edward Aldridge one of the two most prolific lemon strainer makers in London (and indeed anywhere). He had a very long working life, entering his first mark in 1724 and probably dying on the job in 1766, but he must have started late as a strainer maker, as his first that I know of was from 1734 (mentioned under Group 5) and his main period of productivity was from 1743 until 1766, with his commonest style being Group 7 with longer, double-scroll handles. My databases contain 45 of his strainers, in six of the London Groups (e.g. figs 80-83).

Although Aldridge's first mark was a straightforward Roman 'EA', from 1739 onwards he registered one mark in script capitals and used at least six other marks, which were unregistered, three of them in Gothic lower-case letters. This has led to a welter of confusion, from "Benjamin Cartwright" (whose Gothic 'BC' looks like an upside-down version of Aldridge's Gothic 'ea') to "BD (Untraced)" (another upside-down Aldridge) and "SA". I agree with the Canadian antiques dealer who identified in 2013 that the partly rubbed mark on the 1746 strainer he had for sale was Grimwade's unregistered and unidentified mark number 3543 (seen on a pap boat from 1749), and I think this might have been yet another of Edward Aldridge's private marks.

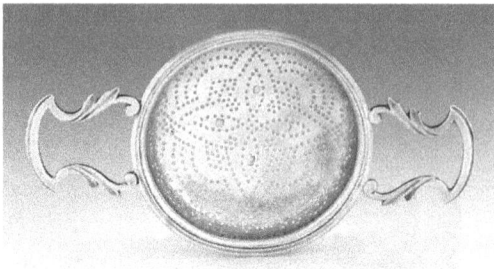

Fig.85: London 1762, Edward Aldridge I & II

Fig.86: London 1770, Charles Aldridge & Henry Green

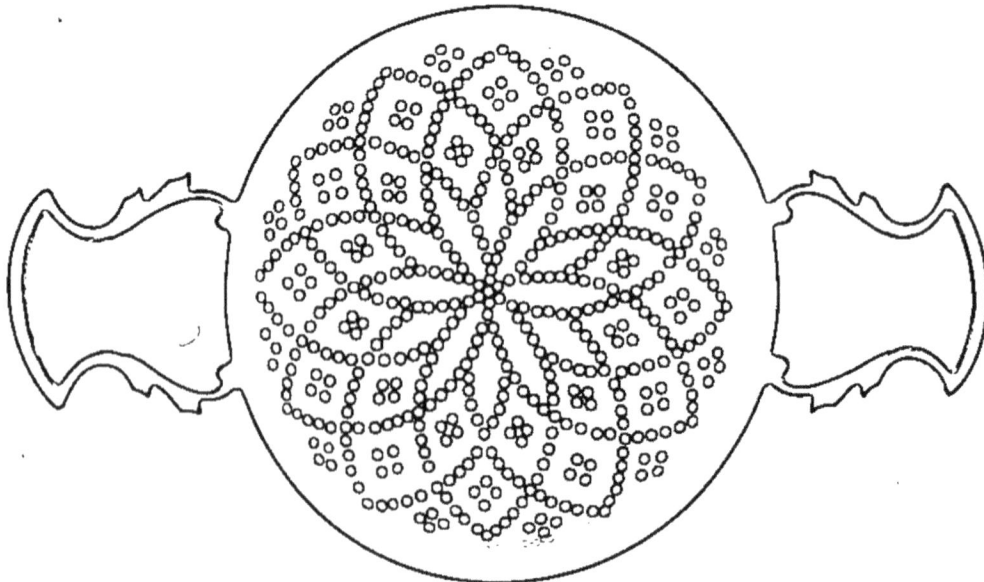

Fig.87: London 1770, Charles Aldridge & Henry Green (stencil of fig.86)

Two of Aldridge's apprentices were believed to be nephews of his, one of whom, Edward Aldridge II, went into partnership with his uncle for a short period (including 1760 and 1762, when three lemon strainers bore their combined mark, e.g. fig.85). The uncle also had a partnership with John Stamper in the mid-1750s, but sending strainers for assay wasn't their forte, it seems, as only three of the six of their strainers that I've come across were hallmarked. The second nephew, Charles Aldridge, had a partnership with Henry Green, whose start date is uncertain but there is a lemon strainer of theirs, in this Group, dated 1770 (figs 86,87); most of their production was of later styles and lasted until the mid-1780s.

In 1766, some silver wares – including a lemon strainer – appeared with an 'EA' in a diamond-shaped punch, the sign of a widow. Elizabeth Aldridge, whom Edward I had married in 1723, presumably wound down the business after his death by registering her own mark (fig.104). Between 1768 and 1771, a few more strainers appeared with 'EA' in a normal rectangle and were invariably credited to Edward Aldridge I, despite his likely decease in 1766; and I've also seen a cake basket from 1772 with this mark. It's possible that his nephew Edward II had a mark of his own before he partnered John Henry Vere, which was either unregistered or lost with the missing register of largeworker silversmiths. Again, most of these strainers belong in Groups other than this Group 6.

Descriptions of Aldridge bowl designs are no easier than any others from the mid-18th century, when bowls were wide enough to sport complex patterns of densely-packed holes. Many are variations on the 'flower petals' theme. In one, 12 overlapping petals create a central 12-petalled flower, and the interstices are filled with quartets of dots. Another has a ring of 6-petalled flowers, with neighbours sharing one petal, their inward-facing petals together forming another 6-petalled flower in the centre. Others still have a hint of the floral, but are largely geometric, for example based on a central 4-pointed star with broad, curved arms and curved, parallel-sided segments between the arms, along with squares or diamonds often divided into four compartments. In some cases 'lollipops' – straight lines ending in clusters or rings of dots – form part of the pattern. The area outside the main piercing pattern is 'filled in' with clusters, semicircles and triangles.

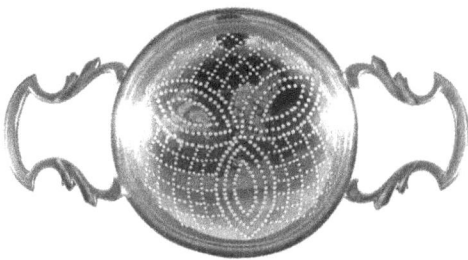

Fig.88: London 1755, William Plummer   *Fig.89: London 1774, William Plummer*

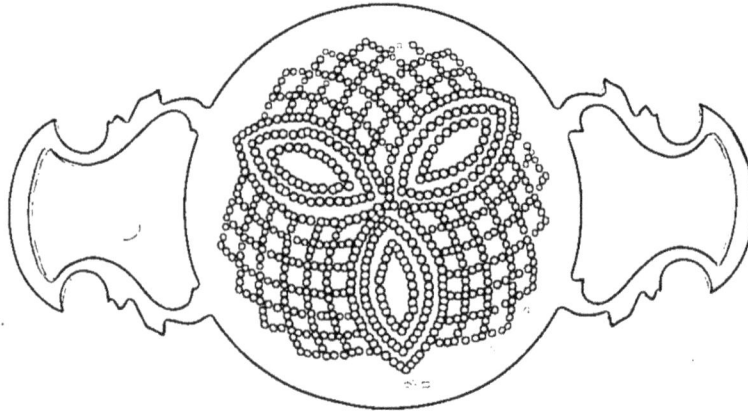

Fig.90: London 1755, William Plummer (stencil of fig.88)

Equally as productive a London lemon strainer maker was William Plummer, also with 45 to his name in my databases, who – like Edward Aldridge I – had a very long career. His master during his apprenticeship was none other than Edward Aldridge I (who was some 30 years older than Plummer). He entered his first mark in 1755 and was still working in 1793. All three of his marks bore a simple Roman 'WP' but he did give his cartouche a flourish with four indentations. Like Aldridge, he specialised in pierced silverware.

Although the great majority of Plummer's lemon strainers were one-handled (in Group 8), the earliest of his that I know of (from 1755; figs 88,90) belongs in this twin-handled Group 6 and has a unique bowl pattern with a central three-armed star, set in a net-like lattice. It has, under its rim on the outside of the bowl, a crest under a viscount's coronet, most probably pertaining to Lionel Tollemache of Helmingham Hall, Suffolk, who was 21 years old in 1755 and fifteen years later became the 5th Earl of Dysart.

Fig.91: London 1752, Samuel Herbert & Co.

Another prolific strainer maker was Samuel Herbert, who entered his first mark in 1747, but whose second mark (1750) revealed that he had gone into partnership with someone whose initials were 'HB' but who has never been identified. The partnership (given as 'Samuel Herbert & Co.' by Grimwade, but I would have preferred 'Samuel Herbert & partner') lasted for the rest of Herbert's career, until at least 1768. They are represented by 26 lemon strainers in my databases, including seven in this Group ranging from 1752 to 1765, all of which had standard bowl designs not dissimilar to Edward Aldridge's (fig.91).

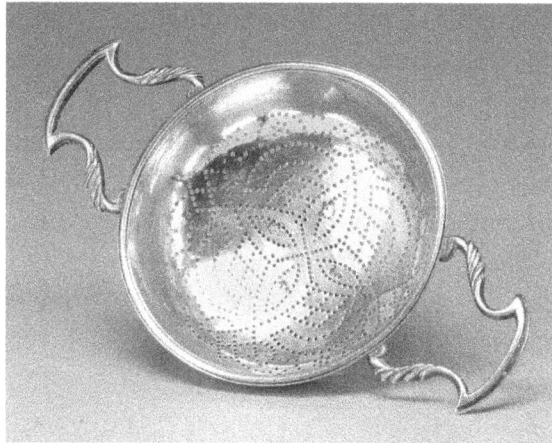

Fig.92: London 1750, possibly David Hennell I

David Hennell I was the first of what turned out to be three generations of London silversmiths in the family: one of his sons (Robert I), three of his grandsons (David II, Samuel and Robert II) and a great-grandson (Robert III) followed in his footsteps, some of whom had temporary partnerships with each other. David I, Robert I and David II all left lemon strainers for posterity, made between 1736 and 1799. David I's later strainers in this Group used standard floral and geometric patterns (fig.92), but his earliest one (1739) had a unique arrangement of small floral scrolls in one central and four peripheral groups, separated by four curved lines of dots and dashes (fig.73).

Fig.93: London c1778, Hester Bateman

Fig.94: London ?c1790, maker's mark rubbed

The Hester Bateman lemon strainer in this category (fig.93) has no hallmarks, but the well-known ornate script initials 'HB' appear in a punch under one of the handles. The London dealer who had it for sale claimed that this dated the piece as "c1774" because the mark ("Hester Bateman's earliest recorded") was registered in 1774. Actually the mark is subtly different from the 1774 one and was registered in 1778 (and her first mark had been entered back in 1761). For more on Hester Bateman, see p. 92.

The great majority of these two-handled Group-6 strainers, from the late 1730s onwards, had plain rims to their bowls, made of a flat (or slightly curved) ring soldered to a broader, moulded band below. Only occasionally was the uppermost ring beaded (Aldridge 1761 and 1762) or gadrooned ('W.T', probably William Tuite, 1768; 'RM', probably Richard Meach, 1771; and 'RN', possibly Richard

Norman, 1775). The 'RM' was attributed by a London dealer to Richard Mills, but Richard Meach – who is known for ten other lemon strainers – is, I believe, the more likely silversmith.

Needless to say, the rule about Group-6 strainers having outward-curving bowl rims after the 1730s has at least one exception. A large example, completely unmarked and with a bowl pattern reminiscent of two of David Hennell I's, probably made in the mid-1750s, has a plain, vertical top to its rim and its strengthening has an exterior 'fillet' arrangement like all strainers had before the 1730s. It is doubly unusual because it has an extra ridge and channel – it could be called 'triple-fillet' – which was maybe necessary because of the particularly heavy gauge of the strainer. Why it wasn't marked, goodness knows, but it does bear a (probably) contemporary cipher, 'AML', so it obviously had a good home.

Similarly, the anomalous strainer (fig.94) with a piercing pattern of concentric rings and rubbed marks, tentatively dated by two dealers as 'c1760' and 'c1750', also has a double-fillet rim, but its handles are soldered *below* the channel rather than within it; the handles, with their long end-arcs, are the same as those used by Peter & Ann Bateman in 1793 and I'm inclined to date this strainer at c1790.

Fig.95: London 1768, W.T (possibly William Tuite)

Finally, I return to the theme that silversmiths whose existing lemon strainers are 'one-offs' or very rare tended not to toe the 'party line', as it were, in terms of their designs, in this case in their bowl piercings. 'RN''s solitary strainer with its heavily gadrooned rim was unusual in its simple pattern of concentric rings of dots in its bowl (*and* its handle scrolls, instead of protruding stylised leafage, merely have parallel incisions across the struts). The 1768 'William Tuite' strainer, also a one-off and also with a gadrooned rim, has a three-petalled flower in the bowl, bisected by a large double triangle, itself 'cut through' by double semicircles of dots: a completely unique pattern (fig.95). And one of Walter Brind's scarce strainers (1760) has its own eccentric pattern of a central dot-filled 6-pointed star surrounded by three rings of six joined arcs. It seems as if the main strainer makers 'compared notes' with each other, so that their designs – albeit varied – had more shared characteristics than the patterns created by the 'outsider' makers. This is reminiscent of the observation I made earlier about handle patterns in Group-3 strainers, some of which were shared between the most productive strainer makers but ignored by other silversmiths who only made the odd strainer (p.68).

LONDON GROUP 7: TWO OPEN, TWO- OR THREE-SCROLL-SIDED, ARC-ENDED HANDLES

The lemon strainers in this Group differ from the previous Group only in having the side-struts of their (cast) handles made of *two* (or rarely *three*) scrolls in series, which make the handles longer. Typical handles in Group 6 are 33-42 mm long (along the mid-line from bowl rim to arc end), while the longest in Group 7 is 93 mm and the average is between 60 and 70mm. As I've suggested earlier, this may not necessarily mean that they were designed to rest on wider receptacles, but merely that they would have been more eye-catching protruding from the container, and handle length may have been seen as a measure of the owner's status. Average bowl diameter was greater, but there was a lot of overlap between the two Groups in this parameter.

Fig.96: London 1752, Benjamin West

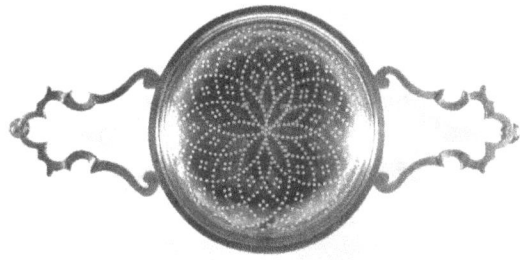

Fig.97: London 1752, Thomas Rush

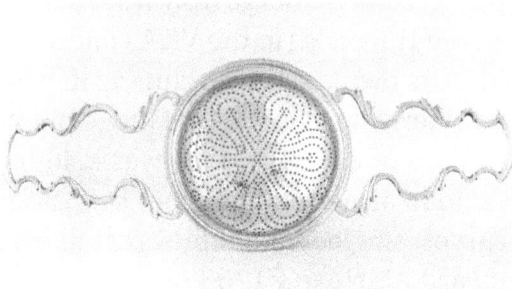

Fig.98: London 1753, Edward Aldridge I & John Stamper

Fig.99: London c1760, maker's mark rubbed

Single-scroll-handled strainers had been on the market for all but twenty years before the first twin-scroll handles appeared in 1749, with familiar silversmiths such as Edward Aldridge I and Samuel Herbert & Co. among the pioneers. But they were few and far between, not as popular as their single-scroll cousins, and – in the 1750s and '60s – a sizeable proportion of them came from workshops better known for silverwares *other than* lemon strainers. The makers' list includes Henry Bailey, Richard Gosling, Benjamin West (fig.96), Thomas Rush (fig.97), Charles Chesterman, George Hunter I, Samuel Wight Welles (fig.100) and the unregistered and unidentified partnership of 'IS and AN' (Grimwade No.3689), whereas the likes of William Plummer, David Hennell and Aldridge & Stamper (fig.98) barely got a look in during this time. There are 62 in my database, compared to 110 in Group 6 with the shorter handles.

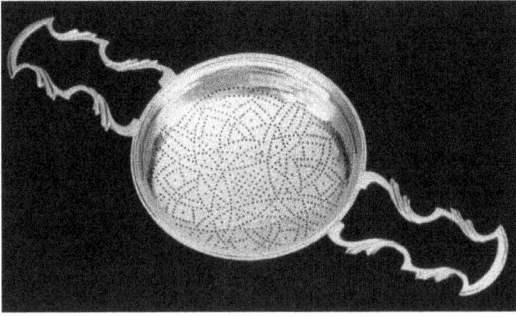

Fig.100: London 1758, Samuel Wight Welles   *Fig.101: London c1765, maker's mark rubbed*

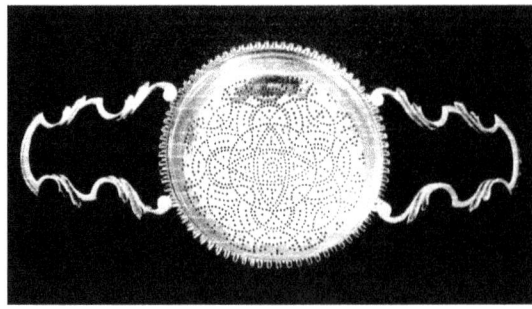

Fig.102: London 1763, Edward Aldridge I

Again, the more unusual bowl piercing patterns came from the least well-known strainer makers, while the familiar names largely used the various designs employed in their single-scroll-handled examples. Samuel Wight Welles's strainer, formerly in the Hyman Collection, has an astonishingly complex geometric design in which four pairs of overlapping 'petals' emerge from a sea of intersecting curves and densely-dotted interstices (fig.100). And George Hunter's (in the V&A collection) has six 'lollipops' radiating from the centre, each head enclosed in its own circle overlapping its neighbours. Perhaps the most intricate dot-patterns of all grace a strainer whose marks are indecipherable (but with lions passant under the handles consistent with a date of c1765), which was sold by a South African dealer at a Cape Town auction in 2019: its central four-armed star and four semicircles inside a single circle are surrounded by a welter of sinuous curves, single and double arcs, all overlapping and infilled with crosses and lines of dots (fig.101). Edward Aldridge's 1763 one with treble-scroll-sided, 93mm-long handles, has a central hexagonal star – made of two intersecting triangles – in a hexafoil surround with an outer area of twirling curves (fig.102).

Fig.103: London 1761, William Solomon (silver-gilt)

A beautiful silver-gilt example, in the Royal Collection, is the only one I know of in this Group with a piercing pattern comprising holes other than plain dots: its central rosette includes six small crosses and radiating from the dot-and-dash ring around it are 12 'splashes'; dots, dashes, crosses and scrolls make up the outer region (fig.103). The maker's mark is rubbed, but decipherable as 'WS with a device above', and is almost certainly one of William Solomon's later creations. The handles are quite unlike his flat, intricately-pierced ones (in Group 2), but they do bear a resemblance to his shell-ended example (fig.59) that was in the Hyman Collection. It is hallmarked 1761 and has the opulent eccentricity of his earlier productions. Silver-gilt lemon strainers are very uncommon and I know of only nine examples, all from London and seven of them made for the King or the Prince of Wales.

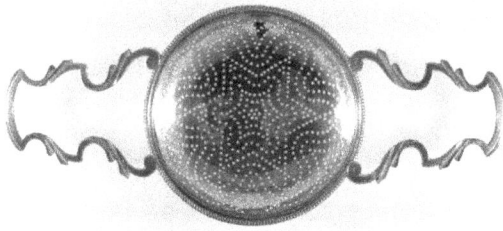

Fig.104: London 1766, Elizabeth Aldridge

Fig.105: London 1767, Samuel Herbert & Co.

Fig.106: London 1769, William Plummer

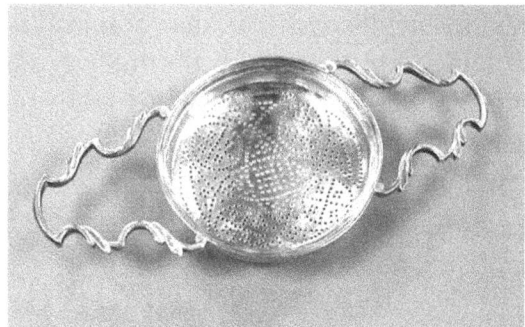

Fig.107: London 1772, probably Thomas Wallis I

Fig.108: London 1774, Richard Meach

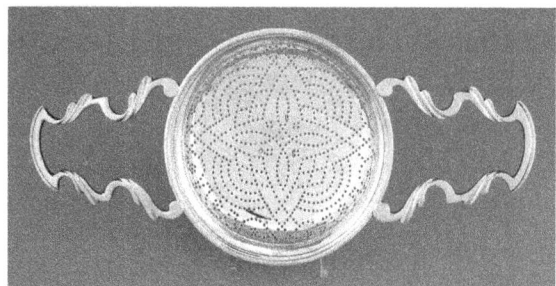

Fig.109: London 1780, Samuel Meriton II

There is relatively little variation in handle shapes in this Group. In the commoner two-scroll examples, the scrolls – particularly the basal one – vary in length. William Plummer's (fig.106) has a particularly short basal section, while the ones from Edward Aldridge's widow Elizabeth (fig.104), 'TW' (probably Thomas Wallis I; fig.107) and Samuel Meriton's (fig.109) have much longer ones. The three-scroll strainers, such as Edward Aldridge I's (fig.102) and Samuel Herbert's (fig.105), have two basal S-scrolls and the extra, third scroll at the end is a shorter C-scroll. The earliest three-scroll-handled strainer that I know of dates from 1753 (Aldridge & Stamper) and both Edward and Charles Aldridge (and their partners) were the main proponents of this type. Another triple-scroll-handle maker's mark was described as looking like 'XX', but this is an artefact of the deeper areas between the makers' letters ('DH and RH') and the star-like punch in which they are set: this strainer was produced by David and Robert Hennell (father and son) in 1764. These extra-long handles with three-scroll sides are prone to distortion and are sometimes seriously skew-whiff.

One minor peculiarity in Group-7 handle design is the lack, in a number of cases, of the inward-scrolling, usually rounded base; instead, the base splays outwards and is often boldly foliate (fig.106).

Only the 1761 silver-gilt strainer, by William Solomon (fig.103), and a 'one-off' by Thomas Rush (1752; fig.97) diverged from the standard handle pattern, the latter dispensing with the typical stylised foliage and having a narrow and semicircular 'arc end', from which an intricately moulded knop-like peg protrudes downwards. Solomon's handles not only bear additional curlicues on their insides and outsides, including at the ends of the terminal arc, but are also joined by an extra, curvaceous framework at the base.

Gadrooning decorated the rims of some of these strainers from about 1760, both a fine, delicate sort (Solomon's silver-gilt strainer is an example of this) and a chunkier form with broader oblique ridges. I know of lemon strainers with the finer type from between about 1760 and 1767 and with the coarser type between 1765 and 1775. In the great majority of cases, however, rims were smooth and unadorned. All these lemon strainers with two- and three-scroll-sided handles seem to have petered out early in the 1780s.

LONDON GROUP 8: OPEN, SCROLL-SIDED (OR LOOP) SINGLE HANDLE

By far the most commonly produced type of lemon strainer, with 152 in my database, this one-handled sort is also the simplest. It probably catered for the 'middling classes' (such as lawyers, teachers, clergymen, merchants, artists and innkeepers) who went along with the fashion for drinking punch at home and could only afford some less showy items of silverware. Production of these single-handled strainers (between 1756 and 1813) overlapped for most of this time with two-handled ones, both single-scroll-handled (Group 6) and double/treble-scroll-handled (Group 7), so there would have been a choice throughout most of the second half of the 18th century and it must surely have been the case that the one-handled strainers were the least expensive to buy.

Admittedly, the Group is artificially large, as it includes three sorts of cast handles, single-scroll-sided, double-scroll-sided and shell-ended, as well as loop handles which were not cast but fashioned from silver strips: in two-handled strainers, these would fit into four separate categories (Groups 6, 7, 4 and 9, respectively). Half of the strainers in my Group-8 database have single-scroll, arc-ended handles; the other three styles (double-scroll, arc-ended; shell-ended; and loop) have almost equal shares of the other half; but single loop handles first appeared (in 1775) 20 years after the first single-scroll one-handled strainers. And, to complicate matters more, shell motifs were popular on the ends of loop handles, more so than they had been earlier on single- and double-scroll, arc-ended examples.

All these single-handled lemon strainers should have a downward-facing clip soldered to the rim, either opposite the handle (more in favour in the late 18th and early 19th centuries) or underneath it (more in favour in the earlier years from 1756). Overall, the two clip placements were almost equally popular. Any such strainer which lacks a clip should be suspected of having had an original second handle (or its original clip) removed. Obviously a one-handled strainer without a clip cannot rest on any receptacle without falling in.

The first genuine one-handled strainer in this Group in my database dates from 1756, so anything purporting to have been made before that should be eyed with suspicion. The earliest single-handled strainer I know of (in the collection of a well-known stately home open to the public) does appear to have a clip, but it is dated 'c.1730' and attributed to Isaac Liger. As he died in 1730 and the bowl's piercing style – with its central panel of crosslets surrounded by splashes and scrolls – did not come on to the lemon strainer scene (in open, cast, two-handled ones) until the mid-1730s, I suspect that the maker's letters were confused with John Luff's; and, since I know of no Group-8 strainers (of any age) with a similar bowl motif, I also suspect that this one started life as a two-handled, single-scroll, arc-ended lemon strainer (Group 6) in the mid-1730s and was modified, maybe in line with the changing fashion 20 years later, by having one of its handles removed and a clip added. Another strainer, dated 1749, with its maker's mark obliterated by the piercing, looks suspiciously as if it lacks a clip.

Sometimes a strainer looks 'right' but its billing arouses doubts, as in the case of the one-handled example, with clip, which came up for auction in 2001 and 2008 (fig.117) and was later sold by a well-known Gloucestershire dealer and listed as 'London 1726', either by Thomas Tombs or Thomas Tearle, but was probably made by an unidentified silversmith with initials 'TT' and hallmarked in 1764 (see p.36 for details of how the 1726 'L' was confused with the Gothic 'I' of 1764).

Fig.110: London probably 1759, possibly Edward Aldridge & John Stamper

Fig.111: London ?1759, David Hennell I

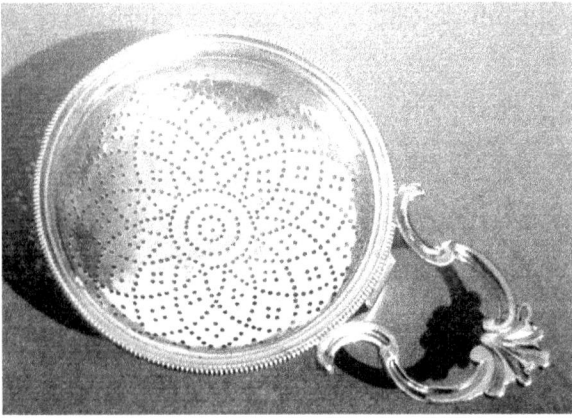

Fig.112: London 1759, William Plummer

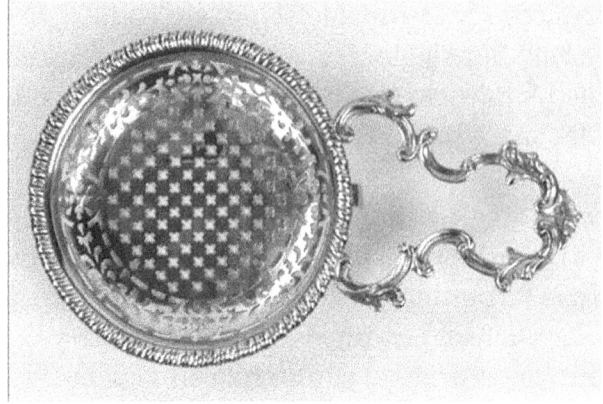

Fig.113: London c1763, Samuel Herbert & Co.

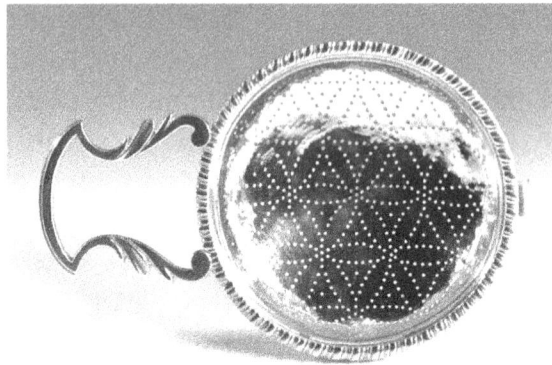

Fig.114: London c1763, Edward Aldridge I

The 'big three' makers of the second half of the 18th century, Edward Aldridge I (figs 114,116,118,120), Samuel Herbert & Co. (figs 113,121) and William Plummer (figs 112,122,123,125,126,133,134,136), were the main exponents of this one-handled style of lemon strainer. The most prolific of all was William Plummer, with 27 of his 45 known strainers belonging to this Group; his long working life started in 1755, soon before single-handled strainers first appeared (his first is from 1759) and he made his last in 1788. Samuel Herbert and his unidentified partner ('HB') entered their mark in 1750 and manufactured these strainers between 1760 and 1768. Edward Aldridge I, as we have seen, began silversmithing long before this; but he adapted to the new style in the last years before his death (1760-1766). As mentioned before, his (probable) nephew of the same name, Edward Aldridge II, may have been responsible for the unregistered 'EA' marks on four of these strainers between 1768 and 1771, before he struck up a partnership with John Vere. David Hennell I (fig.111), Aldridge & Stamper (fig.110) and Aldridge & Green (figs 124,128) are also familiar makers of strainers with representatives in more than one of the Groups.

Among the other makers in this style was the well-known woman silversmith, Hester Bateman, whose fame rests on her romantic story of becoming a full-blown silversmith 'out of the blue' when her watch-chainmaker husband died and she was already in her early fifties; her signature in the Goldsmiths' Company register suggested that she could barely write, yet she founded a highly successful dynasty of silverware makers. She was in charge from 1761 until her retirement in 1790, when two of her sons, Peter and Jonathan, took over. Jonathan died within a year and Peter joined forces with his widowed sister-in-law, Ann Bateman. Later, Jonathan's and Ann's son William entered the partnership as well. Hester has been denigrated as merely an administrator, who permitted the production on her premises of large quantities of thin-gauged silverware; but her lemon strainers – mostly in the loop-handle style, between 1775 and 1789 – have some highly original bowl piercing patterns; these include a central six-petalled flower surrounded by six three-petalled half-flowers and dot clusters in the gaps between, and another one with a six-petalled flower in the middle with a double ring around it and a unique guilloche-like outer ring of joined ovals. Perhaps her loveliest strainer has a handle with single leafy scrolls and an arc end, whose bowl has an 8x8 central panel of crosslets in a ring of dots, outside which are 12 overlapping three-quarter circles creating 12 overlapping petal shapes with single crosslets in the empty spaces (fig.131). As her other types of silverware also show, she must have had her own independent, in-house design team. I also know of two strainers by Peter & Ann Bateman (both hallmarked 1792) with reeded loop handles and interesting bowl designs.

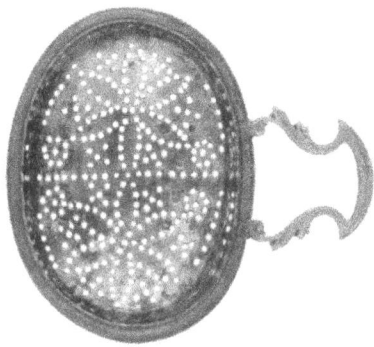

Fig.115: London 1764, Alexander Saunders

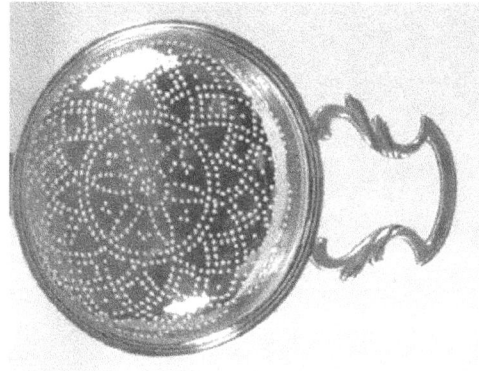

Fig.116: London 1764, Edward Aldridge I

Fig.117: London probably 1764, 'TT'
(unidentified)

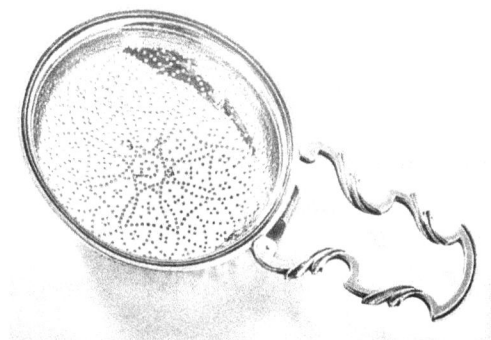

Fig.118: London 1764, Edward Aldridge I

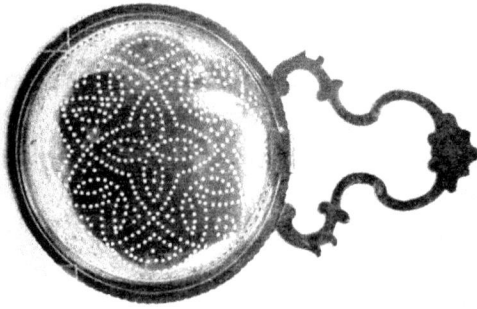

Fig.119: London 1765, maker's mark illegible

Fig.120: London c1765, Edward Aldridge I

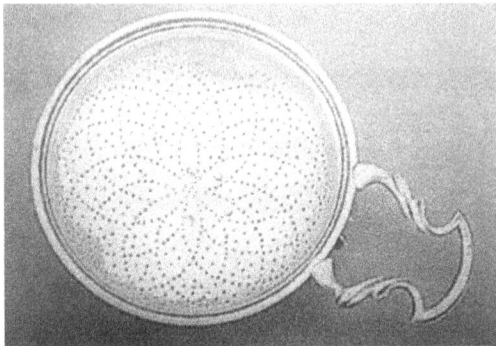

Fig.121: London 1765, Samuel Herbert & Co.

Fig.122: London 1767, William Plummer

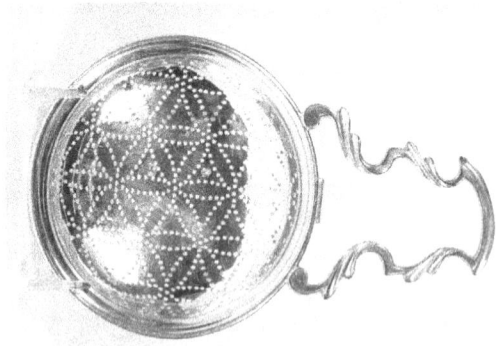

Fig.123: London 1767, possibly William Plummer

Fig.124: London 1768, Charles Aldridge & Henry Green

In the early years of one-handled strainers, the majority of the handles had single-scroll, leafy side-struts and arc ends (figs 116,120,121,124,125,127-133) but all the main makers also produced *double*-scroll, arc-ended handles, from 1759 to 1783. As the clip was designed to fit over the rim of the receptacle, in cases where the clip was fitted *under* the strainer's handle (e.g. figs 118,123), the full length of the handle must have protruded outwards beyond the rim; so their longer double-scroll handles must have been purely for greater show than the single-scroll ones. Figs 119,122 & 134 show *shell*-ended members of this Group, with handle sides whose second scrolls, leading into the shell, are C-shaped.

A couple of lesser-known strainer makers also fashioned some in this Group: Thomas Daniell was quite prolific in the second half of the 1770s: it seems he only made one-handled strainers and most had beaded loop handles; and Thomas Shepherd, working at around the same time and before his double-handled standard offerings, came up with a unique oval-shaped bowl in 1778 and 1779 with a 'midribbed' six-petalled flower and geometric designs between the petals (fig.132). Not the first London maker to produce oval bowls, his was preceded 15 years earlier (1764) by one made by Alexander Saunders, which has a line of dots across the middle of the oval with six-petalled flowers and dot clusters arranged with bilateral symmetry on either side (fig.115). The other two strainers I know of by Saunders have normal round bowls and very different bowl patterns: one has 8 straight lines alternating with 'lollipops' radiating from three central concentric rings. This one and another from the following year were both attributed to Alexander Johnstone, whose script 'AJ' mark is very similar to Saunders's script 'AS' and both are set in shaped cartouches.

Fig.125: London 1768, William Plummer

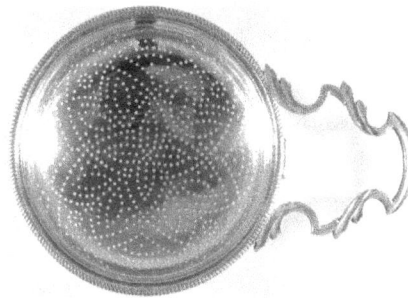

Fig.126: London 1769, William Plummer

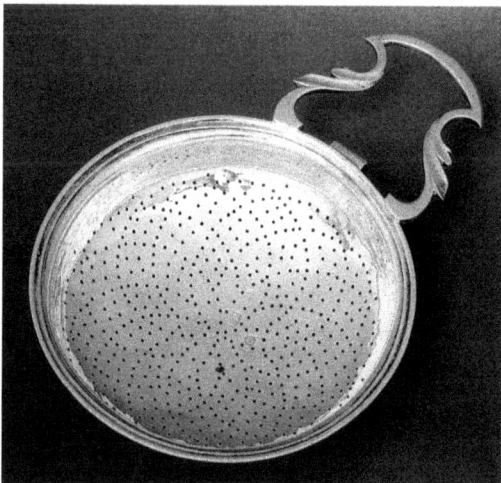

Fig.127: London 1771, Sarah Buttall

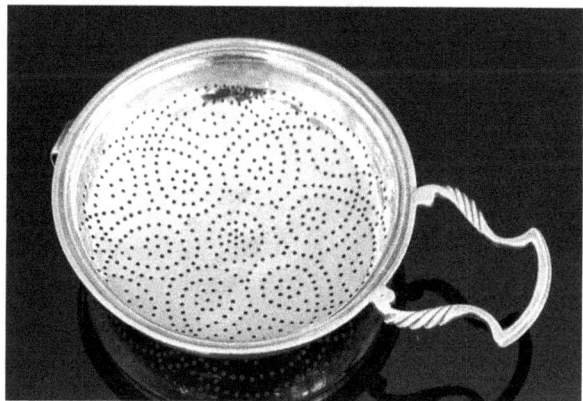

Fig.128: London 1772, Charles Aldridge & Henry Green

Fig.129: London 1774, possibly Richard Meach

Fig.130: London 1774, Richard Meach

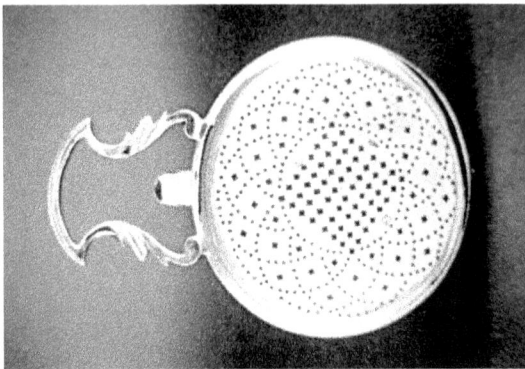

Fig.131: London 1775, Hester Bateman

Fig.132: London 1779, Thomas Shepherd

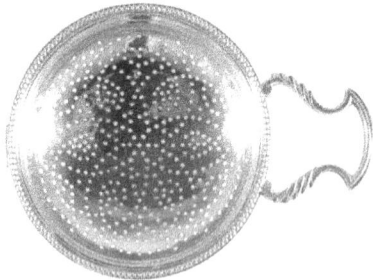

Fig.133: London 1781, William Plummer

Fig.134: London 1783, William Plummer

In the mid-1770s, another silversmith included lemon strainers (both twin- and single-handled) in his repertoire: Richard Meach was fond of small numbers of (three or four) broad 'petals' in his bowl designs, made of three or more parallel curved lines of dot-holes, including 'curlicues' (fig.129), but also made one with 12 triangles outside seven concentric circles (fig.130). Not being well-known as a strainer maker (even though his surviving output numbers at least 10), his marks have been ascribed to other silversmiths such as Richard Mills (who pre-dated Meach) and one with only the second letter 'M' still visible was listed as "possibly Charles Mieg" (fig.129).

I wrote earlier about a one-handled strainer in a stately home which was probably converted from a two-handled one and whose square panel of pierced crosslets gave the game away that it does not date from 'c.1730'. Although this decorative style around the crosslet panel is not found in this category of strainers, I know of three genuine one-handled strainers with a panel of crosslets in their bowls. One, in the Cleveland Museum of Art, is by Samuel Herbert & Co. (1760) and – like a similar one with two handles – it is a lovely expression of the rococo with deeply incised and shell-ended, double-scrolled curvaceous handles, a gadrooned rim and an outer band in the bowl of circles, rosettes and scrolls delineated by rings of dashes. So too is the second, by the same makers and dating from c1763 (fig.113). The third, by William Plummer (1761) is smaller, with single-scroll handles (curving out at the base) and a plain rim, but with a very similar piercing pattern. The clip on the Herbert strainer is under the handle; in Plummer's, it is opposite.

Talking of gadrooned rims (fig.122), they were in fashion between 1759 and 1770, but they would have meant extra cost to the clients so were never as common as rims with no applied embellishments. The relatively delicate beading, however, (applied, not stamped) was used more extensively at the same time as gadrooning when arc- and shell-ended handles were the only single-handled strainers in vogue (figs 125,126,129,130,133 & 134). It became commoner still in the late 1770s and throughout the 1780s, because of its popularity in the later, loop-handled style (figs 135-138). Some of these loop-handled strainers have reeded rim decoration (with parallel incised lines), either just on the rim of the bowl or continuing around the top of the handle: examples are Hester Bateman's oval bowl (fig.139) and Peter & Ann Bateman's round one (fig.142).

Fig.135: London 1777, probably
Thomas Daniell

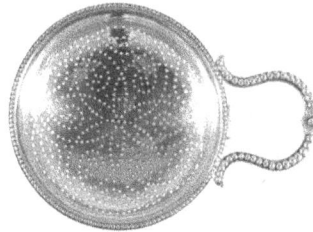

Fig.136: London 1777, William Plummer

Fig.137: London 1782, maker's
mark? rubbed

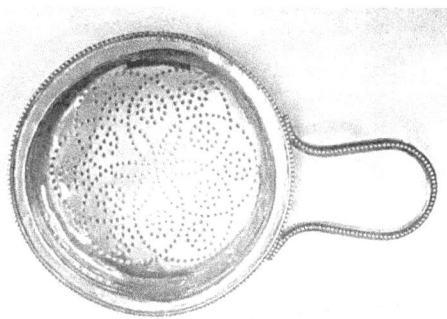

Fig.138: London 1783, William Abdy I

Fig.139: London 1789, Hester Bateman

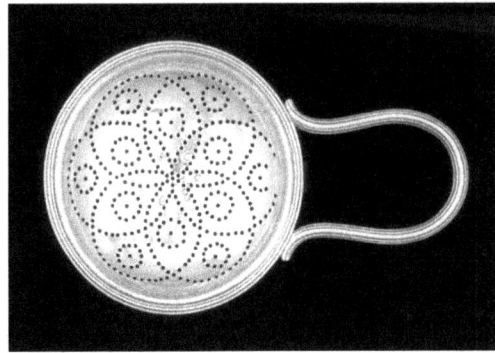

Fig.140: London 1789, Robert Hennell I

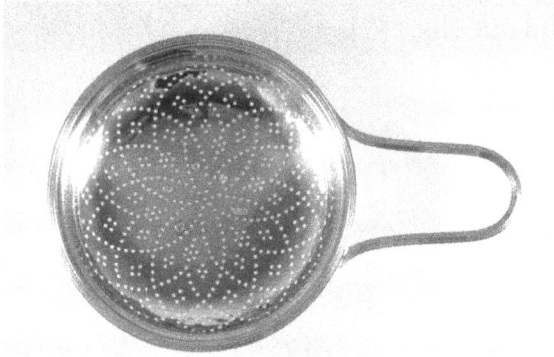

Fig.141: London 1791, Henry Green

Fig.142: London 1792, Peter & Ann Bateman

Fig.143: London 1794, John Touliet

Fig.144: London 1794, Charles Chesterman

Fig.145: London 1813, Rebeccah Emes & Edward Barnard

The first loop handles, made not by casting in moulds but by flattening and bending a thin strip of silver, made their appearance in 1775. Unlike the great majority of scroll-sided handles – which were still being made up to the turn of the 19th century – the bases of the loops tended to curve *outwards*.

Late on in the 'lifespan' of one-handled strainers, between 1788 and 1796, a maker with initials 'IT' had a creditable output of loop-handled ones, mostly with round-ended and deeply waisted loops. The mark on the silver-gilt example in the Royal Collection (from 1788) perfectly fits Grimwade's No.1710 for John Touliet, with its bold serifs and its asymmetrical 'I', as do at least two others, including one with an unadorned loop and a very simple bowl design mostly of parallel straight lines of holes, hallmarked 1794, which was donated to the Royal Ontario Museum in 1993 (fig.143). Dr Peter Kaellgren wrote an article about this strainer in the 2002 Silver Society Journal, occasioned by the fact that the clip has engraved on it the letters 'Ps.AMa.' showing that it belonged to King George III's youngest daughter, Princess Amelia, who lived a life of seclusion because of a debilitating skin condition, fell in love with the much older soldier and member of her household, Charles Fitzroy, but died at the age of 27 with her love unrequited. She was only 11 or 12 years old when the strainer was made and, unless she took possession of it many years later and was a punch drinker, we need to look for another possible use for it. Maybe it was for straining decoctions or milk? Interestingly, the author of the article tried to fit the strainer on a variety of English ceramic containers (in the Ontario museum's collection) and came to the conclusion that only fine Worcester porcelain had narrow enough rims.

It is worth pointing out here that the clips on these one-handled strainers – even though their offset from the strainer was narrow – were generally quite broad and flat, so were better sites for the engraving of family crests and ciphers than either the handle or the curved outside of the bowl.

I don't know of a single one of these looped one-handled lemon strainers with a punched mark on its handle, either a maker's mark or a hallmarked lion passant. This is in sharp contrast to the practice at the assay office of stamping the lion passant (the Sterling purity mark) on many of – but by no means all – the scroll-sided, cast handles in this Group, certainly from the mid-1760s until the late '70s. Usually this was done in addition to a full set of hallmarks (near the pre-existing maker's mark) inside or under the bowl, but in some cases the only marks are on the handle and comprise only the maker's mark and the lion passant (see pp.30-31). Perhaps, as these loop handles were not cast and therefore probably made by the same craftsmen from the same sources of silver as the bowls, there was no need to assay the handles at all?

Other makers whose known Group-8 lemon strainers now total just one or two include Robert Hennell I (fig.140), singly and in partnership with his father David, Samuel Meriton I, his grandson Samuel Meriton II, Joseph Clare II (possibly), Sarah Buttall (fig.127), Burrage Davenport, William Abdy I (fig.138), 'HG' (probably Henry Green after his partnership with Charles Aldridge was dissolved; fig.141), Charles Chesterman (fig.144) and the 19th-century exponents Rebeccah Emes & Edward Barnard (fig.145). Along with Hester Bateman, Sarah Buttall and Rebeccah Emes gave this Group of strainers the distinction of having had the largest number of women makers.

LONDON GROUP 9: TWO OPEN, LOOP HANDLES

Coinciding with the arrival of the new loop-handled style in one-handled strainers in the mid-1770s, two-handled lemon strainers made the same transition. Unlike those with one handle, which continued simultaneously with the old style of scroll sides and arc ends, in two-handled strainers the new style made a more thorough take-over and almost none were made with scroll sides and arc ends after 1780. I know of only 24 lemon strainers in this Group. In silver wares generally, shapes and decorations became more restrained as rococo was replaced, from the 1760s, with the fashion for the neoclassical: the scrolling sides of the earlier strainer handles had been inspired by rococo, whereas the simpler loops with their beaded and reeded decoration were in line with the neoclassical.

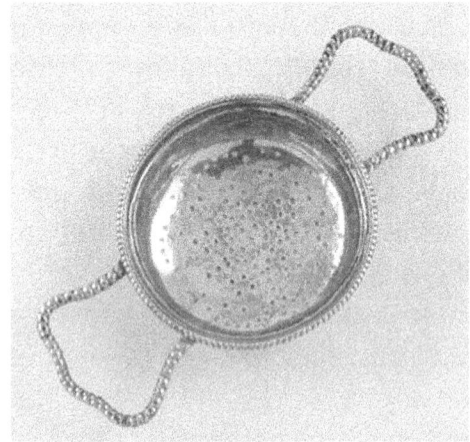

Fig.146: London 1763, possibly Samuel Meriton I   Fig.147: London 1773, maker's mark worn

There were, however, a few 'pioneers' in the loop style which pre-dated the mid-1770s. The earliest may have been wrongly dated as 1760 and its maker's mark was not given. The first genuine Group-9 strainer that I know of came from 1763 with the "possibly SM" mark of Samuel Meriton I (fig.146); its plain handles have a baluster outline, a slight inward notch at the terminal and an inward curve at their base. One, from 1768 and by Edward Aldridge II, is similar but has a finely beaded rim (and lacks the handle's notch). Another, dated 1773, has a unique handle shape, its outline looking like a crown, and both its handles and rim are strongly beaded; its piercing pattern of dot-holes seems formless and its maker is unknown (fig.147).

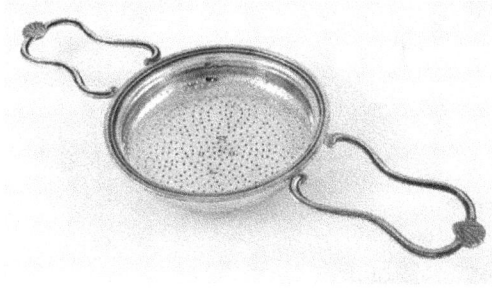

Fig.148: London 1776, John Deacon

From 1776 until the end of the century a steady trickle of these strainers was produced, nowhere nearly as commonly as their one-handled cousins, and Rebeccah Emes and Edward Barnard returned to the theme with heavily gadrooned examples around 1810. The baluster outline was popular until the mid-1780s, after which the handles became consistently less curved along their sides, so that their outlines were less bottle-shaped and more like long noses.

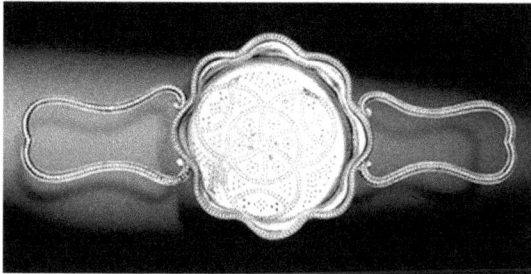

Fig.149: London 1777, Hester Bateman

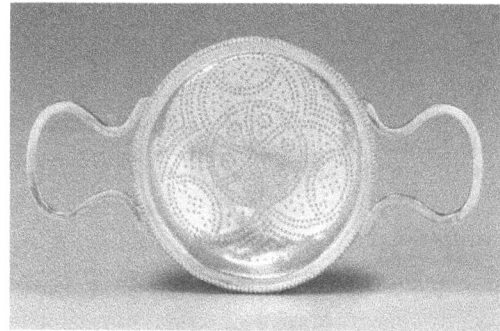

Fig.150: London 1781, Hester Bateman

With the careers of Edward Aldridge I and Samuel Herbert now over and William Plummer seeming to stick to making one-handled lemon strainers, there were no specialist makers of these strainers and a range of general silversmiths were responsible for their production. These included Robert Hennell I (figs 153,154,157), Burrage Davenport, Henry Chawner (fig.155), Crispin Fuller, John Deacon (fig.148) and Thomas Meriton. Standing out because of its very unusual octafoil bowl is a 1777 beauty from Hester Bateman's workshop (fig.149), which is beaded all over its handles and bowl rim and whose bowl piercing is also highly distinctive: three of the 'spokes' of its central 'cartwheel' continue outwards to form three more double-edged circles and all the gaps are filled with clusters of dots. She continued the bowl piercing theme in 1781 but the bowl is circular and the handles short and plain (fig.150).

Fig.151: London 1785, Charles Aldridge & Henry Green

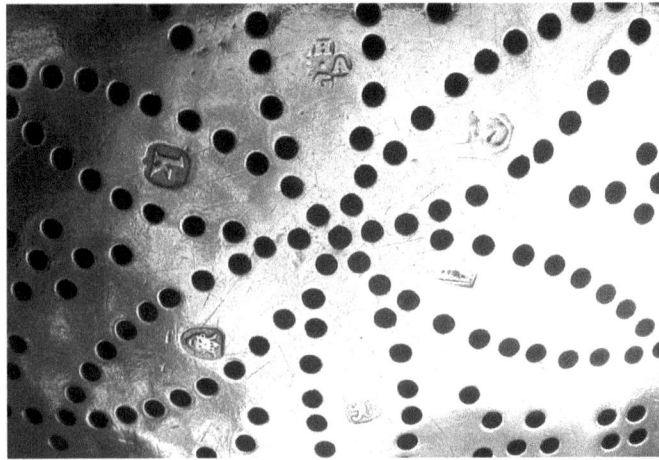

Fig.152: Marks on Aldridge & Green's 1785 strainer (underside of bowl)

Aldridge and Green's strainer of 1785 is a classic of the 'nose-handled' style (fig.151). It is large (282 mm across the handles), its handles and bowl rim are delicately beaded and its piercing design is floral, six large petals overlapping to create a smaller six-petalled flower in the centre and six more 'petal-tips' join in at the periphery. On the underside of its bowl, very neatly punched in each of the inner six petals, are no fewer than six marks (fig.152): the crowned leopard's head and lion passant to show its London-assayed Sterling credentials, the makers' mark (C.A and H.G crossing each other inside a quatrefoil cartouche), the date letter ('k'), the duty mark (George III's head in profile, with its impression sunk into the punch rather than standing out in relief, that is intaglio instead of cameo) *and* the very rare 'duty drawback' mark (the standing figure of Britannia holding a spear and a shield). Not since 1758 had the State levied any tax on silver, but it was reimposed on 1st December 1784 at the rate of sixpence per Troy ounce (about 2 shillings and thruppence on this strainer). This time, a new 'duty mark' was instated to show that the duty had been paid for the assayed item. Until the 1786-87 date letter was first used (May 1786), the monarch's head duty mark was 'incuse' (= intaglio), after which it was struck in relief; so this 'incuse head' is a rarity in itself.

For any piece of silverware that was due to be exported, this duty could be claimed back and the Standing Britannia mark was then stamped to indicate the repayment. As this 'duty drawback' mark caused unwanted damage to some silverware, it was discontinued in July 1785 after a period of less than eight months (see p.27). This means both that the mark is a great rarity nowadays and that this Aldridge & Green lemon strainer must have been hallmarked between the 30th May 1785 (when the date letter 'k' was first employed) and the 24th of July 1785. I don't know of any other lemon strainer with the duty drawback mark.

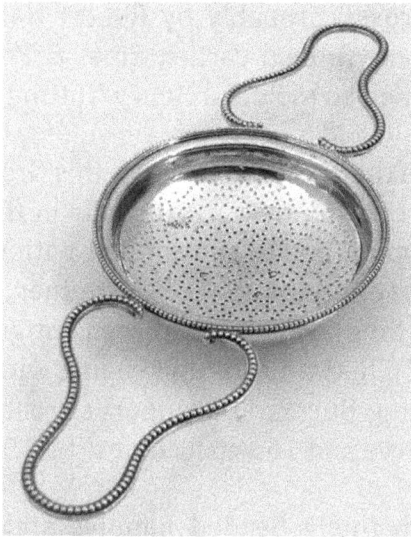

Fig.153: London 1781, Robert Hennell I

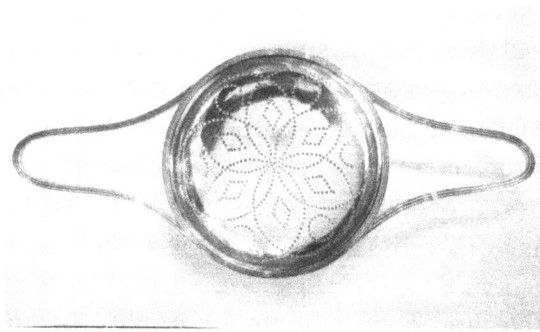

Fig.154: London 1792, Robert Hennell I

Fig.155: London 1795, Henry Chawner

Fig.156: London 1812, Rebeccah Emes &
Edward Barnard

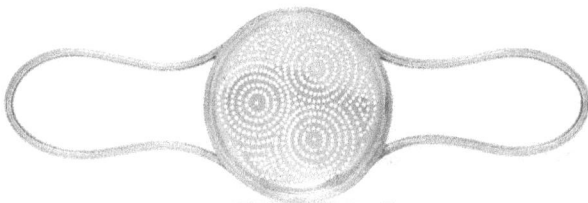

Fig.157: London 1788, possibly Robert Hennell I

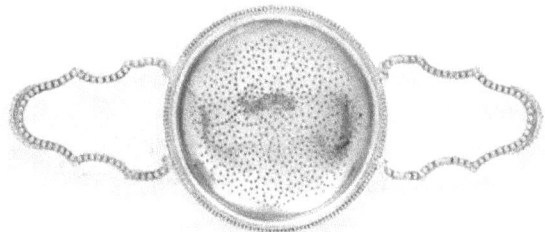

Fig.158: London 1777, Burrage Davenport

The beading of bowl rims (and usually handles as well) was superseded in the late 1780s by reeding, typically involving three parallel and equidistant grooves engraved into the rim and the handles.

A really long-handled example of 1786 (over 27 cm across), probably by Robert Hennell I, was intermediate with a beaded rim but reeded handles. As mentioned earlier, Emes & Barnard used gadrooning in their early 19th-century strainers (fig.156), and so too did a Henry Nutting in 1799.

At the same time as the long nose-shaped handles became the accepted norm in this Group (around 1785), the piercing patterns in the bowls became more consistently floral, usually in the form of a central six-petalled flower surrounded by larger, overlapping petals and infilled with a variety of clusters of geometric arrangements of dots. A marked exception is the 1788 strainer, possibly by Robert Hennell I, of monster proportions (almost 36 cm long), which has three contiguous sets of concentric rings of very densely packed dot-holes (fig.157). In the 1770s, in keeping with the varied handle shapes, bowl designs were often eccentric, including Burrage Davenport's creation of 1777 with its 'ropework' cross surrounded by a long swirling curve and 16 small circles (fig.158).

One attractive and typical member of this Group, with finely beaded handles and rim and a 12-petalled flower at the centre of the bowl's piercing, has an anomaly which I can't explain – and nor could the London dealer who showed it to me: it has a full set of 1790 London hallmarks in very reasonable condition, but the maker's mark has been deliberately defaced by crude gouging. How could anyone be offended by a couple of letters?

LONDON GROUP 10: ODDITIES

'Oddities' include lemon strainers that could be genuine but are highly atypical – sometimes in their bowl piercing design but more often in their handle(s) – as well as those with handles replaced or removed later and conversions from cauldron salt cellars, bowls and wine funnels. It is, of course, not always easy to tell apart the genuine from the conversion.

PROBABLY GENUINE ODDITIES

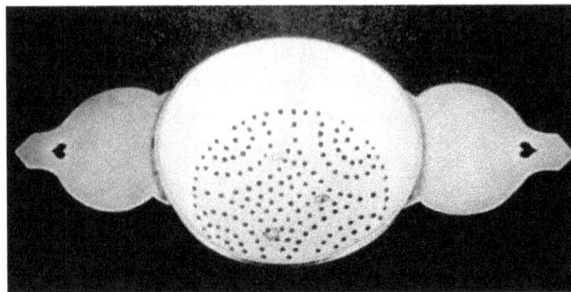

Fig.159: London 1724, James Goodwin

Let's begin with by far the smallest category, of 'whacky but probably genuine' strainers, in chronological order. Most of them were from the workshops of recognised lemon strainer makers. James Goodwin's of 1724 (fig.159) would fit in Group 3 with its two flat, shaped, solid handles, but their shape – and the solitary small pierced heart in each of them – is more redolent of Dublin than of

London: a bulbous base tapering to a pointed 'snub nose'. Yet the bowl – even though its piercing pattern has an unusual geometric pattern – seems to have genuine London hallmarks. Maybe an Irish client of Goodwin's, living in London, requested a special commission? Anyway, someone paid nearly £1000 for it at a 2007 auction.

In the same year another auctioneer offered another unique oddity, this one by the well-known generalist silversmith Edward Feline: it has handles like a child's cut-out of a lady in a billowing skirt, with an applied tapered 'rat-tail' on top, ribbed and opening out towards the terminal. It has no hallmarks but Feline's marks are on both handles. It had earlier (1970) been for sale at Christie's whose attribution of "c.1730" is probably closer to reality than Lyon & Turnbull's 2007 one of "c.1720".

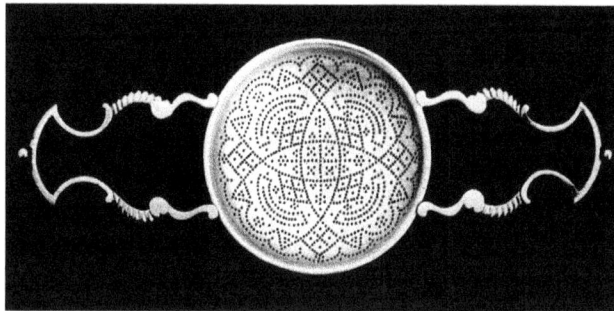

Fig.160: London 1744, William Justis

I've also already described (p.37) the interesting provenance of a William Justis strainer of 1744 with extra long handles (fig.160). It could be a very early example of a Group-7 open, double-scroll-sided, arc-ended strainer, albeit of an unusually large size (35 cm long), with very simplified stylised foliage in the middle of its handles and an extra 'knob' on its arc ends. It could have had its handles extended later, when there was demand from the 1750s for additional handle scrolls, but its particularly wide bowl makes the whole strainer look in proportion; and as Justis was known for breaking convention, at least in his strainer output, I'm inclined to believe this was a 'pioneer' example of Group 7.

Fig.161: London c1750, Thomas Heming

Thomas Heming was the Kings' goldsmith (both George II's and George III's) and the Royal Collection has at least three of his lemon strainers, only one of which is of standard construction. The earliest, unhallmarked but assumed to be from around 1750 (fig.161), is pure rococo with asymmetrical loopy handles embellished with foliage which drapes itself over the rim of the bowl, itself decorated with applied scrolls and foliage; the piercing in the bowl is a unique set of fountains radiating out from the central rosette, with barely a normal dot-hole among the scrolls and squiggles. Heming's mark is on at least one of the handles; and the outside of the bowl has an engraving of the Prince of

Wales feathers and the motto of the Order of the Garter, *Honi soit qui mal y pense*. (Rococo decoration is famous for its asymmetry, which in lemon strainers is not normally a feasible option; this is the only example I know of with truly asymmetrical handles.)

In line with my observation that silversmiths who hardly ever made lemon strainers often created their own handle designs, a 'one-off' by John Alderhead in 1751 has a geometric dot-hole design in its bowl, which wouldn't have looked out of place in an Edward Aldridge production; but its handles, based on Group 6's single-scroll sides and arc end, have the stylised foliage facing *inwards* and extra flourishes added on to the bases and the outside of the arc. I don't know if these handles were hallmarked, but even if they weren't that wouldn't necessarily flag this strainer up as anything other than atypical yet genuine.

Fig.162: London 1763, Edward Aldridge I

Edward Aldridge I's lemon strainer of 1763 (fig.162) is doubly extraordinary as there appear to be two of them in existence, one with crowned crests on both handles and the other with a cipher on one handle; otherwise they seem almost identical, with the same date and the same maker and similar floral dot-hole piercing patterns. Yet their handles are utterly peculiar: very long (the strainers measure nearly 29 cm between their tips), flat and unadorned and with a cut-out central triangle, they taper to a sharp notch and a circular, knobbed terminal. At least one of them has Aldridge's mark on both handles as well as in the bowl; and the handles also bear the lion passant from the assay office. In 1763, lemon strainers came in six styles (Groups 4 to 9) and my databases have more strainers from 1763 to 1765 than from any other year since 1719 (or any later date). So, flexibility of style was the order of the day and contemporary commissions for a simple, yet eccentric, design are no surprise. The handles of these Aldridge strainers, if anything, seem more Irish than London and one of them bears the crest and coronet of the Irish Earl of Drogheda, who may have personally specified the style.

The next oddity appeared on a Dutch website, but is unmarked except for the French import mark struck under both handles (a swan in an oval punch, used from the end of the 19th century for foreign silverware, after being re-tested for purity and before being sold at auction in France – see p.27). It's another large strainer (28 cm in length), whose bowl has curved parallel rows of very densely-packed dot-holes outside a central circle with numerous radii and whose handles have elaborate, cast, curvaceous leafy scrolls and a shell terminal.

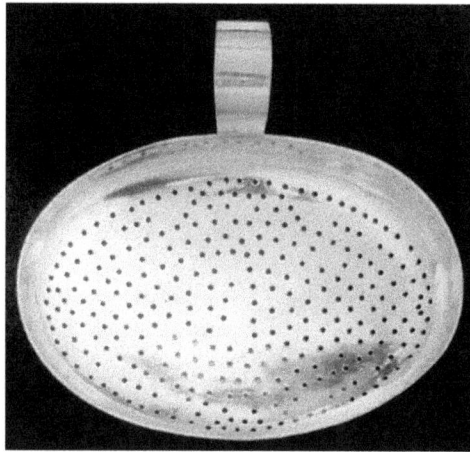

Fig.163: London 1762, 'WC'
(overstriking another)

Two London-made lemon strainers with many of the characteristics of strainers produced in Plymouth are known from the 1760s. Every Plymouth strainer has an oval bowl and almost all of them have a very simple handle made up of a vertical ring with a downward-facing clip below it. Pentecost Symons was the main maker there, for very many years (pp.117-120), and he remained faithful to a particular bowl piercing design (straight radii, alternately ending in 'lollipop' heads). These London 'copies' share the Plymouth handle design, but neither has the Symons bowl pattern: the first, by 'WC' in 1762 (fig.163), has a simple arrangement of equidistant dots in curved lines, and the other, by Aldridge & Green (1768), appears to have overlapping 'petals' with dot clusters in the gaps. The last known silver wares made by Symons date from the mid-1750s, but other Plymouth makers did keep up the tradition of strainer making until the 1770s. Like the case of the 'Irish'-handled oddity mentioned above, these may have been commissioned by West-country gentlemen in London feeling nostalgia for their country home.

The 'WC' was attributed to William Chatterton by Christie's in 2006 and to William Cripps by a Wiltshire auction house in 2008; the strainer had been in the Albert Collection and Robin Butler's description hedged its bets and stuck with 'WC', adding – as Christie's had done – that it was 'overstriking another'. This means that the strainer's original maker's mark was deliberately obliterated by a second maker's mark stamped on top of it, a very rare occurrence on lemon strainers. It's conceivable that this strainer was actually made by a Plymouth maker and found its way to London, where a local retail silversmith superimposed his own mark; but – even if it could – the London assay office would not overstrike any of the Exeter hallmarks which a Plymouth piece would carry, so they would still be visible. It's more likely that either Chatterton or Cripps (neither is known for making other lemon strainers) sold this one as his own after adding to his stock by buying from another maker. A final twist to this strainer's story is that the Wiltshire auction house gave it a date two years earlier than Christie's and Butler, an easy mistake as the Gothic 'E' for 1760 and 'G' for 1762 are alike.

Henry Hayens, known for his rococo and rustic silverware creations from 20 years earlier but not for making lemon strainers, came up with an extraordinary single-loop-handled one in 1772 (which was in the Hyman Collection from 1988 but too off-beam, perhaps, to be illustrated in John Davis's article about it). Instead of the dot-holes in the bowls of all strainers of the time, he made a mesh of narrow slits radiating from a central solid button, intersected by strips of silver in the form of 15 overlapping 'flower petals'.

Fig.164: London ?c1800, maker's mark indistinct

I have no reason to suppose that Samuel Meriton II's 1794 strainer, with its peculiar flat bottom which allows it to fit snugly into its own unique fully-hallmarked stand, was converted from anything else. Its piercing pattern appears to be uncontroversial, involving several six-petalled flowers, and its bowl has a standard diameter (11 cm); it has a single handle, tubular and silver at its base and turned wood outside that, and a clip on the opposite side of the rim. Nor am I suspicious of the weird ribbed, 7-sided handles on the strainer with rubbed maker's mark but visible lion passant and duty mark (fig.164). The duty mark dates the piece from after 1784, when loop handles were in fashion and they weren't always smoothly curved.

CONVERSIONS – REPLACEMENT HANDLES

The remaining lemon strainers in this Oddities section are conversions, which almost certainly looked different when they were first made. Either they started life as strainers but with different handles from the ones they now bear, or they were originally salt cellars or wine funnels (or a bowl) and subsequently transmogrified into lemon strainers.

Replacing original handles with new ones is quite an easy matter for a silversmith, especially as the area of soldered contact between the rim of the bowl and the handle or handles has never been large. In Groups 2 and 3 with their broad, flat handles, the contact is longer but narrower than in Groups 6 to 9 with their scroll-sided, openwork handles meeting the rim in only two places. Handles come undone by mistake, due to manhandling, and to remove them deliberately would merely involve heating, removing the remains of the solder and tidying up. Only on strainers with applied extra ornamentation, for example around their rims, would this be awkward as it would probably be impossible to melt the handle solder without softening the solder under the applied parts.

Fig.165: London 1724, James Goodwin

When openwork handles first appeared in the 1730s and quite quickly superseded the broad, flat handles, both pierced and solid, it would have been tempting to keep up with the times and ask for new handles in the new fashion. As bowl shapes and designs didn't alter for several years, it would have been easy to hide the alteration, but only if the old handles were removed cleanly. I know of one strainer by James Goodwin (1724) with a beautiful piercing pattern of splashes, scrolls and curved dashes (fig.165), in which the sides of the rim between the handle contact points must have been damaged by removal of the original flat handles, as a crude attempt seems to have been made to reshape the 'double fillet' strengthening there. The fact that the bowl was hallmarked some 6 or 7 years before the first open-handled strainers came on to the scene is another giveaway that this lemon strainer, attractive though it is, has been modified, probably in the 1730s.

Fig.166: London 'c1710-15', John Chartier

The "Queen Anne Silver Lemon Strainer by John Chartier", which sold well at a West London auction house in 2017, is an interesting conundrum (fig.166). Its flat, solid, shaped handles do bear the (very worn) Britannia mark of John Chartier, suggesting a possible date of between 1697 and 1720 (the auction house thought "c.1710-15"). Stylistically, however, they are mid-1720s at the earliest; Chartier didn't register a Sterling mark until 1723, so he presumably continued using the Britannia standard until then (and maybe after that year as well). The bowl is completely unmarked and its style is most unusual, neither from the Britannia period nor any time in the first half of the 18th century; I suspect it was made in the late 18th century at the earliest. Not only that, but the handles have been engraved with an acanthus motif *and* they bear a deeply-struck (but also worn) mark of another maker, 'FB' or 'FR', which – despite its highly distinctive shaped cartouche and the two pellets above the letters – is unidentified. Because such cartouches are rare after 1739, I tentatively believe that the 'FB/FR' mark was added not more than 15 years after the manufacture of the handles, perhaps at the same time as the engraving, but that the handles were added to a new bowl much later on.

Fig.167: London 1728, maker uncertain ('-B')

The chamberstick handles attached to a beautifully pierced bowl hallmarked for 1728 could well be contemporary, so this strainer (fig.167) – which was sold on eBay from the USA in 2012 – may be an original construction, made as a special commission, but as the seller conceded that both handles may have had "solder repairs", they are more likely to have been part of a later 'marriage'.

Fig.168: London 1773, Charles Aldridge & Henry Green

It is similarly suspicious when a lemon strainer has a handle which clearly belonged to a spoon, as with the one sold by a Boston, Massachusetts auction house in 2018, whose bowl is hallmarked for London 1773 and bears the Aldridge & Green makers' mark (fig.168). Its description doesn't reveal if there are any marks under the spoon handle which could give away the 'mongrel' status of this piece.

And when an auctioneer's photograph shows that a pair of very unusual 'three-tier' openwork handles were in effect riveted to the bowl of an unmarked lemon strainer, and the bowl's size, shape and piercing pattern are similar to a London strainer by Thomas Rush from 1752, it suggests the later replacement of the handles on a George II bowl. The auction house was non-committal, describing it as "19th century white metal continental".

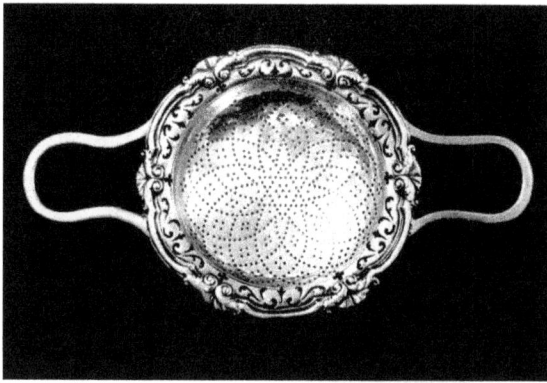

Fig.169: London c1752, maker's mark rubbed

Fig.170: London c1770, 'IW over TB'
(unidentified)

In the next example (fig.169), the plain loop handles are completely out of keeping with the applied rim of shell, scroll and piercings: a mismatch of later-added neoclassical handles and a rococo bowl, which – although it has no decipherable maker's mark nor date letter – is in the one of the styles used by Edward Aldridge, Samuel Herbert and Paul de Lamerie in the first half of the 1750s. The lemon strainer with the unidentified makers' marks of 'I.W over T.B' (fig.170) is also almost certainly a 'mongrel': the 'IW/TB' marks are very crisp and clear on both handles (which are open, double-scroll and arc-ended, but unusual in having attractive bifurcated bases), but what the four auction houses that put it up for sale between 2017 and 2019 neglected to point out are the very worn hallmarks in the bowl, which include a lion passant in a punch used between 1751 and 1755. The bowl is surely much older than the handles, as judged by the differential wear to their marks.

CONVERSIONS – HANDLES REMOVED

Fig.171: London 1722, possibly James Goodwin

Single-handled lemon strainers without clips would have fallen into any receptacle on which they were placed, so the assumption must always be that such strainers originally had two handles and one has come off since. They come up for sale more often than they should. When the handle is of a type which was *never* used on one-handled strainers (except possibly in Philadelphia in 18th-century America), there can be no doubt about a strainer's history. For example, one from 1722 and possibly made by James Goodwin (fig.171), with a Group-2 flat, triangular, pierced handle, was sold at auction in Cumbria in 2015 and appeared on eBay the following year (with a price tag almost nine times the hammer price).

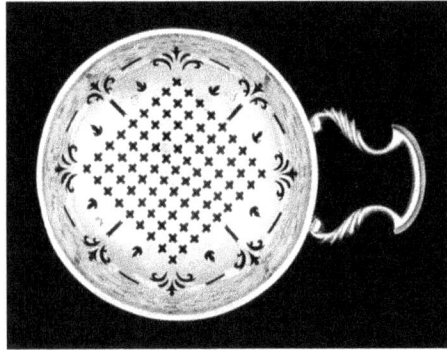

Fig.172: London 1733, George Greenhill Jones

Other clip-free one-handled strainers include ones from 1733 (fig.172) and 1740, both by George Greenhill Jones and with crosslet-and-scroll piercing, in which the hallmarks can't hide the fact that they pre-date the fashion for one-handled strainers by about 17 and 10 years respectively. Another one, by William Justis, has no give-away date letter as it is worn, but the bowl style suggests c1750; so, if it weren't for its cliplessness, it might have been genuine.

One of the pieces in the Hyman Collection, illustrated but not in its entirety in John Davis's article (Pl. IV, left), looks like an example of a 1740s two-handled London Group-2 strainer, with a lovely bowl piercing design of crosslets, squares and scrolls and ornate semi-openwork handles (as occasionally used in the 1730s and '40s by Edward Aldridge I and Gurney & Cooke); but Shrubsole's description gave the game away that it only had the one handle visible in the illustration – and a clip opposite. Matters are confused by the fact that it is unhallmarked and the maker's mark (D:D) has not been identified, but scroll-sided, one-handled strainers only appeared in the late 1750s and this handle style pre-dated that time. I suspect that it had had one handle removed and a clip added, perhaps to conform to the new fashion for single-handled strainers in the 1760s.

CONVERSIONS FOR OTHER USES

Fig.173: London 1758, ?no maker's mark

I know of two strainers which, though probably genuine, have been converted for another use. One, a Group-7 strainer made in 1758 (maker unknown), came up at auction in 2008 with a pale yellow glass dish snugly fitting into the bowl (fig.173); the dish has a 24-arm cut star in the centre. The other is a Group-8 single-handled strainer, with a clip, whose bowl has been coated by thin layers of silver both on the outside and (in silver-gilt) on the inside; the original dot-hole piercing is still visible from above but there is no sign of hallmarks in the bowl and the handle is unmarked. In both cases, considerable trouble must have gone into the conversion, but I can only guess at their new functions.

CONVERSIONS FROM OTHER OBJECTS

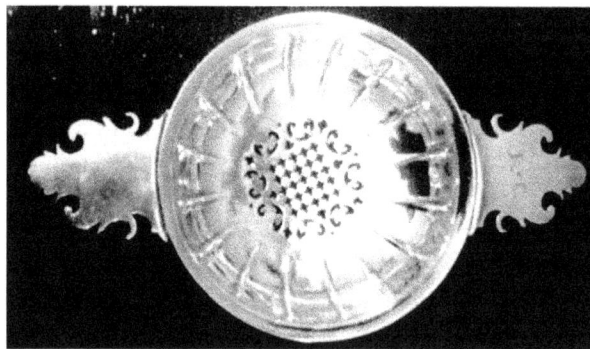

Fig.174: London 1737, Paul de Lamerie

The last category of 'oddities' comprises the conversions into lemon strainers from what originally were other items of silverware, beginning with a converted 1737 fluted bowl with pedestal foot by Paul de Lamerie (fig.174), now bearing two handles of a slightly earlier style (late 1720s?) and a group of pierced crosslets and scrolls in the bowl, in a pattern that could be contemporaneous but is anomalously restricted to a small area in the centre because of the presence of the foot below. The online seller went to some lengths to give the piece a semblance of plausibility, comparing it both with the orange strainer lent by Jaime Ortiz-Patiño (of similar weight and diameter, but with little else in common) and the strawberry dish (with fluting "just like" [sic] the one for sale) that were in the 1990 de Lamerie exhibition at Goldsmiths' Hall. The asking price started at £4,450.

Fig.175: London 1736, Edward Wood

I've come across two strainers that had originally been circular 'cauldron' salt cellars, with their legs removed, their bowls pierced and handles added. The earliest was dated 1736 and the maker was the well-known salt-cellar maker, Edward Wood (fig.175); its handles were shaped in a style and thickness never seen before or since, the hallmarks and maker's mark were on the base of the bowl (usual for salts but uncommon in strainers) and the dot-holes seemed too crisp to have been drilled nearly 300 years ago. The second one dated from 1783 with the mark of Pratt & Humphreys, who produced a wide variety of silver wares including salts but not – it seems – any lemon strainers: the bowl was almost hemispherical, in contrast to the shallower, nearly flat-bottomed strainer bowls of the time, it had a much smaller diameter than contemporary strainers and its dot-holes had no discernible pattern (unheard of in the 1780s); finally its handles – solid, shaped and stumpy – were unlike any others on real lemon strainers.

The demise of lemon strainers' popularity at the end of the 18th century coincided with a marked upsurge in production of silver wine funnels, but since wine funnels were first made in the mid-1760s there was quite an overlap and the earliest conversions I know of date from the 1770s. A number were made, initially simply by discarding the detachable spout. What was left would have been a circular bowl, already perforated with small holes, usually with an applied circular foot at its base but sometimes footless with a very flat bottom. All that was needed was to solder one (or usually two) genuine lemon-strainer handles just below the rim of the bowl. The two surest indications of a wine-funnel-to-strainer conversion are the small area of pierced holes in the middle of the bowl and the bowl's foot and/or flat base. Also diagnostic is the hallmarking around the outside of the bowl (or on the outside of its base) rather than inside it.

Fig.176: London ?c1771, maker's mark rubbed

Fig.177: London 1779, William Plummer

Fig.178: London ?c1800, maker's mark rubbed

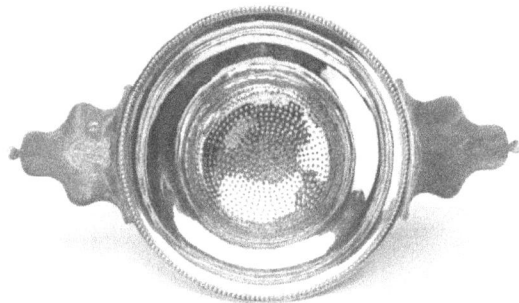

Fig.179: London 1779, Thomas Heming

One that I know of, but was withdrawn from auction in 2019 by the Antique Plate Committee of the Goldsmiths' Company, even still had its spout attached, which – if Georgian in origin – would suggest it was intended for use on quite a tall receptacle rather than a porcelain slop bowl (fig.176). The others are spoutless and would rest steadily on a flat surface as well as suspend themselves on the rim of a bowl. An example with open, single-scroll, arc-ended handles is by William Plummer (1779; fig.177). One with a solitary but similar handle has rubbed marks but probably dates from the turn of the 19th century (fig.178). Another with reeded loop handles to match the reeded rim of the wine funnel's bowl is by 'Moses Brent' (1796). One, from 1799, was given a long handle, largely of turned wood but with a bifurcated tubular silver base, and a small, shaped, horizontal clip opposite. My final example, of 1779, which dates from Thomas Heming's later years as Principal Goldsmith to King George III and remains in the Royal Collection, looks like a converted wine funnel bearing small, flat, 'snub-nosed' handles (fig.179). One might doubt that such plain but idiosyncratic handles were Heming's work if it weren't for the fact that one of them is engraved with George III's coat of arms and cipher.

Chapter Three
ENGLISH PROVINCIAL LEMON STRAINERS

Most of the identifiable crests and coats of arms engraved on the handles and bowls of London-made lemon strainers belonged to families whose main residences were in the provinces rather than London itself. The noblemen and gentry who had their country estates all over England – and some of them in Wales, Scotland and Ireland – may have generally bought their lemon strainers during the summer season in London when they spent months in their London homes, because strainers made in England outside London are very few and far between. Apart from the substantial output from Plymouth (in its own very distinctive style), I know of a total of only nine other provincial English lemon strainers, made in Norwich, Newcastle, Liverpool, Birmingham and Sheffield.

Chester, Exeter and Newcastle were the only places outside London which had their own assay offices throughout the 18th century (York having a long gap without one between 1713 and 1778). Exeter was the hallmarking destination for all the Plymouth wares, but I don't know of any lemon strainers made in Exeter itself. Norwich ceased assaying operations in 1701. Liverpool never had an assay office, but two strainer makers are known to have worked there, one of whom used the Chester office for hallmarking. Both the Birmingham and Sheffield offices first opened in 1773.

STRAINERS FROM ENGLISH PROVINCES
OTHER THAN PLYMOUTH

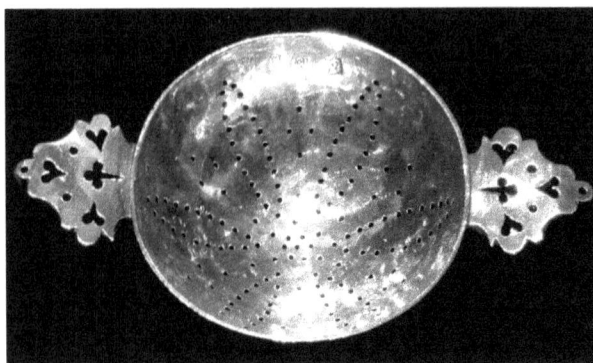

Fig.180: Norwich 1691, Thomas Havers

The only known English provincial lemon strainers from the 17th century both came from Norwich. One was referred to in a Sotheby's 1942 catalogue, with no additional information available now, as "a Rare Norwich Lemon Strainer, 1690". Maybe it had the same maker, Thomas Havers, as the other one (from 1691) which is on show in the Norwich Castle Museum (fig.180)? Havers's strainer is small, with a six-petalled flower as its pierced motif in the bowl and flat, shaped handles pierced with three hearts, three dots and a stalked trefoil. It is fully and clearly hallmarked with the crowned rose and 'castle over lion passant' Norwich town marks, the Gothic 'd' date letter and Havers's maker's mark; it is a highly valuable treasure.

One of the earliest 18th-century provincial lemon strainers is from Newcastle, dating from 1724 by John Ramsey, which was referred to by John D. Davis in his article on the Hyman Collection as an example of the later provincial use of the early London style of two-handled strainers. Its handles look like the Thomas Kedden strainer's from the 1690s (Group 2; fig.23); and its deep bowl with its concentric rings of perforations is also 1690s London in shape, but many of the dot-holes are uniquely replaced by hearts, four-pointed stars and diamonds. It was advertised in an arts magazine in 1964 by a prestigious London silver and jewellery dealership now associated with Fabergé and fabulous gold boxes.

Fig.181: Newcastle c1750, Isaac Cookson

A second Newcastle strainer – with open, single-scroll-sided, arc-ended handles with a shell and scrolls on the arc – bears its maker's mark (for Isaac Cookson) under one handle and a lion passant under the other, but no town mark nor date letter (fig.181). Bonhams in 2012 put its date as c1750 and I'm inclined to agree, given the strong resemblance of the handles to a London-made strainer by Benjamin West in 1749 (Group 4; fig.52). Its bowl piercing is, however, not so imitative: its central floral 'star' surrounded by alternating groups of bold scrolls and panels of nine crosslets, with a single ring of dots around the outside, is quite unique.

Fig.182: Newcastle, date & maker's marks invisible

A third strainer from Newcastle could easily pass for a London Group-8 single-handled one, except that it bears the three – separated – castles mark for Newcastle and a lion passant (but sadly no signs of a date letter nor a maker's mark). This is a piece (fig.182) that, between 2107 and 2019, did the rounds of auction houses from Woking to Derby to Honiton, selling on four occasions.

Fig.183: c1720, Benjamin Brancker of Liverpool

The only example of a strainer hallmarked in Chester that I know of is mentioned by Jackson (in the 1921 edition). I don't know what it looks like, but it was from the workshop of Joseph Walley in 1780. In Jackson's later edition (the third, from 1989), Walley is given as a Liverpool maker, who was clearly strongly connected to Chester as he is also listed as a member of the Chester Goldsmiths' Company. The Liverpudlian Benjamin Brancker, however, who made a strainer with quite a simple piercing pattern but beautifully 'pierced' triangular handles with open diamond-shaped terminals (fig.183), never used an assay office, content merely to punch his own mark and sometimes a 'Sterling' mark, also his own. This one, which Woolley & Wallis sold in 2006, dates from the 1720s.

The only sure reference I have to a lemon strainer by a Birmingham maker comes (thanks to Craig O'Donnell) from the Plate Register of the Birmingham Assay Office: a heavy 'punch strainer' (nearly 6oz, 185g) by Matthew Boulton and John Fothergill which was assayed in its first year (1773-74). Unfortunately such registers didn't give detailed descriptions. G. Bernard Hughes (1968) reported that Matthew Boulton submitted punch strainers for assay in Birmingham "from 1770", but this would anyway have been impossible for the first three years (Chester may have been their destination) and I have no further evidence of the existence of these strainers.

I know of only one lemon strainer from Sheffield, hallmarked for 1799 and possibly the work of Samuel Kirkby & Company. The piercing in its bowl takes the form of six overlapping circles of dots forming a six-petalled flower, with infills including six sets of four unusual kite-shaped holes. It lacks handles: instead, it has two quite long, shaped, downward-facing clips, meaning it could rest only on a purpose-made bowl with a diameter of about 11 cm.

PLYMOUTH LEMON STRAINERS

Pentecost Symons had an extraordinarily long working life as a Plymouth silversmith, entering his first mark at the Exeter assay office in 1706, making communion cups and patens in 1716 and 1717 and lemon strainers between 1730 and 1750 before dying in 1758, having had his last spoon hallmarked in 1757-58. Despite this longevity, his output – at least of strainers – was remarkably conservative, in that he pioneered a highly distinctive style of simple and lightweight strainer and remained faithful to it for twenty years. Other Plymouth makers used a similar style in the 1750s and even in the 1770s little had changed in the design. As a result, all Plymouth lemon strainers can be instantly recognised.

Fig.184: Exeter 1733, Pentecost Symons of Plymouth

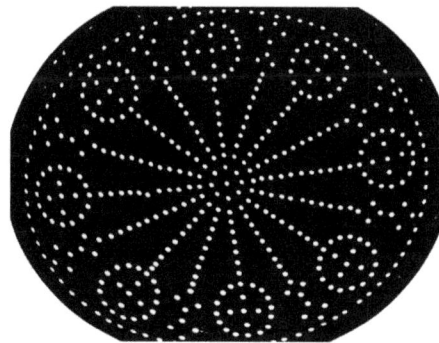

Miles Harrison's book on Exeter and West Country silver (2014) illustrates one of Symons's lemon strainers (fig.184), but although its bowl has the classic Pentecost piercing pattern its handle is very different from all his others and quite unique: apparently cast, it is flat, shaped and pierced through with tear-drops and semicircles, engraved with a possibly contemporary married couple's initials. This strainer was offered in 2002 by a Nottingham auctioneer, who recognised it as having been hallmarked in Exeter in 1733 and made by Symons. In 2014 in Darlington, another auction house listed it as "London 1784", which would share the lion passant, crowned leopard's head and date letter 'i' but should have an incuse king's head in profile rather than the Exeter castle. A Devon dealer came by it, realised its true origin and slapped a price tag on it more than ten times greater than its latest hammer price.

Fig.185: Exeter 1736, Pentecost Symons of Plymouth   *Fig.186: Detail of Symons's 1736 strainer*

All but one of the other 11 Symons lemon strainers I've come across have a much simpler handle, shaped as a broad vertical ring with a small clip facing down from its lower surface (fig.185). They all have a rounded oval bowl with maker's marks and hallmarks on the outside under the unstrengthened rim. Their piercing pattern always comprises 16 radii emanating from a small central double circle, every other one of them terminating in a 'lollipop' of a cross within a circle (fig.186). The radii in between end in a simple pair of crosses and the whole design is surrounded by a single ring of dot-holes.

One other anomalous strainer by Pentecost Symons, sold by a Massachusetts auction house in 2009 without knowing where it was made, nor by whom, has the typical bowl motif but the handle seems to have been replaced by a tiny vertical ring with another ring suspended from it. Its date letter may be the 'n' of Exeter 1737, but as with the majority of Symons's strainers, the marks are far from crisp through years of polishing and manhandling of thin-gauge silver.

Some of his strainers have initials engraved on their handle and one manages to fit a crest and a motto on it; at least one has a crest under the rim at 90° from the handle.

Fig.187: Exeter c1755, probably Richard Bidlake of Plymouth

Two strainers indistinguishable from Symons's carry the Exeter hallmarks for 1753 and 1755 and each has the mark of Joseph Freeman, another Plymouth silversmith, who began his career in 1753. Richard Bidlake was also a Plymouth maker who faithfully copied the same style in the mid-1750s. One of his (fig.187) was identified by a top Somerset auction house as "possibly by Robert Bowers, Chester", sold for £460 and then appeared at the Antiques for Everyone fair at the National Exhibition Centre later in 2014 and found its way to a Devon dealer who knew its true origin and gave it a price tag of over £3000. And from about 1760 comes very similar strainers with the mark of Pentecost's son, Roger Berryman Symons. The two of his that I know of have one feature that distinguishes them from his father's: in the bowl, there is an extra outermost curvy ring of dots.

Fig.188: Exeter c1775, Jason Holt of Plymouth

The final Plymouth strainer in my database has the same shape again and the same handle and clip, but its piercing design has taken a revolutionary new turn! It has eight concentric circles in the middle, beyond which is a pattern of broad and strongly overlapping 'flower petals' (fig.188). The bowl's rim is also distinct, having a 'double fillet' of applied strengthening, like the London strainers until the 1730s. It was the work of Jason Holt in about 1775, bearing only his maker's mark and an Exeter lion passant.

Chapter Four
IRISH LEMON STRAINERS

Throughout the 18th century, the Kingdom of Ireland is run by an Anglo-Irish Protestant landowning class who make up just 5% of the population and who control the economy, most of the agriculture, the legal system, both Houses of the Irish Parliament and local government. The last uprising by the Catholic Jacobite supporters of the deposed King James II brought King William to Ireland to crush James at the Battle of the Boyne in 1690, and now the Catholic majority – mostly peasants – are dispossessed and the law will enshrine discrimination against them until their emancipation in 1829. Ireland has its own peerage and its own Church of Ireland, but many of the landowners are absentee Englishmen.

Although Ireland will have its own Parliament and legislature until its Union with Great Britain in 1801, it has very limited autonomy, ruled as it is from London, whose monarchs appoint a series of (mostly absentee) English Viceroys. Ireland is largely treated like a backward colony.

Despite a famine in 1740 and 1741, following two very cold winters, which kill some 400,000 people and force 150,000 to emigrate, but helped by general peace in the country until the 1780s, the population doubles in size during the century to more than 4 million.

Ireland is not usually credited with having had its own Enlightenment, mainly because the continued religious tensions prevent political reform, but its capital city Dublin is an important seat of culture and social change. Even as early as 1700 its population is exceeded in the British Empire only by London's, comprising a mix of Catholics, mainly of ancient Irish origin, and Protestant descendants of English settlers. Its ancient university, Trinity College, maintains an excellent reputation for learning – and for its extensive library (where the famous illuminated manuscript of the Gospels, the Book of Kells, *has resided since 1654). The satirist Jonathan Swift, Dean of Dublin Cathedral, has his* Gulliver's Travels *published in 1726.*

It is in Dublin (in 1742) that Handel's Messiah *is first performed and cultural life in the city from the middle of the century revolves around its theatres, libraries, book-shops, coffee-houses and taverns, where liberal sentiment is aired aimed at improving education, encouraging civilised behaviour, supporting entrepreneurs and doing charitable works. The old narrow medieval streets are replaced with broad roads, elegant squares and new residential Georgian properties, on both sides of the river Liffey. The Guinness Brewery is founded in 1759. Immigration from rural areas of Ireland results in a Catholic majority in the city, but it is not involved in the Irish Rebellion of 1798 against British rule which is quickly put down by British forces.*

Both the medieval walled and castled cities of Cork in the south-west of the country and Limerick, Ireland's main port on its western seaboard, are also gentrified with new Palladian architecture in the mid- and late 18th century, helped by income from trade. Cork – through its port on one of the largest natural harbours in the world – exports mainly butter and beef; and Limerick – with its access to transatlantic trade – exchanges exported foodstuffs with timber, coal, tar and iron. Cork is Ireland's second city and Limerick its third. Both have been besieged by the Williamite forces, Cork taken by the Duke of Marlborough in 1690 and Limerick finally suing for peace in 1691: the Treaty of Limerick marked the end of the Jacobite uprising.

Throughout Ireland, the absence of any successful bank until the Bank of Ireland's establishment in 1782 acts as an incentive for the purchase of silverware, not only by the aristocracy but also by an increasing number of 'middling gentry' including merchants and small landowners.

Douglas Bennett, the main authority on antique Irish silver, may be correct that Dublin's "designs in silver often followed those of London, with a time lag of a few years". Yet Irish silver, especially in the first 60 or 70 years of the 18th century, has numerous recognisable peculiarities of its own: think, for example, of the embossed rustic scenes on dish rings, milk jugs and sugar bowls, the harp-shaped handles on cups, the little counter dishes and the Celtic-point terminals on spoons. Irish lemon strainers, until the 1750s, are instantly identifiable, particularly in their handle shapes, and it seems that any direct design influence from London was minimal: the numerous Irish silversmiths shared a distinctive Irish style of strainer handles and, although it evolved subtly as the century wore on, they stuck to it. Most of their clients would have been Anglo-Irish Protestants with homes in England as well as in Ireland, many with a fond nostalgia for Irish ways.

Far fewer lemon strainers were made in Ireland than in England. The total of 59 surviving Irish strainers (46 of them from Dublin, 12 from the provinces and one of uncertain Irish origin) that I know of is more than ten times smaller than the English total. This is despite the fact that Dublin was the second-largest city in the British Isles after London and the Irish silversmiths' clients were enjoying a very comfortable lifestyle in the Irish 'Age of Elegance'.

Hallmarking in Dublin had been in the capable hands of the Company of Goldsmiths since 1638, involving a Sterling purity mark specific to Dublin (the Crowned Harp) and a date letter, which were stamped by the Assay Office at the Goldsmiths' Hall on every piece of silverware submitted for assay, to accompany the maker's mark already on it. The obligation in England (between 1697 and 1720) to fashion silver wares in the purer, Britannia standard was never imposed in Ireland. After a tax (of sixpence per ounce) was introduced in 1730, a new punch was added, as proof of payment: the figure of Hibernia (not to be confused with the English Britannia). For unfathomable reasons, however, from that time onwards, the Dublin Assay Office omitted to stamp date letters on virtually every silver item except for flatware. Fortunately for today's collectors, however, the assay office often changed the designs of both harp and Hibernia and by comparing these with dated spoons and forks, the National Museum of Ireland was able to publish a guide (Ticher *et al*, 1968) to Dublin marks between 1730 and 1772.

Most of the Irish lemon strainers in my database lack a date letter, so they have 'circa' dates estimated by dealers and auctioneers, and without being able to see – in most cases – the assay marks in detail, I cannot verify them and knowledge of when the makers flourished and stylistic comparisons are all one can use to help to narrow down the date ranges.

The Irish provincial towns, Cork and Limerick, included a small number of lemon strainers in their production, most of which are very out of the ordinary and include some of the most beautiful ever made anywhere. Neither place had its own assay office (Cork tried several times during the 18th century but met with implacable opposition from Dublin's Assay Office) and the roads to Dublin were long, slow and unsafe for travel with valuable silver, so not one of the provincial lemon strainers made the journey for assay in Dublin. Nor does any town mark appear on them, as Cork and Limerick makers agreed merely to stamp their own mark and – but not always – the word 'STERLING'. Date letters were never used. I have included the Cork and Limerick lemon strainers along with the Dublin ones in the two Irish categories, 'nose-handled' and 'other'.

The earliest Dublin lemon strainer in my database dates from 1714, the earliest from Cork is c1725 and the first ones from Limerick were made in c1750. Two Dublin strainers believed by important authorities on antique silver to date from "1696" and "1696-98" were, I believe, both made in 1730 when the date letter was the same (see next page). By the 1740s, numbers were already dropping and only a few are known from after 1770; I know of only one strainer from each of the 1780s, 1790s and 1800s.

With one exception (which is of questionable Irish origin), every Irish lemon strainer that I know of has two handles: the most popular of all the London styles, the Group-8 one-handled strainers, didn't get a look in on the other side of the Irish Sea. The great majority of the earlier ones have flat, solid handles, broadest in the middle and tapering to a terminal 'nose'; a few of these are pierced. From about 1750, they became longer and more triangular. As far as I know, all were hammered from sheets of silver, rather than cast. A very small number of Irish handles have their topsides engraved or flat-chased (in the latter cases with the decoration extending around the rim as well).

The rims of their bowls never had the 'double fillet' strengthening that pre-1730s London ones had; instead, their strengthening was applied as a broader ring, giving the rim a 'reeded', gently everted look. As in London, gadrooning, beading and true reeding of rims only appeared after 1760. Flat handles on London strainers fit neatly into the channel within the 'double fillet'; on Irish ones, the bases of the handles are fully visible underneath where they were soldered on to the rim.

Bowl piercing patterns are almost as varied as London ones, with virtually no two looking alike. There are concentric rings, central rosettes, various flower-petal designs, panels of crosslets, as well as scrolls, splashes, fountains, squiggles and curved dashes: each silversmith seems to have had his own patterns and none are direct copies from London strainers. I say "his" because all the makers in my database were men, the only attribution to a woman maker (Jane Daniell) probably being incorrect.

The overwhelming majority of Irish lemon strainers have an engraved crest, usually on top of one of the handles. Each strainer, it seems, would have been valued as a family treasure. As evidenced by their strong representation in Fairbairn's Book of Heraldic Crests, Irish families were particularly fond of heraldry and these would have included the purchasers and users of lemon strainers, proud of their station in society.

Needless to say, because of their relative rarity, Dublin lemon strainers tend to fetch more than their London counterparts and Cork strainers more still. Among the highest prices ever paid for lemon strainers were for two of the three known ones fashioned by Joseph Johns of Limerick. Dublin ones with maker's marks only are less desirable than those with full hallmarks (even if the date letter is absent).

IRISH WITH FLAT, 'NOSED' HANDLES

This category covers most of the lemon strainers made in Ireland. Only in the second half of the 18th century did deviations from the norm appear, many based on contemporary London designs, which are described under 'Irish Other' from p.132.

Michael Clayton's *Dictionary* (1971) gives a Dublin 'orange strainer' with a hallmark "for 1696", which would be by far the oldest known Irish strainer. The illustration is good enough, however, to show that the maker's mark tallies with Jackson's mark for George Cartwright seen on a hash spoon from 1726. The Gothic (or Olde English) 'L' date letter for the years 1696-98 was virtually indistinguishable from the one used in 1730 and 1731, and the latter was used *without* an accompanying Hibernia stamp until 20th April 1730 (when the silver duty was imposed), so it is likely that this strainer – which lacks the Hibernia – dates from the first four months of 1730. The same may well be true – for the same reasons – for Jackson's reference to a David King lemon strainer from 1696-98, especially as Jackson also cites a communion paten of 1730 by the same David King with a very similar mark.

Fig.189: Dublin 1714, maker's mark pierced through

That would give the honour of the oldest Irish lemon strainer that I know of to the one sold by Bonhams in 2013 with the Olde English 'x' date mark for 1714 (but its maker's mark is "lost in the piercing"). Its design is unusual, both in its handles and its bowl piercing: the handles have a 'thick-stemmed mushroom' shape with a large cut-out heart at the base, and the bowl has a central rosette of scrolls with nine radii of straight-line dots (fig.189). Another strainer, in the collection of the National Museum of Ireland, is by David King and from 1715. Delamer & O'Brien (2005) described it as "1716-1718", probably because the museum's list gives two descriptions of the same strainer, one with those dates and the other referring to the correct Olde English 'y' mark for 1715-16 (seen by me on photographs kindly sent by Edith Andrees, Curator of Silver at the museum). The central rosette in its bowl is not dissimilar to the 1714 example, but it has no fewer than 32 lines of pierced dots radiating from it; its two trefoil flat handles are pierced with a unique assortment of hearts, scrolls, dots and crescents with a terminal fleur-de-lis. Apart from these very early examples, handles seem not to have been pierced again until the middle of the century. Delamer & O'Brien point out that the Dublin Assay Office sometimes described lemon strainers as 'orange' strainers.

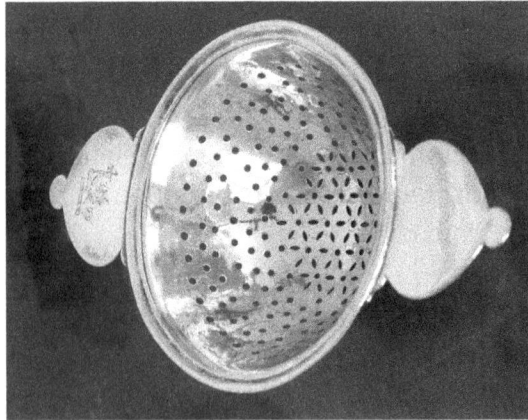

Fig.190: Dublin 1717, John Hamilton

John Hamilton's lemon strainers of 1715 and 1717 (fig.190) represent the most common theme of handles until the mid-1730s: plain, flat and 'bulbous', narrowed at or near the base and tapering to a 'snub nose' terminal. These two examples, however, have very different bowl piercings, one being a riot of scrolls and the other having dots around a central panel of 14 interlocking six-armed stars. Another of Hamilton's came up for sale at a Maryland auction in 2012 (with its snub noses bent awkwardly downwards). Its description dated it as "circa 1720", which fits the photograph of the crowned harp, whose design was used for four years from 1720 until 1723; it seems that even then (before 1730), not all silverware was given a date mark.

Fig.191: Dublin 1719, Philip Kinnersly   *Fig.192: Dublin c1725, Thomas Bolton*

There were no specialist makers of lemon strainers in Ireland. I know of 14 silversmiths who produced strainers up until the 1740s (and Jackson lists three others), most of whom are known to have been generalist makers of all sorts of silver wares. They include those already mentioned (George Cartwright,

David King and John Hamilton (fig.194)) as well as Thomas Bolton (fig.192), Matthew Walker, Philip Kinnersly (fig.191), Erasmus Cope (fig.195), Thomas Isaac [or Isaacs] (fig.198), Isaac d'Olier (fig.199) and (in Cork) William Newenham (fig.193). Most of them served as Master of the Goldsmiths' Company of Dublin (Bolton in 1692-93, King in 1699, Hamilton in 1714-15, Cope in 1715-16 and 1722-24, Walker in 1724-25, Kinnersly in 1727-28, Cartwright in 1738-39, and d'Olier in 1752-53; Thomas Isaac held the lesser post of Warden from 1742-45). Thomas Bolton, who became Lord Mayor of Dublin and has Bolton Street named after him, is widely considered to have been the finest of all Dublin's silversmiths (but apparently was in poverty when he died in his late 70s). His work was described in a Sotheby's catalogue as "versatile and avant garde with unique flourishes of ornament" and, although he made a very traditional lemon strainer in 1718, he branched out in the 1720s with two strainers which dispensed with snub noses and had handles shaped and engraved to resemble scallop shells. The history of one of these (fig.192), marked only (in the bowl and on both handles) with his maker's mark, was given on p.35; the other was fully hallmarked for 1723 and forms part of the excellent Assheton Bennett Collection of silver at the City of Manchester Art Gallery.

Fig.193: Cork c1725, William Newenham

The earliest nose-handled strainers from Cork are by William Newenham and date from c1725 and c1730. The first (fig.193) is unusual in having a sharply pointed 'nose' at the end of its handles, which are pierced with a diamond and two bean-shaped cut-outs. Its bowl is pierced with 15 concentric rings of dots. (An almost identical strainer bearing the mark of William Clarke of Cork is illustrated by Bowen & O'Brien (2005).) The second Newenham one also differs a little from contemporary Dublin strainers, in this case having broadly triangular, shaped handles with no constriction near the base; its bowl piercing pattern comprises five concentric rings of dots and alternating groups of three and seven dots outside them. Newenham was Master of the Cork Company of Goldsmiths in 1726 after promotion from his position as a Warden. This Company flourished from the mid-17th century until at least the 1720s, although it was never allowed its own assay office.

An intriguing Dublin strainer from c1730, belonging to a private collector who kindly sent me photographs, appears to be the very same one that Jackson mentions under 'Unascribed Irish Provincial Marks' with the maker's mark ('crowned I+F') "stamped four times on a lemon strainer", dated from "about 1780". Its handles and bowl piercing design all cry out Dublin 1730, however, and there was a Dublin maker at that time by the name of John Freebough who completed his apprenticeship in 1722 and worked until 1748. His mark illustrated by Jackson is a different 'crowned I.F', but it's possible that he registered or used more than one mark. Jackson's earlier (1921) edition adds that this strainer was "noted by Mr. Dudley Westropp" [probably M.S. Dudley Westropp who was Keeper of Art & Industry at the National Museum of Ireland] and the current owner believes it came from the 'Westropp dispersal Belfast/Glasgow c1990'. The crest on one of its handles may pertain to Sir John Banks KCB of Golagh, co. Monaghan (c1815-1908), a prominent Irish physician and professor.

Fig.194: Dublin 1730, John Hamilton

John Hamilton had a long working life and in 1730 he produced another strainer (fig.194), with typical handles and a lovely piercing pattern of scrolls and alternating dots and dashes arranged in a circle and in a square with inward-curving sides. Like the Cartwright example mentioned above, it bears the 'L' date letter for 1730 but not the Hibernia mark, so it was made before the imposition of the tax in April of that year. It seems that the tax was advertised in advance and there was such a rush to pre-empt it that more wares were hallmarked in the first three months of 1730 than in the nine following months! Another pre-tax model came up for sale in 2013 (from the Crichel Estate in Dorset) which is so similar in shape and bowl design that, even though it has no maker's mark, one could safely credit Hamilton's workshop for it. It found its way to the prestigious New York dealership, S.J. Shrubsole.

Fig.195: Dublin 1731, Erasmus Cope

Fig.196: Dublin 1732, Matthew Alanson

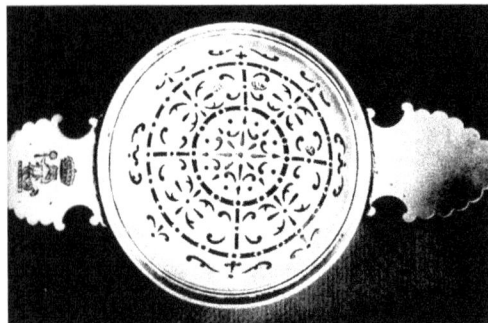

Fig.197: Dublin 1732, Matthew Alanson

After the 1730 start of the tax and before the change of date letter in 1732, two more lemon strainers in my database were produced. One is attributed to Jane Daniell, whose only reference in Jackson dates from 1740; Henry Daniell, however, whose conjoined 'HD' mark is almost identical, was working in the 1710s and died in 1738, so is a more likely candidate; he was Master of the Dublin Goldsmiths' Company in 1730 and Jane Daniell gets no mention at all in Bennett (1984). The other is by Erasmus Cope, with a variation on the theme of radiating lines of dots from a central rosette in the bowl (fig.195). A heavy strainer by Matthew Alanson (fig.196) is fully hallmarked under both handles, but lacks a date letter; its Crowned Harp design places it between 1729 and 1732, and its Hibernia between 1732 and 1738, so it was most probably produced in 1732. Its engraved crest (a goat passant) is set within an elaborate baroque cartouche of swirling foliage and could possibly be for John Russell, the 4th Duke of Bedford, who inherited the dukedom in 1732 and later became Lord Lieutenant (Viceroy) of Ireland and Chancellor of Trinity College, Dublin. Another by Alanson, from the same year, has a geometric arrangement of scrolls, dots and dashes in its bowl and handles reminiscent of Bolton's scallop shells (fig.197).

Fig.198: Dublin c1740, Thomas Isaac

Fig.199: Dublin c1750, probably Isaac d'Olier

The first signs of lengthening handles came in the late 1730s with two strainers by Thomas Isaac, the main changes being a longer, shaped nose and more small protrusions from the sides; the first is from 1736 and the other (fig.198) is undated but probably broadly contemporary (c1740). The latter not only has a particularly beautiful piercing design of crosslets, scrolls, squiggles and splashes, but one of its handles sports a unique notched rib attached to its underside, which may have prevented the strainer from sliding lengthways while straddling wide receptacles of different sizes.

One other long-handled lemon strainer has unwaisted triangular handles with multiple ogee sides and is hard to date. It was sold by a respected dealer as by Joseph Walker, who was active between 1694 and 1717, but it is stylistically more in keeping with the 1740s and there was a John Walker – with an almost identical 'script IW' mark – who features in Jackson in the 1739-40 year. Another with a long triangular handle, but with smoother edges, was – according to a Miller's Buyer's Guide in 2002 – credited to Michael Smith and dated 1793 by no less an authority than the Dublin dealership of J.W. Weldon. Smith's working dates were between 1732 and 1754, and the Roman 'W' letter for 1793 may have been confused with the Olde English 'W' in use between 1741 and 1743. Understandably, a strainer estimated as 'c.1750' by Sotheby's in 2019 was attributed to James Douglas, but at least one of his marks is – according to Jackson – interchangeable with one of Isaac d'Olier's, who was a known strainer maker, and I would hazard a guess that this one is also by d'Olier (fig.199). All these uncertainties over ascription and dating highlight the greater difficulties presented by Georgian silver from Dublin compared with London silver of the same age.

Fig.200: Limerick c1750, Joseph Johns

The most desirable of all Irish lemon strainers – and including the two most valuable non-London lemon strainers ever sold – are those made by Joseph Johns of Limerick. Spoons from Limerick are so rare that very ordinary ones fetch many hundreds of pounds; any other Limerick silverware is extremely unusual and even more sought after. A coffee pot by Joseph Johns fetched £70,850 at Christie's in 2008 and a cream jug and a sugar bowl, both by the same maker, realised 13,000 and 21,500 Euros, respectively, at Adam's auction house in Dublin in 2014. Another of his coffee pots had been 'Victorianised' with dense and extensive foliate and floral chasing, which greatly reduced its monetary value, but it was expertly (and no doubt expensively) dechased to return it to its original smooth-bodied glory and offered for sale by a top Dublin silver dealership in 2014. Johns had a long and successful working life, from 1731 to 1774, becoming Sheriff of Limerick in 1756 and later Chamberlain and Mayor of the town.

Fig.201: Joseph Johns's mark on Limerick lemon strainer

His three surviving lemon strainers were probably made between 1750 and 1760. All have similar handles, broad at their base with curvaceously shaped edges and tapering to a rounded end containing a pierced heart or tear-drop. Unusually and beautifully, they are all flat-chased with scrolls, sunflowers, roses and baskets of flowers, highlighted by delicate matting, and the chasing continues around the rim of the bowl, here with curving stems bearing leaves and tendrils. The bowls are wide (12 cm across) and pierced with dot-holes and a variety of small scrolls, commas, crosses, crescents and squiggles, each strainer having its own design. Overall they are 28 to 28.5 cm in length and they are all marked under each handle with Johns's mark of 'II' with a lion rampant between, in a shaped punch (fig.201). The first one also has the 'STERLING' punch.

One of them (the heaviest, at 5oz 17dwt = 182g) was in the John A. Hyman Collection of lemon strainers on loan to the Colonial Williamsburg Foundation in Virginia, after selling at Sotheby's in New York in 1987; three years before that, it seems to have been up for sale at Christie's in London. Its bowl design is of dense 'splashes' and arabesques within a broad six-armed star of dots and one of its handles has an engraved crest. This is the one illustrated by Douglas Bennett in 'Irish Georgian Silver' (1972). After the Hyman Collection was dispersed, it was sold by S. J. Shrubsole and *via* J. & W. Duvallier to a private collector.

Another has eight lines of alternating commas and squiggles radiating from a central embellished rosette, each terminating in one of two starburst motifs; the segments between the lines are filled with dots. This one (fig.200) sold in 2015, in Lawrence's auction room in Crewkerne, Somerset, for a hammer price of £14,000, to a local private collector who outbid telephone bidders in Ireland.

The third sold at Christie's in New York in 2001 for $32,900 (equivalent to £21,100 at that time) and was loaned to the Hunt Museum's exhibition in 2007-8, *A Celebration of Limerick's Silver,* and was illustrated in Bowen & O'Brien's catalogue. It has a bowl pattern similar to the second one and its handles bear two crests, one of which is for the Massey family of County Limerick. Its current owner, I believe, is also a native of County Limerick.

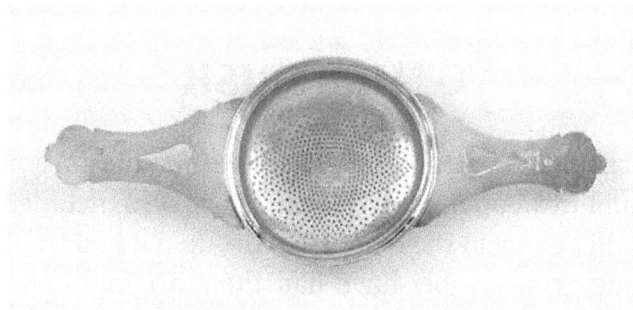

Fig.202: Dublin c1752, John Letablere

At around the same time as Joseph Johns was fashioning his lemon strainers in Limerick, a handful of Dublin silversmiths favoured very long, shaped and tapering handles with substantial pierced areas in them. Matthias Brown and John Letablere in around 1750/1752 used very similar, narrow-waisted handles with a large cut-out heart; Brown's bowl has a large panel of 'bottony' crosslets alternating with dots surrounded by a ring of swirling scrolls, while Letablere sticks to dots in and around a large four-petalled flower with quadruple borders (fig.202).

Fig.203: Dublin c1755, Richard Williams

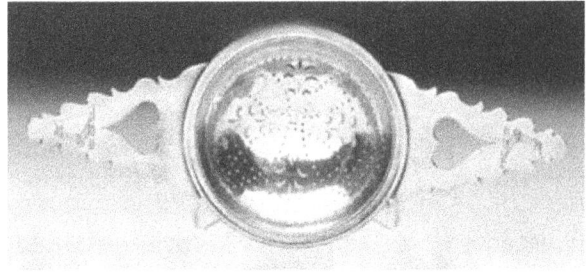

Fig.204: ?Dublin c1755, perhaps Richard Williams

Richard Williams's fabulous lemon strainer of c1755 (fig.203) has the long, shaped, triangular handles of the period but pierced in a unique, bold 'splash' design. Its bowl is a masterpiece of uncluttered rococo ebullience, on a par with the best of the elaborately pierced London strainers from the late 1710s into the 1730s but on a larger scale, using a strictly geometric arrangement of Maltese-like crosslets, four-petalled flowers, scrolls, curved dashes and fountains to give a kaleidoscopic effect. It has only the maker's mark ('RW') under one handle, a scratch weight (of 5oz 5.5dwt = 164g) and a crest of a 'boar's head erased' on top of the other one. It is 26.2 cm long and its (particularly shallow) bowl has a diameter of 12.2 cm. It now weighs 162.4g. I'm inclined to believe, from the shape and outline of the handles, that a strainer described in 2004 by Christie's in Melbourne as "A Georgian Sterling Silver Lemon Strainer, Unmarked" (fig.204) comes from Williams's workshop. It has a single large heart cut out of its handles, a crest on top of one of them, and a bowl with four scroll fountains between dot petals and with outer concentric rings.

OTHER IRISH

Into this category go the Irish lemon strainers whose two handles are *not* cut from a flat sheet of silver but are cast instead and in an openwork design. I have also included a single-handled strainer of uncertain origin that would belong in the main Irish Group if it had two handles. The earliest ones, from the 1730s and 40s, may conceivably have had their original handles replaced, but without having handled them myself I can't tell; they are certainly eccentric.

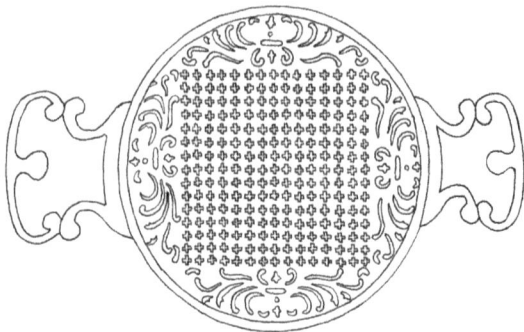

Fig.205: Dublin c1730, John Hamilton (outline hand-drawn by the author)

Fig.206: Dublin c1740, maker's mark obscured (shown upside-down)

The first, by John Hamilton in about 1730 (fig.205) – now at the National Museum of Ireland – has C-scrolls at the sides and an E-scroll at the end of each handle, with the central stroke of the 'E' facing inwards; the bowl piercing is reminiscent of the c1740 strainer by Thomas Isaac (mentioned on p.129, fig.198), with a panel of crosslets surrounded by splash-like scrolls. The second, from c1740, sold at Sotheby's in London in 1967 (fig.206): its maker's mark is "obscured", its bowl has an attractive design of crosslets, scrolls, dashes and splashes and each handle has double-scroll sides, a connecting bar across the middle and a baluster knop at the end. The catalogue photograph of the underside suggests that the original handles may have been cut away. George Cartwright, who made the snub-nosed 1730 strainer wrongly dated as 1696, made another (possibly c1735) with unique, pierced handles with a central oval medallion held in place by scrolls coming in from the sides and a fleur-de-lis at its base; the bowl has a central panel of dots and crosslets surrounded by three concentric dot rings.

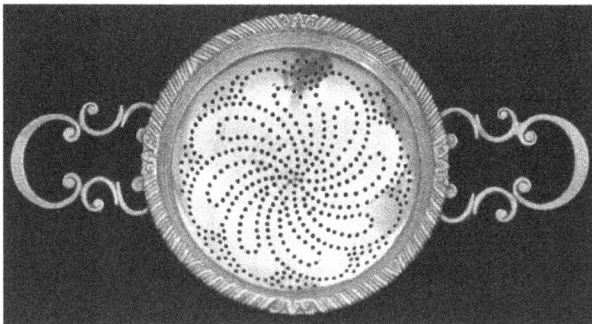

Fig.207: Limerick c1760, Samuel Johns

Fig.208: Cork c1760 or later, Stephen Walsh

By about 1760, the fashion for flat, shaped handles had passed and Irish lemon strainer production went into decline. Not surprisingly, therefore, tradition went out of the window and whimsical designs were employed, sometimes influenced by contemporary London styles. The Limerick silversmith Samuel Johns (not believed to have been directly related to Joseph Johns) made a splendidly eccentric strainer in c1760 (fig.207) with a swirl in the bowl of eight curved, radiating arms, a gadrooned rim with four acanthus motifs and each handle comprising five dainty scrolls (and with the maker's mark underneath). This one is housed in Limerick Museum. Probably in the early-to-mid-1760s, Stephen Walsh produced a lovely lemon strainer in Cork (fig.208) with rococo, leafy double-scroll handles, an applied shell-and-scroll rim and a complex geometric design of pierced dots. John Nicolson, also of Cork, used a very similar pair of handles and applied rim, but with a simpler geometric bowl pattern and extra piercing on the rim, on his strainer which was in the Albert Collection. London makers were using very similar handles in the mid-1760s, so maybe Butler, in his 1999 catalogue of the Collection, was correct to date it as c1770. Whether he was also right to suggest that Nicolson had bought the handles and rim from London, I don't know, but if he didn't buy the handles he certainly copied them.

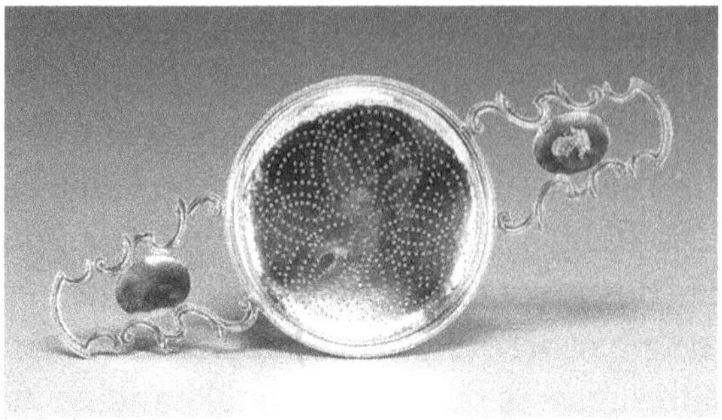

Fig.209: Dublin c1770, maker's mark rubbed   *Fig.210: Dublin c1770, possibly James Graham*

Triple-scroll-handled strainers, from the workshops of an unknown Dublin maker (with a rubbed mark; fig.209) and of Carden Terry of Cork, probably made in the 1770s, were inspired by or copied from London equivalents. Another one differs in having an oval medallion nestled between the sides (fig.210), one of them bearing a crest; this was sold by a Cork auctioneer in 2013 as by "J. Gumley, Dublin c.1750", but John Gumley's last mention as a silversmith was in 1739 and the strainer is stylistically of the 1770s, when a James Graham was working in Dublin.

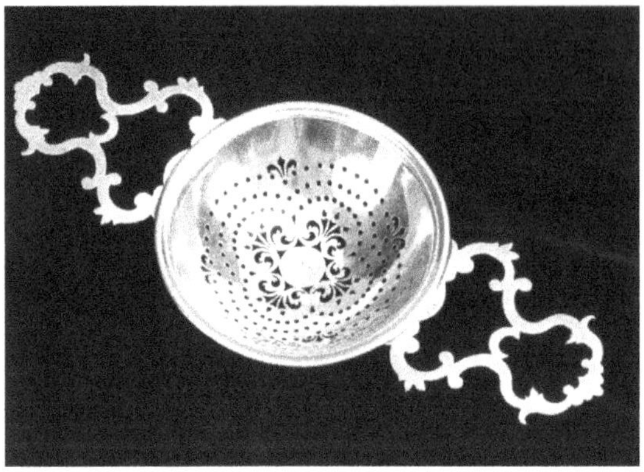

Fig.211: Dublin c1765, probably Richard Williams

Richard Williams has already been mentioned and praised for his independent designs: his 1750s flat-handled strainers were bold and luxurious, so his later lemon strainer with openwork handles was probably an original creation as well (fig.211). The handles have double-scroll sides with bold vestiges of stylised leafage, an arc end with a central shell-like motif and a crescent-shaped mid-connector; the maker's mark ('RW') is on top of the base of one handle. The bowl has four scrolling splashes near the middle and four smaller ones outside, with three concentric, indented circles of dots. A circular medallion in the centre of the bowl bears the engraved crest of a griffin's head erased, under the motto *Grip Hard*, probably for the Leslie family of County Monaghan, now part of Northern Ireland.

Fig.212: Dublin 1789, William Bond

In the late 18th and early 19th centuries, the very few Dublin lemon strainers that were produced mimicked the London fashion for loop handles. William Bond made one in 1789 (fig.212) with reeded handles and rim (and very old-fashioned concentric dot-rings in the bowl), and Robert Breeding's of 1808 has plain handles and a 12-petalled flower bowl design. By this time, the Dublin assay office was giving silverware full hallmarks, including date letter and the king's head duty mark. Gustavus Byrne's 1797 lemon strainer, in the collection of Dublin's National Museum of Ireland, has an old-fashioned arrangement of five concentric rings of dot-holes in its bowl, a reeded rim and distinctive (but fully marked) shaped triangular openwork handles with a longitudinal strut down the middle; it even has a snub-nosed terminal, harking back to the Dublin of the 1750s and earlier.

Fig.213: Possibly Irish c1740, unmarked

My final Irish lemon strainer is a (completely unmarked) curio (fig.213). It came from the silver dealer and generous donor to Oxford's Ashmolean Museum, Michael Wellby, and was sold at auction by Woolley & Wallis in 2012, listed as "18th century Continental". It appeared the following year at the Art Antiques London fair on a stall manned by the great silver dealer Brand Inglis, nearing the end of his distinguished life at the time, who stated with confidence that it was Irish, from c1740, based on its bowl piercing design, its handle shape and the decoration on the handle. The decoration is reminiscent of Joseph Johns's Limerick creations, with its scrolls, flowers, foliage and matting, and no-one else in Ireland or England has made anything like it; but it is engraved not chased and has been cut out of a pre-engraved piece of silver. The bowl has Irish motifs like the crosslets with bulb-ended arms, but the central rosette and splash-like scrolls were universally used both in London and Ireland. The underside of the bowl has been engraved as well, with small crosses, leaves and diamonds, to enhance the pierced design, a flourish I've not seen on any other strainer. Its single-handledness is genuine, as there is a clip opposite, yet there is no other known Irish one-handled lemon strainer. And the rim of the bowl is strengthened by a 'double fillet' of two protruding rings and a channel between them, into which the handle fits; yet every other Irish strainer – as far as I know – lacks this arrangement, which was used in London until the 1730s. It is an exquisite piece, but I reserve judgement on its origin.

Chapter Five
SCOTTISH LEMON STRAINERS

At the end of the 17th century and until the middle of the 18th century, Scotland has its own aristocracy but is generally a poor, rural society based on quite primitive agriculture. A slump in trade, a series of failed harvests and the subsequent famine lead to a major investment, largely by the middle classes, in a scheme to forge a new trade route by colonising Darién in Panamá, whose failure bankrupts the nation in 1700. It also results in the Scottish Parliament agreeing to political Union with England, and the creation of Great Britain, in 1707. At this time, Scotland has a population five times smaller than England's and is 16 times less wealthy.

The succession of Protestant monarchs in London after the overthrow of the Catholic King James II (James VII of Scotland) is not universally popular, especially outside the main towns, and James's son (the 'Old Pretender') and grandson ('Bonnie Prince Charlie') try – and fail – to lead uprisings against George I and II, respectively. These 'Jacobite' rebellions end with the battle of Culloden in 1746.

Edinburgh before 1750 is a small town, but very densely populated because of the confinement of its perimeter walls: many of the houses are up to 12 or more storeys tall. There are often water shortages and sanitation is poor. But it does engender social cohesion because families from very different classes live in the same houses and can't help passing one another on the stairs. The Union with England means politicians have moved to London, but lawyers, teachers and doctors remain and Scotland has four universities (compared to England's two).

Glasgow – with its Atlantic port – takes advantage of the legalisation of trade with America after the Union and it booms by exporting Scottish linen in exchange for cotton and sugar – and particularly American tobacco, the province of the 'Tobacco Lords', nouveau-riche entrepreneurs whose aristocratic behaviour includes financing the town's growing infrastructure. By 1760, Glasgow's tobacco trade is greater than London's; but when it collapses because of the American Revolution the town's merchants successfully diversify into West Indian sugar and rum. Scotland's largest firm is the British Linen Company, exporting to England as well and becoming the British Linen Bank.

After Culloden there is an upsurge in Scottish participation in political, military, economic and intellectual life, heralding the 'Scottish Enlightenment'. Edinburgh builds, to the north of the castle, its elegant Georgian residences of the 'New Town' and the long Presbyterian tradition north of the border lends itself to a new and modern 'liberal Calvinist' ethic, exemplified by the philosopher David Hume and the economist Adam Smith, responsible between them for the first statements of the scientific method and of modern economics. Romantic poetry begins with James Macpherson's adaptations of ancient Scottish Gaelic ballads (Ossian) and is continued by the national poet of Scotland, 'Rabbie' Burns, *immortalised by* Auld Lang Syne. *James Watt designs the first steam engine, in use from the 1770s, and the Scottish portrait painters Allan Ramsey and Henry Raeburn leave permanent records of the great and the good (and many of the middle classes too).*

Industrialisation begins in Scotland late in the 18th century, starting with the spinning and weaving of cotton, which has recently supplanted linen. Glasgow's population outgrows Edinburgh's by 1820 and is at the forefront of iron founding, coal mining and shipbuilding. Scottish soldiers fight in Wellington's victorious Anglo-Allied army at Waterloo in 1815 and Walter Scott writes his historical novel Ivanhoe *in 1819, in the year that Glasgow opens its own silver assay office.*

The smaller eastern Scottish towns Aberdeen, Perth and Dundee – known for the handful of lemon strainers produced outside Edinburgh and Glasgow – have their own enterprises in the 18th century, fishing and paper-making in Aberdeen, linen, leather and whisky in Perth and linen in Dundee.

Other than two extraordinary examples from Aberdeen made in c1685 and c1730, Scottish lemon strainers had a first, brief appearance in Edinburgh in the early 1740s but were only produced in numbers after c1765. Then, rather than dying out at the end of the 18th century as in London and Ireland, they continued from strength to strength in Scotland until the 1830s. The fashion in London for lemon strainers for the first fifty years after 1713 clearly didn't filter up to Scotland, probably because punch only became popular north of the border during the Enlightenment along with a general rise in prosperity.

By far the greatest numbers of Scottish lemon strainers were made by Glasgow silversmiths (four times as many as by Edinburgh makers). Glasgow had its own unofficial town mark (a tree bearing a fish, a bell and a bird) throughout the 18th century, but only inaugurated its own Goldsmiths' Company and Assay Office in 1819. Before the mid-1780s at the earliest, the main Glasgow makers – Adam Graham and Robert Gray – punched their own maker's marks (very rarely with the Glasgow town mark) and did not send their strainers to the only official Scottish assay office, in Edinburgh. After the mid-1780s, Robert Gray did use the Edinburgh office and, for the first time, the Glasgow strainers were properly date-stamped. From 1819, of course, the Glaswegians used their own assay office and their wares bore full sets of marks including date letters.

Edinburgh's silversmiths made few lemon strainers, but generally did send them for assay. Glasgow is considered to have been 'Scottish Provincial' prior to 1819, but other towns continued to retain their provincial status by never opening their own assay offices; those known to have produced lemon strainers (in very small numbers) are Aberdeen, Dundee and Perth. Silversmiths in these towns usually struck their own unofficial town marks along with their maker's marks: 'ABD' (or 'AB') for Aberdeen, a pot of lilies for Dundee and a double-headed eagle for Perth.

My database of Scottish lemon strainers contains 78 examples. Janice & Rodney Dietert's 2007 *Compendium of Scottish Silver, Volume 2* contains 51 'Strainers & Squeezers', of which some are doubled up, two are only 'possibly Scottish' and one is a lemon *squeezer*. There are only 17 in their list of which I have illustrations; the descriptions of the others – taken from auction, museum and collection catalogues – are so brief that I cannot do them justice: I can't even assign them to their respective Groups, so I have not included them. Similarly, there are two lemon strainers mentioned by Jackson which I do not know of, one by Robert Gray & Son (1832) – a partnership which features heavily in my database – and one by Robert Duncan (1822), also of Glasgow. This last maker, along with six listed by the Dieterts (James Dempster and James Douglas of Edinburgh, Robert Dickson of Perth, George Jamieson and Alexander Thompson of Aberdeen and the partners James Newlands & Philip Grierson of Glasgow) are unknown to me otherwise. My database has just five Edinburgh makers, six from Glasgow (assuming 'DM' to have been a Glaswegian), two each from Dundee and Aberdeen and one from Perth, making only 16 makers in total. All of them were men.

I have divided up the Scottish strainers into seven Groups, separated by their handle shapes. They are briefly described below with the numbers of examples in my database and their dates:

1. Two flat, shaped handles (3)   *Edinburgh 1740-42*

2. One or two handles with scroll sides, ringed arc-end and shell cross-piece (5)
                                                 Edinburgh 1774-98; Glasgow c1780-c95

3. One single-scroll-sided, arc-ended (or loop) handle (25)
                                   Glasgow c1765-1826; Edinburgh 1773 & 74; Perth c1810

4. Two scroll-sided, arc-ended handles (12)
                                   Dundee c1750; Glasgow c1763-1817; Edinburgh c1825

5. Two loop handles (11)   *Edinburgh 1784-1818; Glasgow 1819-29*

6. Two ornate, usually lyre-shaped, handles with shell (18)
                                                 Glasgow 1818-33; Edinburgh 1811

7. Scottish oddities (4)   *Aberdeen c1685, c1730; Dundee c1770*

Note that most of the strainers hallmarked in Edinburgh were made by Glasgow silversmiths.

Three of these Groups are uniquely Scottish in the design of their handles. The first (Group 1) have handles that are vaguely Irish but have broader ends. Group-2 examples are unlike any others: if the ring protruding from their arc ends suggests Boston (see American lemon strainers, pp.154-168), their cross-struts with central shell decoration are unique. The best-known distinctively Scottish strainers are the Group-6 lyre-shaped ones with large, heavy, usually oval bowls and very long, cast handles, made after lemon strainers had virtually disappeared in England and Ireland.

Yet even many of the strainers with handles similar to London examples have one Scottish peculiarity, in the pattern of their bowl piercing: a central *unpierced* six-petalled flower which is outlined by dot-holes and the sectors *between* its petals are filled with dot-holes, contrasting with the plain petals so that the flower stands out boldly. (Interestingly, this is stylistically similar to the bowl of a Greek strainer from the Archaic Period about 500 BC, probably used for wine.)

SCOTTISH GROUP 1: TWO FLAT, SHAPED HANDLES

I know of only three of these, made in Edinburgh in 1740, c1740 and 1742. They have different dot-hole piercing patterns in their bowls, and different – or no – engraving or chasing designs on their handles, but their handle shapes have a very similar flat-cone shape with blunt ends and ogee-like sides. By 18th-century standards and despite being of average length (e.g. 18.7 cm), they are of quite a heavy gauge, weighing between 3 and 4oz (= 93-125g).

The simplest is by Dougal Ged, hallmarked for 1740, with apparently plain handles and eight radii opening out at their ends to join a single circle around the bowl and with eight half-radii between them. According to the Dieterts, Ged made at least one other strainer, this one unhallmarked with an engraving of a shell under one handle and the maker's mark under the other.

Fig.214: Edinburgh 1742, James Ker

James Ker also made two which survive, one unassayed and the other fully marked. The first has two lines engraved around the handles on top, parallel and close to the edge, and a crest under a baron's coronet on each, probably representing George, 13th Lord Ross of Hawkhead, who had recently inherited the barony (in 1738) and had become Governor of Edinburgh Castle (in 1739) ; the centre of the bowl has a five-spoked wheel, a ten-pointed star and two concentric circles, from which emerge the ten 'petals' of a flower, itself surrounded by three circles, one wavy. This lemon strainer belonged to Major Ian Shaw of Tordarroch, was sold by Christie's in Edinburgh after his death and was purchased by the National Museums of Scotland in 1983 or 1984.

The second by Ker (fig.214) has a very finely gadrooned rim to its bowl and its handles are beautifully flat-chased with scrolls, flower, shell and foliage on a matted background; under one handle are four marks: 'I.K' for James Ker, 'crowned EL' for the assay master Edward Lothian, the Edinburgh town mark (a three-turreted castle) and the date-letter 'N' for 1742. Edinburgh was unique in punching its assay master's initials as a guarantee of purity, between 1681 and 1759 (after which a thistle was used instead); during those 78 years there were only seven masters, Edward Lothian being the penultimate one. Interestingly, the fifth master was Dougal Ged, who took on the job temporarily for less than two years between 1740 and 1742 and was permitted to use his maker's mark ('GED') to double up as maker and assay master.

The bowl piercing motif is not unlike Ker's other strainer's; the crest in the bowl is of a greyhound sejant, collared, under a tree, which Dreweatts identified in its 2015 sale catalogue as pertaining to Kynardsley or Kinnersley, but I don't believe that the fit is close enough. Sadly I can't find a better match.

SCOTTISH GROUP 2: ONE OR TWO HANDLES WITH SCROLL SIDES, RINGED ARC-END AND SHELL CROSS-PIECE

Fig.215: Edinburgh 1782, William Davie

Fig.216: Edinburgh c1795, probably Robert Gray (of Glasgow)

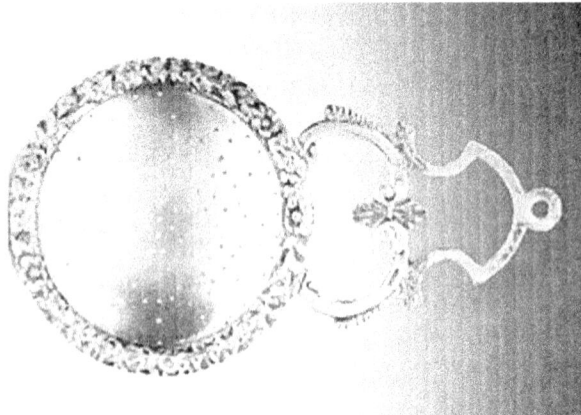

Fig.217: Edinburgh 1798, W.& P. Cunningham

William Davie of Edinburgh was the first silversmith to come up with this unusual handle design, in 1782 (fig.215). Robert Gray of Glasgow made his first one (as far as I know) after 1791 (fig.216), when he first started using the Edinburgh assay office (even though Bonhams, in 2002, 2003 and 2012, dated it as 'circa 1770'). Davie's is the only strainer with two handles, the other three in my database having just the one. Ironically, the only illustration which clearly shows a clip is of Davie's *two*-handled one.

The handles differ from those in the London Group 6 (two-handled) and Group 8 (one-handled) in having the end-ring and the scroll-&-shell cross-piece, both of which add to the strainers' attractiveness. Credit for the bowl piercing design in three of the four representatives of this Group has to be given to Patrick Robertson of Edinburgh, who was the first to use it in two lemon strainers in Group 3, hallmarked 1773 and 1774, some 20 years before these two by Robert Gray. As already mentioned, the idea of making the flower motif stand out from its background, by leaving it unpierced, was Scottish and remained uniquely Scottish.

The bowl of one of Gray's strainers in this Group is circular; the other is pointed oval and with a broader rim; the extra triangular segments on either side of the central circular motif in its bowl are filled with concentric part-rings of dots. The final (Edinburgh) member of the Group dates from 1798 and was made by William & Patrick Cunningham (fig.217). What it lacks in its very simple bowl piercing pattern it more than makes up for in its cast and applied floral and foliate rim, as well as the extra flourishes on its handle.

SCOTTISH GROUP 3: ONE SINGLE-SCROLL-SIDED, ARC-ENDED (OR LOOP) HANDLE

These lemon strainers, based very much on the Group-8 strainers in London, are by far the commonest known from Scotland, manufactured in numbers between the mid-1770s (20 years after openwork one-handled ones first appeared in London) until the mid-1820s. They tend to have smaller bowls than their London counterparts, with simpler piercing designs, while the Scottish and London handles and clips are indistinguishable from each other.

With the exception of the earliest ones made by Patrick Robertson in Edinburgh (fig.218), mentioned above, and one by a Perth silversmith, all the rest come from the workshops of Adam Graham and Robert Gray (later Robert Gray & Son) in Glasgow. As in London, they would have been cheap to buy and therefore available to the middle classes who wanted to follow the fashion in England and Ireland of drinking punch at home.

Adam Graham first used his 'AG' mark in 1763 and had a monopoly on lemon strainer making until Robert Gray was admitted to Glasgow's Incorporation of Hammermen in 1776. Both makers were generalist producers of silverware and Gray's reputation for high quality has given him the epithet of 'Scotland's Paul Storr'. Because neither of them – before a law in 1784 forced them to send their wares for assay in Edinburgh – used date letters, and there was no obvious evolution of strainer handle or piercing designs, it is difficult to guess at their dates of production. The only one of Graham's which bears Edinburgh hallmarks dates from 1783; all the others pre-date that, probably beginning in the 1770s. (Even the ascription of hallmarked pieces with an 'AG' maker's mark to Adam Graham is not 100% certain, as Alexander Gairdner of Edinburgh had a similar – but smaller – punch; although Gairdner entered his mark back in 1754, he was – according to Jackson – still going strong in 1789.)

Fig.218: Edinburgh 1773, Patrick Robertson

Fig.219: Glasgow c1775, Adam Graham (backlit)

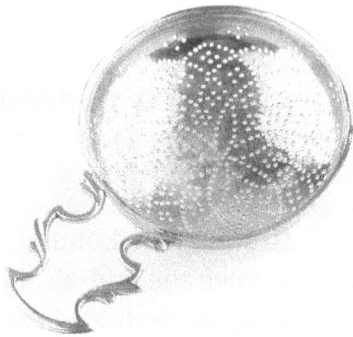

Fig.220: Glasgow c1780, Adam Graham

Fig.221: Edinburgh 1794, Robert Gray (of Glasgow)

Fig.222: Edinburgh 1809, Robert Gray & Son (of Glasgow)

Fig.223: Glasgow 1826, Robert Gray & Son

Graham's one-handled strainer bowls have a variety of dot-hole designs, mostly involving variations on the six-petalled flower motif, in one case with the flower created by larger overlapping petals (fig.220). One of his is unique in having eight curved and blunt-ended 'petals', giving a swirling effect of movement (fig.219). The only pre-1784, unhallmarked strainer I know of by Robert Gray (estimated by an Edinburgh auctioneer as 'c1780') has a very simple piercing pattern which can only be described as 'random dots, more or less equidistant from one other'. Some of the strainers he sent for hallmarking now have rubbed marks, but any sign of an 'R' or a 'G' points to him as the maker. Later ones favoured the stand-out six-petalled flower, but because of a paucity of dot-holes between the petals the contrast is never as stark as in the Robertson examples. Others were more geometric with 12-pointed stars.

In 1784 and 1785, the head of George III stamped by the Edinburgh assay office (to show that tax had been paid) was (as in London) 'incuse' or cut away down into the mark. From 1786, it was in normal relief or cameo style in an oval punch. In 1797 the tax was increased and from that year until 1823 the monarch's head in Edinburgh was set in a shaped punch (either with a 'double cusp', meaning indentations on either side, or a 'triple cusp' with a third notch in the base). This all helps to date strainers which have worn or missing date letters (and to show that some auctioneers are nearly 40 years out when they date a strainer with a double-cusped duty mark as 'c1760'). One such worn example with a clear triple-cusped duty mark has the rare distinction of delicate engraving on the top of its handle, involving double edging and a tapering foliate motif.

Robert Gray's eldest son William completed his apprenticeship to his father in 1802 and joined him in a very successful and long-lasting partnership. The firm 'Robert Gray & Son' continued beyond Robert's retirement in about 1825 and his death in 1829 and produced its last silverware in 1849. Both father and son had become stalwarts of Glasgow society, Robert helping to found what is now the University of Strathclyde and William becoming Chairman of the Glasgow Goldsmiths' Company. More will be written about them under Scottish Group 6, but their Group-3 output extended from 1809 (with no earlier ones listed by the Dieterts) to 1826. The earliest one has a very simple pierced motif of a seven-pointed star and no dot-holes between the points (fig.222) and their designs rarely developed beyond six-petalled flowers even into the 1820s (fig.223). Later ones have rims embellished by gadrooning.

Fig.224: Edinburgh 1813,
Robert Gray & Son (of Glasgow)

Fig.225: Edinburgh 1816, 'DM' (unidentified
of Glasgow?)

The solitary example by a Perth silversmith (Robert Keay) probably from c1810 repeats the Scottish stand-out six-petalled flower, has a reeded rim and a clip – but no handle at all; it has been struck five times with the 'RK' maker's mark. In London, single-handled lemon strainers with *loop* handles were commonly made from 1775 until the end of the century; in Scotland they seem to have been much rarer. One by Robert Gray & Son from 1813 (fig.224) has a long and pointed loop with an unusual lozenge-shaped cross-plate near its base: this gives room for the engraved crest and motto of Stirling of Keir. (In Scotland – and sometimes also in Ireland but never in England – mottoes appear above the crest, rather than below.) Interestingly, this strainer has a 'twin', an identical one with identical heraldry, which was made in London in 1793 by Henry Chawner; I presume that Robert Gray & Son were commissioned to create a second one for the family, using the original as the template, and the two did remain in the same ownership until very recently.

The only other loop-handled strainer in this one-handled category has the unidentified maker's mark 'DM' (fig.225; see p.149); it bears Edinburgh 1816 hallmarks, has a simple arrangement of concentric circles of dot-holes in its bowl and its loop is plain and rounded.

SCOTTISH GROUP 4: TWO SCROLL-SIDED, ARC-ENDED HANDLES

With the exceptions of an 'early' one from Dundee and the last one (probably by an Edinburgh maker), all the lemon strainers that I know of in this Group came from the Glasgow workshops of Adam Graham and Robert Gray (with and without his son William). Those few by Robert Gray & Son have distinctive bowl piercing designs and the non-Glasgow strainers have either pierced patterns or handles of non-standard sorts, but otherwise they could all have been in London Group 6 (with single-scroll sides to their handles) or Group 7 (with double- or triple-scroll sides).

A single-scroll-handled one, rare and desirable because of its full set of (unofficial) Dundee marks, sold at Bonhams in Edinburgh in 2009. The auction catalogue suggested that the letter 'W', punched along with the Dundee pot of lilies and John Steven's maker's mark (struck twice), may represent the Edinburgh date letter for 1751. The shape of the 1751 letter 'W', however, differs from this one and Richard Turner (2014) reads it (on a similarly-marked spoon) as 'M' and gives it no credence as a date letter, because Scottish provincial silversmiths often added letters to their sets of punches, apparently at random and without any date connotations. Considering that this style of strainer with two open, scroll-sided cast handles first appeared in London just before 1750, and the first Glasgow ones appeared in the mid-1760s, it is unlikely that Steven's one is any earlier than the others: he worked until 1775. His dot-hole bowl piercing comprises a delicate ring of six overlapping circles, the overlaps forming six separated 'petals' – a design that gives no stylistic hints to its age.

Fig.226: Glasgow? c1765, Adam Graham   *Fig.227: Glasgow c1765, Adam Graham*

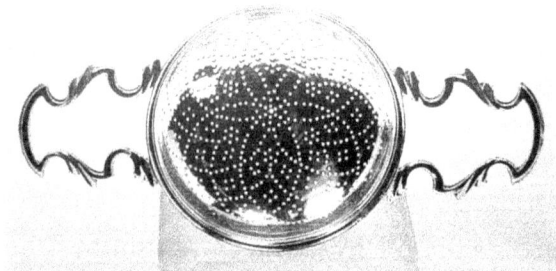

I know of three Adam Graham double-handled strainers, two with double-scroll and one with triple-scroll handles. All carry his maker's mark and the Glasgow tree mark under one or both handles and probably date from between 1765 and 1780. Those with the shorter handles have 12 overlapping 'petals' of dot-holes in their bowls with clusters of dots in between them (fig.227); the triple-scrolled one has a geometric arrangement based around two overlapping 'squares' with inward-curving sides, whose edges are delineated by triple rows of dots in parallel (fig.226).

Fig.228: Edinburgh c1800, Robert Gray
(of Glasgow)

Fig.229: Edinburgh 1804, Robert Gray & Son
(of Glasgow)

Fig.230: Edinburgh 1817, Robert Gray & Son (of Glasgow)

There seems to have been a gap of at least 15 years after Graham ceased production (in around 1784) before Robert Gray came up with a few single-scrolled strainers with very simple, concentric-ring dot piercing, all of which have the post-1797 cusped duty mark (fig.228). Soon afterwards, in 1804, Gray & Son made one with double-scroll handles and an interesting variation on the typically Scottish piercing design: instead of a six-petalled flower, theirs is eight-petalled; and instead of leaving the petals unpierced but highlighting them by a dense arrangement of dots around them, here they are pierced and the area around is left unpunctured (fig.229). The visual effect is similar, but I think the citrus juices would have taken an impractically long time to drip through. Another of theirs dates from 1817 and has a boldly gadrooned rim and single-scroll handles (fig.230).

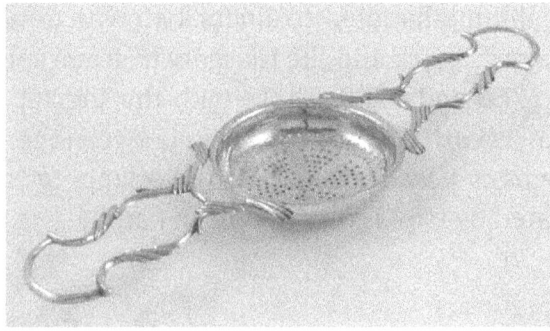

Fig.231: possibly Edinburgh, probably Glasgow c1825, 'DM'

The last of this Group is an oddity whose probable Scottish origin is assumed because of its piercing pattern, the classic Scottish six-petalled flower standing out from the background of concentric rings of dots (fig.231). The Wiltshire auctioneer who offered it for sale in 2005 thought it was 'probably American', because it is struck only (twice) with a maker's mark, 'DM', and there was a silversmith in Boston called David Moseley (whose marks actually all used his full surname). The style of its handles is not found elsewhere among either American or Scottish strainers: they are based on the usual double-scrolled sides with an arc at the end but the struts are round in section, the arc is very curved and the stylised foliage is extensive and made of short, parallel cylindrical strips; there is also a short cross-strut near the base. The 'DM' mark is found on two other Scottish lemon strainers and I provide evidence on p.149 that, although unidentified, this maker was from Glasgow.

SCOTTISH GROUP 5: TWO LOOP HANDLES

These lemon strainers, known from Edinburgh and Glasgow between 1784 and 1829, share with the London Group 9 their simple curved handle shapes, cut from strips of silver rather than cast, starting about ten years after they became fashionable in London. If it weren't for the typically Scottish 'highlighted' six-petalled flower design in their bowls, they could easily be confused with London examples: even the first ones, made in Edinburgh until the turn of the 19th century, with their incurved handle bases and central inward-facing notch in the terminal, had their counterparts in 1760s and 1770s London.

Fig.232: Edinburgh 1784, Patrick Robertson

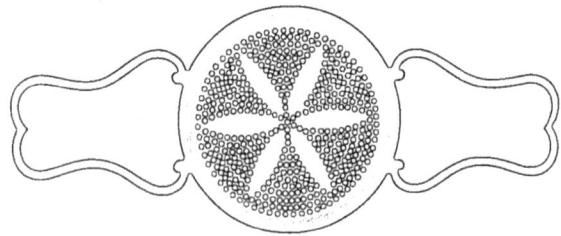

Fig.233: Robertson's 1784 strainer (stencil)

Fig.234: Edinburgh 1789, W.& P. Cunningham

The earliest, by Patrick Robertson, has a full set of Edinburgh marks for 1784 (figs 232,233), including the incuse duty mark, as well as a crest (of a goat's head erased) under the motto *Spare Nought*, which may be for George Hay, 7th Marquess of Tweeddale, who married Lady Hannah Maitland (daughter of the 7th Earl of Lauderdale) in April 1785, before the change of date letter at the end of May 1785. He didn't inherit the title until two years later, explaining the lack of a marquess's coronet over the crest. Another, from 1789 by William & Patrick Cunningham (fig.234), is similar but has a cross-piece mirroring the scalloping at the end. This one's crest (of a hand holding an eagle's leg erased) may have belonged to the Scottish Napier family.

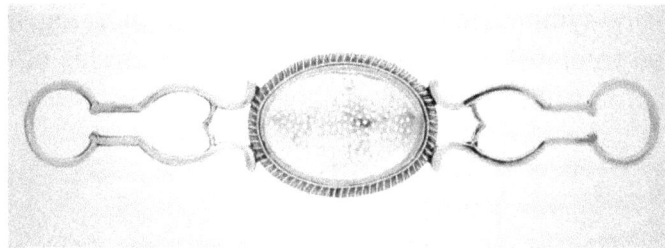

Fig.235: Edinburgh 1818, maker's mark indecipherable

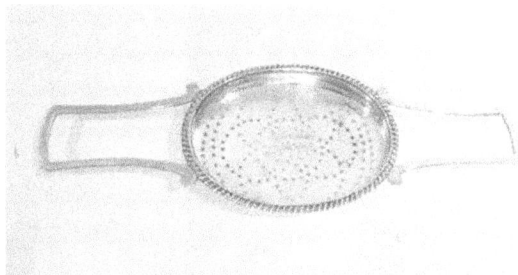

Fig.236: Glasgow 1821, Robert Gray & Son

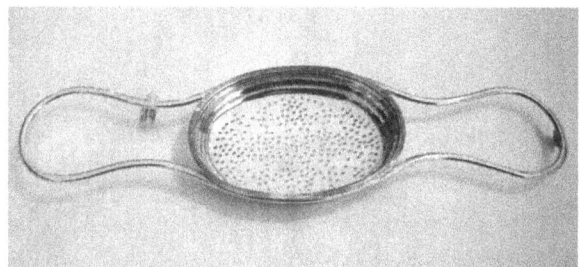

Fig.237: Glasgow ?1829, Mitchell & Son

The 19th-century examples in this Group are varied and each has its own idiosyncrasies. Ranging in length from 28 to 34.5 cm (11-13.5 in), they would all have been comfortably long enough to straddle a punch bowl and one, by Mitchell & Son and probably from 1829 (fig.237), has downward-facing shell-shaped lugs under the tips of its handles, presumably to stop the strainer from sliding lengthways and falling in. Like many of the others in this section of the Group, its bowl is oval in shape (helping to increase the overall length of the strainer), in common with most of the 19th-century strainers in the next, lyre-handled Group.

Handle shapes range from almost rectangular (fig.236) to narrow-waisted curvy loops, ornamented with reeding, and from long narrow loops with a single outward-pointing scallop on either side to those looking like the outline of a bottle with a large, circular stopper (fig.235). Most of the rims of these strainers are gadrooned.

SCOTTISH GROUP 6: TWO ORNATE, USUALLY LYRE-SHAPED, HANDLES WITH SHELL

If, in early 19th-century Glasgow, the one-handled, the two scroll-handled and the two loop-handled lemon strainers were purchased by the middle classes, only the wealthiest would have been able to afford the large, heavy and highly ornate strainers in this Group. Although made by at least five different Glasgow silversmiths, there was a consistency to their design, nearly always involving a long oval bowl with an applied, decorated rim and long, boldly curving, cast handles with relief shell motifs. The handles, with their sides curving inwards at the base and outwards at the end, are reminiscent of the classical Greek musical instrument, the lyre. To quote John D. Davis, writing about the Hyman Collection in 1991, "Just as punch strainers were going out of fashion in London they experienced an extraordinary efflorescence in Glasgow". The shape of the bowl generally meant dispensing with the radially symmetrical six-petalled flower piercing motif (although it is still present in a few cases) and the most common pattern involves circles of dot-holes, overlapping or side-by-side, with curves as 'end-fillers'.

Fig.238: Edinburgh 1811, Robert Gray & Son (of Glasgow)

I'll begin, though, with the exceptions which don't fully conform to this generalised description. The first is the earliest, made in 1811 by Robert Gray & Son (fig.238) and one of five in this group once owned by John A. Hyman. Its bowl is of typical shape and size but with a highly experimental piercing pattern, which is attractive but defies description (unless opting for the tenuous suggestion that the main components represent flying birds in profile). Its handles are exceptionally fanciful, with shell-ended solid tongues flanked by very leafy scrolls which curve inwards and touch each other at their ends. On both 'tongues' the crest and motto (and the 'helm' or helmet set in its own foliage) of the Langlands family are relief-stamped.

The second exception is the last Scottish strainer that I am aware of (by D.C. Rait in 1833); it is described and illustrated on pp.150-151.

Fig.239: Glasgow 1819, Robert Gray & Son

Three of those with typical lyre-shaped handles in my database have a private-die armorial crest built into the relief pattern of the handles, a different one in each case. Each would have been built into a bespoke casting mould, an expensive extravagance if only one or a few lemon strainers were cast by commission from the family. Two are the work of Robert Gray & Son, from 1818 and 1819, featuring (separately) a head in profile and (fig.239) a 'sand-glass' timer; in the first case, the head takes the place of the shell at the end, and in the second the sand-glass nestles within the shell. The first strainer has a sort of 'twin': another one of the same shape and size, also by Robert Gray & Son and from 1818, with handles very similar (including a leopard's head in relief at the base) but having a standard terminal shell in lieu of the private-die profiled head.

The third strainer with a built-in armorial bears the maker's mark of the mysterious 'DM' but has no hallmarks and the end shell is replaced by the boar's head of the Campbell clan. This was sold by Christie's in London in 2013, as 'probably (by) Daniel McLean, Edinburgh, circa 1825', but their case is weakened by the fact that McLean's mark seems to have been 'DMcL', not 'DM'. According to the website *silvermakersmarks.co.uk* there is an unidentified Edinburgh 'D.M' mark, seen on pieces made between 1815 and 1828, two of which (dated 1822 and 1825) also bear the mark of James & Walter Marshall who had a long Edinburgh silver-making pedigree. But the 'DM' on lemon strainers lacks the dot between the letters and there were no other Edinburgh silversmiths at the time with those initials. Because all the other lyre-handled strainers hail from Glasgow, it is very likely that this one by 'DM' is also Glaswegian and that the other two are by the same silversmith. Jackson lists three Glasgow silversmiths whose first pieces dated from the 1810s: Donald McCallum, Duncan McFadyen and David McDonald; any of these may have used the 'DM' initials, but unfortunately none of their marks are known.

Fig.240: Glasgow 1823, Mitchell & Son

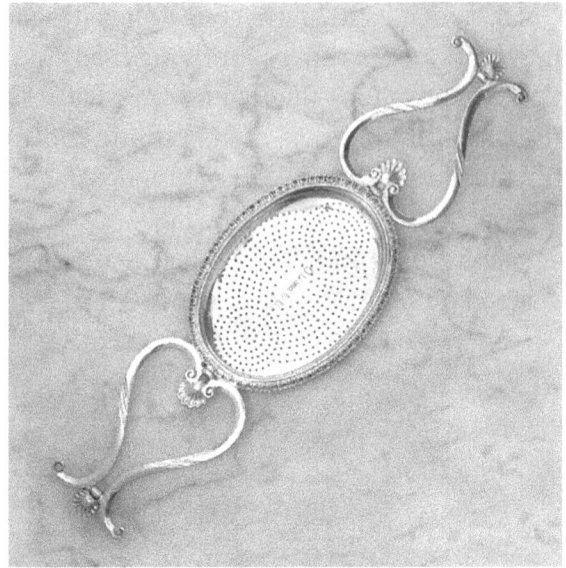

Fig.241: Glasgow 1827, D. C. Rait

Three others in this Group have round, rather than oval, bowls (but still with applied gadrooning around their rims). Two are similar, by Mitchell & Son in 1823 (fig.240) and Mitchell & Russell in 1833, with handles more delicate than the heavy-set ones by Gray & Son: they have thinner scroll sides and lack the reeded central strut. Only the relief shell components were cast; they were then soldered to the scroll sides which were hammered from silver strips. The third strainer, lacking any maker's mark but with Glasgow hallmarks for 1824 and direct provenance going back to the time of its making (remaining in the Ferguson-Buchanan family of Auchentorlie, Dumbartonshire until the 1970s), has handles so shortened that they comprise only the final third of the lyre with the outward-curving end of the scroll sides and the shell between them. This short-changing of the handles was reflected in the low hammer prices when the strainer came up for sale, three times between 2007 and 2010.

Another strainer with (full-sized) similarly delicate handles, but with the standard hefty oval bowl, came from David Crichton Rait, who had been producing lyre-handled strainers in Glasgow since its year of manufacture, 1827 (fig.241).

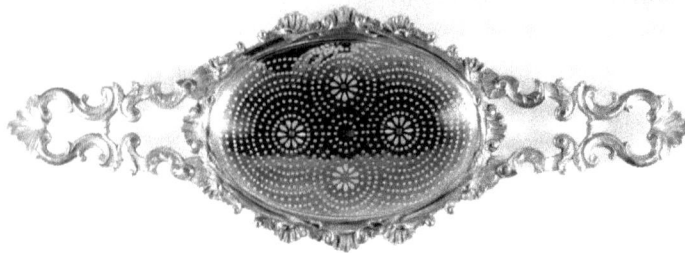

Fig.242: Glasgow 1833, David Crichton Rait

The final example of the ornate-handled theme – but with no trace of a lyre – was perhaps a 'final fling' by D. C. Rait (fig.242). This one, from 1833 – also purchased by Hyman and then sold by the major New York dealer S. J. Shrubsole (and by another New York dealership, Robert Lloyd), to reappear at a Somerset auction in 2020 – has extremely ornate and long triple-scroll handles terminating in a shell; its bowl has a splendid shell-&-scroll applied rim and the piercing pattern has four sets of incomplete concentric circles centred with rosettes of tear-drops – maybe the only Scottish example of piercings other than dot-holes. It could be described as archetypically 'Rococo Revival'. In the perfect, unpierced centres of the rosettes are the four Glasgow hallmarks, the town mark, the lion rampant, the king's head duty mark and the date letter 'O', undoubtedly punched by the assay office *after* the bowl pattern had been pierced.

All the strainers in this Group, except for the one with truncated handles, are consistently between 29 and nearly 32 cm in length, long enough to have been able to rest comfortably across the top of a typical punchbowl and, from the mid-1820s onwards, many of them had downward-facing, short, cylindrical pegs near the tips of their handles, making their purchase safer by acting as a brake to side-slippage. Maybe the Glaswegian punch drinkers of the time squeezed lemon or orange juice into them directly over the punchbowl and then put them to one side to allow the punch to be ladled out?

It's hard to know why lemon strainer production in Glasgow seemed to cease after 1833. In London, where lemon strainers had almost entirely died out by the end of the 18th century, their place was taken over by wine funnels which probably had dual functions for filtering wine and citrus juice. Yet in Glasgow, wine funnels and lemon strainers co-existed throughout the early decades of the 19th century and Robert Gray & Son included both in their repertoire; but both seemed to have died out in the 1830s. Perhaps punch itself lost its glamour at that time?

SCOTTISH GROUP 7: ODDITIES

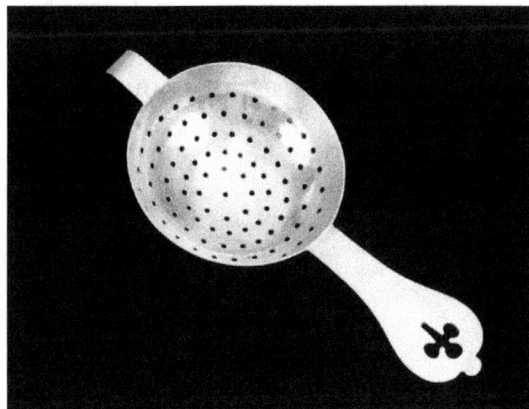

Fig.243: Aberdeen c1685, William Scott I

The first Scottish oddity is the only 17th-century Scottish strainer that I know of (fig.243) and one would be forgiven for thinking that it was made in London if it weren't for the 'AB' mark for Aberdeen in addition to the maker's mark of William Scott I. This – an understated star of the Hyman Collection

– was dated as c1685 because Scott moved away from Aberdeen (to Banff) in about 1689. Its concentric rings of dot-holes and simple flat handle, broader at the end and with a single pierced motif, are typical of the period during the reigns of Charles II and James II. The cut-out stalked trefoil on this one was also used by the London maker 'RB' (possibly Robert Butterfield) on one of his two-handled strainers. The whole piece is only 11 cm long, considerably smaller than its London counterparts.

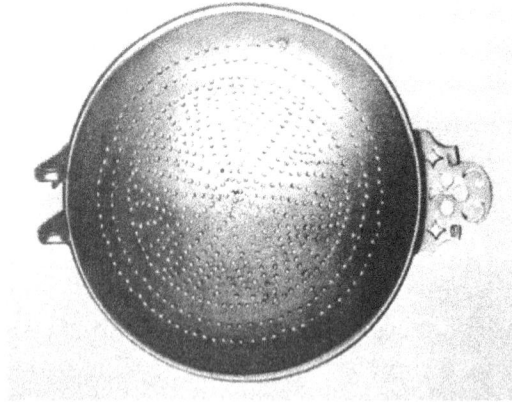

Fig.244: Aberdeen c1730, George Cooper

The same trefoil piercing – along with scrolls and diamonds – graces the tiny, shaped handle of the next strainer in this 'misfit' Group (fig.244), identified by Christie's of Glasgow in 1984 as by George Cooper of Aberdeen and dated 'c.1730'. Cooper was active between 1728 and 1748 and tended to use his own punch of three towers as well as his 'GC' maker's mark. The clip opposite the handle is intriguing, as it has a unique internal flange to grip the rim of the (necessarily small) bowl the strainer rested on. The bowl piercing design is a forerunner of the Scottish six-petalled flower, but the petals have internal dot-piercing. This is the second-oldest Scottish lemon strainer that I know of.

Another oddity is presumed to be Scottish, partly because it bears a crest which could pertain to the Drummond or Williams-Drummond family and partly because its extraordinary handles have a shape reminiscent of the Scottish Fiddle spoon-handle pattern. Nearly 34 cm from tip to tip, its handles look like ice-lolly sticks, slightly swollen in the middle. Its bowl piercing comprises radiating lines of dots, each one slightly curved. It was interesting enough for John Hyman to buy it.

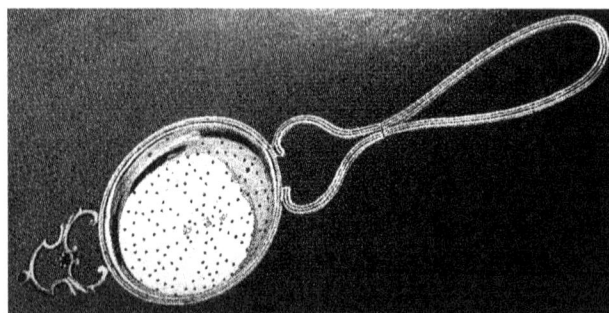

Fig.245: Dundee c1770, James Steven

The final unusual strainer from Scotland (fig.245) has one handle which belongs in Scottish Group 2, with its scroll sides, cross-strut with shell, and ring on its arc end. But its other handle is totally unique: a very long reeded loop, waisted about one-third of the way along, so tightly that the sides come together and, where they do, there is a hinge allowing the longer end of the loop to fold back over. The marks ('JS' flanked by two pots of lilies) are stamped in the bowl and belong to James Steven of Dundee (not to be confused with his contemporary, John Steven of Dundee, mentioned in Group 4 on p.144), who worked between 1740 and 1775. The shorter handle style is known from Edinburgh from the early 1780s, so probably existed there in the 1770s and was copied by Steven in his later years. Although the reeding on the folding handle matches the lines on the bowl where its strengthening was applied, I think it is likely that this handle was added later, when loop handles were in vogue, possibly as late as the 1820s. Maybe its owner took it with him to other people's punch gatherings – or to the local tavern or coffee-house – folded up in his pocket?

Chapter Six
AMERICAN LEMON STRAINERS

By 1730, when the first lemon strainers are produced in Boston, Massachusetts, the 13 British colonies along a 1200-mile stretch of the eastern seaboard of America have been established for the best part of a century. Despite the depredations of malaria in the south and diphtheria and yellow fever further north, and benefiting from further immigration from Europe, their populations are growing and most people – whether small-time farmers, plantation owners or land-owning middle-class professionals or tradesmen – have voting rights, are able to read and write and live in reasonable comfort. The exceptions are the black slaves (who make up 40% of the population in the southern colonies of Georgia, the Carolinas and Virginia) and indentured servants as yet unable to pay off their debts to secure their freedom.

Some of the land still belongs to the French and Spanish, but wars between the 1740s and 1760s result in British gains of all the territory east of the Mississippi river. The colonies are administered by the Board of Trade in London and each one has its own Colonial Agent. A strong democracy exists in America, with most important public and private bodies peopled by elected representatives, who live in the same neighbourhoods as the rank and file and there is no aristocratic ruling class. Education is well established and universities such as Yale, Harvard and Virginia are already decades old. The ingrained Puritan and Quaker morality encourages a spirit of equal rights (at least for the whites) and a distrust of elitism and corruption. The people still consider themselves as British, follow British tastes and conduct most of their trade with Britain.

By the time of the first rumblings of republicanism in the 1760s, the American colonies are flourishing. Endless timber supplies mean cheap house construction and the building of sturdy ships for export. Farm surpluses (tobacco, cotton, rice and indigo in the southern colonies and corn, wheat, barley and hay in the north) foster successful trade, including with the West Indies for their sugar and molasses, and there is a prospering sea-fishing industry. There is little in the way of literature, other than histories, newspapers and pamphlets, and theatre is considered ungodly in the northern colonies, but the spirit of the Age of Enlightenment in Europe does have a strong influence, particularly in the fields of science, economics and politics, best exemplified by the American 'Founding Father', the scientist, publisher, fighter for colonial unity, University president and Governor of Pennsylvania, Benjamin Franklin.

Britain continues to levy external taxes on the American colonies and this, together with attempts by British parliamentary laws and military force to stamp out dissent, leads to the American Revolution in 1775. All 13 of the colonies unite to form a Provincial Congress which wrests power from the British colonial authorities and forms the Continental Army under General George Washington (who has been trained 20 years earlier by British officers for the fight against the French). The Declaration of Independence, drafted by Thomas Jefferson, creates the United States of America on 4ᵗʰ July 1776, but

Independence, drafted by Thomas Jefferson, creates the United States of America on 4th July 1776, but *the war that follows only ends in 1783, with a victory for the Patriots and the establishment of a Constitution, a national government, a centralised executive and judiciary and the two Houses of Congress. The first President George Washington takes office in 1789. Most of the Americans who supported the defeated Loyalist cause stay put and friendly trade relations are quickly established with Britain.*

So few American lemon strainers come across the 'pond' to the UK that, of the 86 American strainers in my database, only one has been sold recently at a British auction and only one is lodged in a museum in Britain. The great majority of the rest of them are housed in numerous museums in the USA (45) or appeared for sale at New York auction houses, mostly Sotheby's and Christie's (26); the remaining 15 are in private collections, were on sale by US dealers, or appeared in a guide book or on an online blog.

The first silversmiths in Colonial America, the Englishmen John Hull and Robert Sanderson, plied their trade in Boston from the early 1650s. A hundred years later, there were silversmiths in every sizeable town in the northern colonies on the eastern seaboard and in the southern cities, while northern cities such as Boston, New York and Philadelphia had dozens of silver shops. But not one of these towns and cities was permitted, by the British authorities, to have its own assay office (like Cork in Ireland, Philadelphia made repeated, unsuccessful requests for permission to create one), so there were no American hallmarks in existence during the years when lemon strainers were made (except in Baltimore between 1814 and 1830). Nor did the silversmiths add their own town punches: they simply stamped their maker's mark, usually just as initials but sometimes the full surname.

This means that the only ways of assessing the production date of an American lemon strainer are from the working years of its maker and from its style. The stylistic method of dating is difficult as certain designs were maintained for decades with little change. Fortunately, US scholars have unearthed or surmised the makers' working dates and identified their marks.

The earliest strainers that I'm aware of (today's Americans tend to call them 'punch strainers') date from about 1730 and the majority were made between 1740 and 1770; much smaller numbers were produced from then onwards until the first decade of the 19th century, with two 'stragglers' in my database from the 1840s. The fashion for strainers was therefore at its height during the Colonial Period before the American Revolution and there is no reason to suppose that they were used in ways substantially different from London's or Dublin's. Some were long enough to straddle a punchbowl, but the majority were too short and must surely have been placed on smaller receptacles while citrus juices were squeezed into them.

Some of the American lemon strainers were clearly influenced by pre-existing styles in London and Dublin, but a number of handle designs are very characteristically American, notably those with end-rings, including the Boston 'bell-loops'. Others are quirky and different, but didn't seem to catch on. I have classified American strainers into six Groups based on handle shapes, listed below with their respective numbers in my database and their dates and places of production:

1. Two triangular, pierced handles (4)
Philadelphia c1740; Rhode Island c1765

2. Two open, ring-&-knop-ended, bell-shaped handles (19)

Massachusetts: Boston c1745-c1780;
Newburyport c1770; Hartford, Connecticut c1761-c1787

3. Two open, ring-ended, double-scroll-sided handles (18)

Stratford or New Haven, Connecticut c1750;
Massachusetts: Boston c1750-1792; Medford c1780-1800

4. Two open, arc-ended handles (10)

Boston c1740-c1770; Charlestown,
Massachusetts c1750-65; Philadelphia c1760;
New York c1765; New Haven, Connecticut c1770

5. Others with two handles (9) *Boston c1730, 1724-58, 1742-44; Charleston,*
South Carolina c1745; Providence, Rhode
Island c1790; New York c1770, c1800; Philadelphia c1800

6. One handle (26) *New York c1745-1802; Albany, New York 1760-80; Boston*
c1740; Philadelphia c1765, c1770- c1800; Mobile, Alabama
c1840; Baltimore, Maryland 1846

The United States museums with lemon strainers illustrated in their searchable online collections are as follows, with the numbers I have found in each:

Museum of Fine Arts, Boston, Massachusetts (10)
Philadelphia Museum of Art, Pennsylvania (7)
Yale University Art Gallery, Connecticut (6)
Winterthur Museum, Delaware (6)
Metropolitan Museum of Art, New York (5)
Art Institute of Chicago, Illinois (2)
Cleveland Museum of Art, Ohio (2)
The Heritage Foundation, Old Deerfield, Massachusetts (2)
Worcester Art Museum, Massachusetts (1)
Detroit Institute of Arts, Michigan (1)
Charleston Museum, Charleston, South Carolina (1)
Minneapolis Institute of Art, Minnesota (1)
Massachusetts Historical Society (1)

There is also one Boston-made strainer on display in the American Museum in Britain, at Claverton near Bath.

Among the more important collections containing American lemon strainers, sold by Christie's and Sotheby's in New York, have been the Cornelius Moore Collection (1986), the Collection of Mr & Mrs Walter M. Jeffords (2004), the Collection of Roy & Ruth Nutt (2015) and the Iris Schwartz Collection (2017). Seven American lemon strainers from the Hyman Collection were sold by S J Shrubsole in New York in the early 2010s.

The surviving lemon strainers for which I have data were made in 15 different towns and cities in what are now eight different States of the USA. By far the most prolific was Boston, Massachusetts (41), followed by New York (14) and Philadelphia, Pennsylvania (12). Two towns are represented by two (Providence, Rhode Island and Albany, New York) and 10 others by one strainer each (Newport, Rhode Island; Charlestown, Medford and Newburyport, Massachusetts; Hartford, Stratford and New Haven, Connecticut; Charleston, South Carolina; Mobile, Alabama; and Baltimore, Maryland). That leaves 6 strainers whose origins are unknown or uncertain.

They represent the output of no fewer than 51 silversmiths, 33 of them known from only one strainer. The most prolific makers were all from Boston: Jacob Hurd (5), Benjamin Burt and Daniel Parker (4 each); John Coburn and Paul Revere I (3 each) and Samuel Edwards and Paul Revere II (two each). Most American silversmiths were assiduous about punching their maker's marks, but there are six in my database without such marks or with an unidentified mark. It seems that American silversmiths were held in high esteem in the 18th and 19th centuries, having a social status comparable with that of doctors and lawyers.

One of them became famous for reasons other than fashioning silver: Paul Revere I (son of a French Huguenot immigrant, Apollos Rivoire) was one of the ringleaders in the 'Boston Tea Party' in 1773, the revolutionary gesture against the British monopoly on Chinese tea (not helped by the imposition of a new tax on the commodity), in which an entire shipment was dumped into Boston harbour by American patriots, many disguised as Mohawk Indians. Revere gained greater fame as a patriot two years later for his night ride on horseback (after rowing across the Charles river) from Charlestown to Lexington in Massachusetts to alert the colonial militias along the way to the imminent approach of British forces. This was before the battles of Lexington and Concord, in which the first shots were exchanged between Americans and British in the American Revolution. Revere was captured by the British and his horse confiscated, but he was released when his captors retreated, and he continued to flourish as a metalworker and entrepreneur for the rest of his long life.

AMERICAN GROUP 1: TWO TRIANGULAR, PIERCED HANDLES

This very small Group is represented by two 'pairs' of lemon strainers separated in time by some 20 years. The first, by Philip Syng II of Philadelphia and dating from between 1740 and 1750, have handles which were obviously inspired by the London Group-2 handles of the 1710s and 20s, the 'piercing' leaving a design of multiple connected scrolls. As in London, the gaps between the scrolls were not cut out but created in the casting from a pre-formed mould. Their bowls are deep (almost hemispherical) and densely pierced with concentric rings.

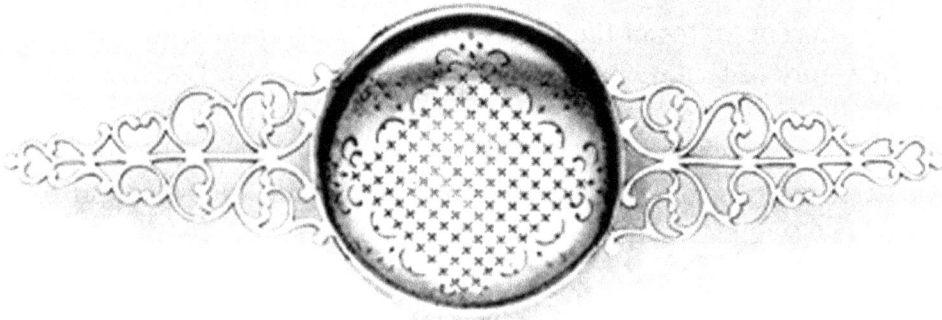

Fig.246: Newport, Rhode Island, c1760, Thomas Arnold

The later pair, by Jonathan Clarke of Providence and Thomas Arnold of Newport (fig.246), both in Rhode Island, were made in the 1760s. Their handles – almost identical save for the extra terminal projection on Arnold's – are much longer than Syng's but are still based on a series of scrolls and a central longitudinal strut. Clarke's is famous (and unique) for its dot-pierced circular inscription outside the 12-petalled flower motif, reading (for its owner, later the Deputy Governor of Rhode Island) "JABEZ BOWEN PROVIDENCE JANUARY 1766".

Like so many of the American strainers made outside Boston, the ones in this Group were 'maverick' creations, seemingly uninfluenced by other American styles and not repeated elsewhere.

AMERICAN GROUP 2: TWO OPEN, RING-&-KNOP-ENDED, BELL-SHAPED HANDLES

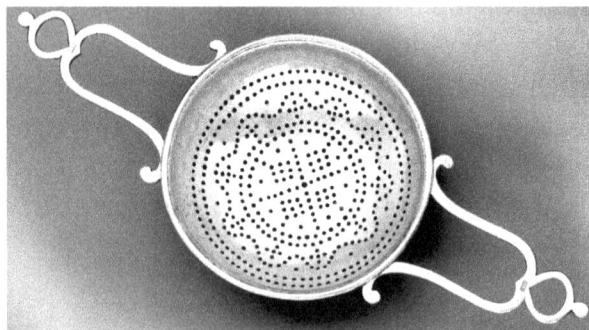

Fig.247: Boston c1745, William Simpkins   *Fig.248: Boston c1760, Daniel Henchman*

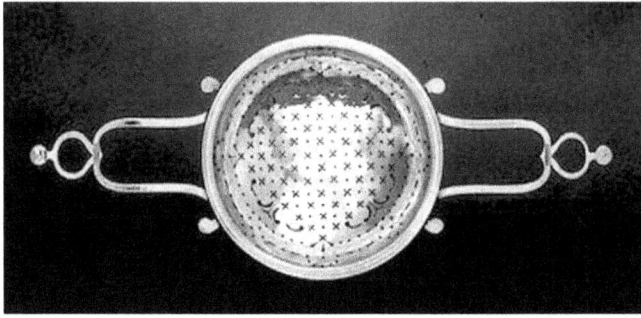

Fig.249: Boston c1740-50, Paul Revere I

Fig.250: Boston c1765-70, Joseph Edwards II

These large strainers with their bell-shaped handles are the most characteristically American of all, partly because more of them survive today than strainers of any other American style and partly because their handles are genuinely distinct from any others. Made almost exclusively in Massachusetts and almost entirely in Boston, by at least twelve silversmiths including William Simpkins (fig.247), Daniel Henchman (fig.248), the brothers Thomas & Samuel Edwards, their nephew Joseph Edwards II (fig.250) and Paul Revere I (fig.249), and dating from between the 1740s and the 1760s, they had already ceased production ten years before the loop-handled (Group-9) strainers became fashionable in London; so, if there was any design influence, it would have been eastwards, from Boston on London. The London loops, however, never had end-rings nor the flamboyantly everted scrolling bases of the American bells. The one example that I know of from outside Massachusetts was made by Ebenezer Austin in Hartford, Connecticut.

These strainers are large (typically 26-28 cm in length and therefore perfectly able to straddle a punchbowl), but quite shallow-bowled. Despite being made by so many different silversmiths over a 20-year period, there was remarkable consistency in their handle design: the ring (in every case except one) being knopped and always shaped like a squat tear-drop, the point of the ring indenting the top of the 'bell' to which it is attached.

The bowl piercing patterns were more varied, but the prevailing theme was a large square panel of crosslets, with or without dots in alternating rows within it, surrounded by various arrangements of dots and scrolls. Others have dot-holes in geometric patterns varying from simple lattices to complex central circles surrounded by rounded or pointed multi-armed stars; in one case the centre comprises the ubiquitous six-petalled flower.

Americans love provenance and nothing satisfies more than the full possession history of a lemon strainer. Sometimes the connecting links are left to the imagination, such as "Provenance: Deacon Thomas Greenough (1710-1785) of Boston; then by descent to the present owner". But two of the strainers in this Group, both at the Museum of Fine Arts in Boston, do better than that. The history of one reads: "Isaac and Elizabeth (Storer) Smith, m. 1746; their son William, m. Hannah Carter; their son Thomas, m. Frances Barnard; their daughter Frances Barnard Smith, m. Thomas Davie Townsend; their son William, father of the donors." The other's entry is: "Patrick Tracy (b.1711, Ireland), m. first 1742/3 Hannah Carter (1723/4-1746), second 1749 Hannah Gookin (1723/4-1756), third Mary (1713-1791), widow of Michael Dalton; Hannah (daughter of Patrick and Hannah Gookin Tracy), m. Johnathan Jackson, 1772; their daughter Mary, m. Henry Lee, June 21, 1809; to Elizabeth Caboe Ware and the donor." (The fact that a 'Hannah Carter' crops up in both of these provenances is a coincidence.)

One of these bell-handled strainers appeared in Margaret Holland's *Silver: an illustrated guide to collecting silver* (1973) as a "tea strainer" by an unspecified maker and dated "c1780", but I believe it belongs fairly and squarely among all the others from the 1740s to the 1760s (and that it was too large to have been used for tea).

AMERICAN GROUP 3: TWO OPEN, RING-ENDED, DOUBLE-SCROLL-SIDED HANDLES

Lemon strainers in this Group are still recognisably American, because of their large size and the rings at the ends of their handles, although the sides of their handles owe a lot to the open, double-scroll-sided ones of the contemporary Group-7 strainers of London. With one exception they also share the 'arc' which joins the far ends of the side-scrolls. Sometimes the end-ring has a rounded knob, but sometimes it's lacking.

All bar two that I know of were made by Boston silversmiths, between the 1750s and the 1790s, so there was an overlap with the bell-handled Group-2 strainers. Interestingly, although my database has Group-2 and Group-3 strainers by 17 different Boston silversmiths, only four of them (John Coburn, Jacob Hurd, Daniel Parker and Paul Revere II) have representatives from *both* Groups; so it seems that from the 1750s onwards, although both styles were popular in Boston, most makers specialised in one or the other.

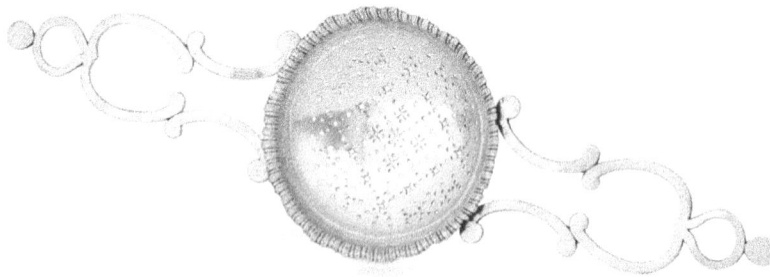

Fig.251: Stratford, Connecticut, c1750 or New Haven, Connecticut, c1770?, Robert Fairchild

One lemon strainer that belongs in this Group, but differs from the others in having simple scrolls (without stylised foliage), everted at the base and curving round, horseshoe-like, at the end, was made by Robert Fairchild in Connecticut (fig.251). Christie's dated it as c1750, believing it to come from Fairchild's years (1747-1767) working in Stratford, CT. But the 2007 revised edition of Bohan & Hammerslough's 1970 book on early Connecticut silver suggests not only that *all* Fairchild's surviving pieces date from his New Haven period (1767-c1790) but also that there were probably two separate

Robert Fairchilds. The one born in 1738 in Durham, CT, who fathered a son in New Haven in 1777 and who died in New Haven in 1794, was the New Haven silversmith, *not* the one born in 1703 who worked firstly in Durham and then in Stratford. The latter would already have been 64 years of age when the successful New Haven business was set up, whereas the former was at a much likelier age, in his late twenties. Yet there *are* silver wares purporting to be by the second (older) Fairchild during his days in Durham (a sword hilt) and Stratford (a chafing dish), so it seems that both men were silversmiths. All the same, it is probable that Christie's date of c1750 for this strainer should be revised to a time after 1767 (and the place of manufacture from Stratford to New Haven) – which would make the earliest strainers from this Group those by Bostoners Jacob Hurd (Fig.254) and Benjamin Burt in the 1750s.

Fig.252: Boston c1760-75, Benjamin Burt

Fig.253: Boston c1760, Daniel Parker

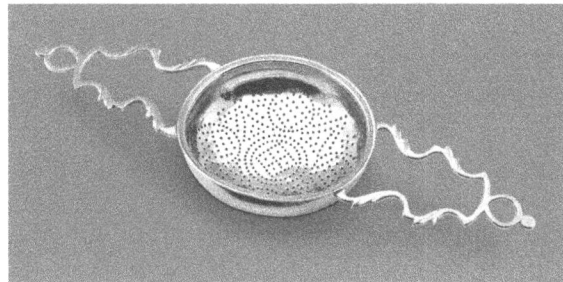

Fig.254: Boston 1749-59, Jacob Hurd

If there is a theme to the piercing patterns in their bowls, it is groups of circles – sometimes separate, sometimes overlapping and sometimes with inner concentric rings (figs 252,253,254). There are of course exceptions: the one (by Samuel Minott) in the American Museum in Britain is entirely pierced with short, curved scrolls, and the one made by a Massachusetts silversmith (William Gowen of Medford) has four triangles pointing out between four two-ringed circles.

John D. Davis's article on the John A. Hyman's collection of 'punch strainers' is excellent; but two of the images were inadvertently confused. His cover page illustration of 9 strainers included two American ones with ring-ended handles, but the captions were the wrong way around: the one labelled 'D' (with bell-shaped handles) was attributed to 'Daniel Parker c1760' and the one labelled 'F' (with double-scroll-sided handles) to 'Daniel Henchman c1765'. The first one, however, is clearly punched twice with David Henchman's initials ('DH') on top of its handles and the second presumably bears Daniel Parker's mark, as the Colonial Williamsburg inventory identifies them correctly (and S.J. Shrubsole did so too when it put them up for sale after Hyman's death).

The latest strainer in this Group was made by Paul Revere II, son of the famous silversmith-cum-revolutionary, as part of a 'tea service' commissioned by the Boston merchant, John Templeman, and his wife Mehitable in 1792, held by the Minneapolis Institute of Arts since 1956. It accompanies the teapot and stand, tea caddy and stand, sugar urn, cream pitcher and sugar tongs, which were all marked by Revere, and the caddy spoon which – like the strainer – was not marked; all except the tongs are engraved with the initials T over JM (or JMT) and most were included by Revere in his account book, the strainer listed as a 'punch strainer'. The description by the MIA suggests that the "sieve was used for straining punch, a beverage often served along with tea". Its bowl piercing pattern is complex, with four densely-dotted circles on radiating stalks and triangles between them, facing both inwards and outwards.

All these strainers are as long – if not slightly longer – than the American Group-2 strainers, ranging from 26.5 to 29.5 cm.

AMERICAN GROUP 4: TWO OPEN, ARC-ENDED HANDLES

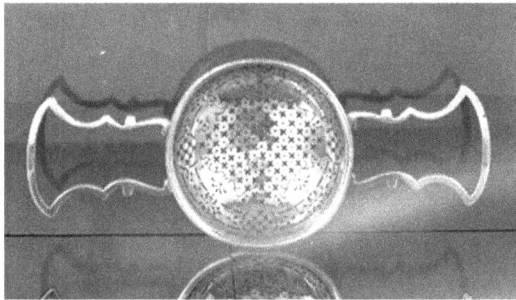

Fig.255: Charlestown, Massachusetts c1750-65, Josiah Austin

Fig.256: Philadelphia c1760, Philip Syng II

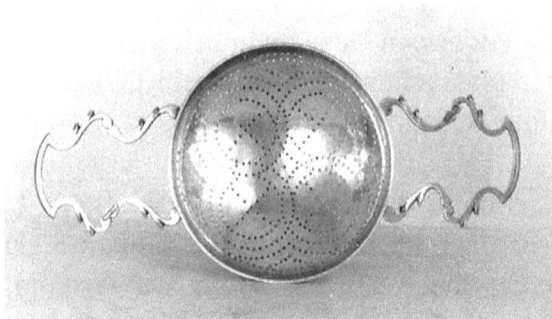

Fig.257: Boston c1770, Benjamin Burt

Fig.258: New York c1765, Myer Myers

Small numbers of American lemon strainers with scroll-sided, arc-ended handles were made which lacked the terminal ring, many of them indistinguishable from London strainers of the mid-to-late 18th century. Some, like Philip Syng II's of Philadelphia in about 1760, have leafy single-scroll sides (fig.256); others, like Benjamin Burt's of Boston in c1770, have handles almost twice as long, with double-scroll sides (fig.257). One, by an unknown maker and therefore from an unknown city, has an extra stirrup-shaped projection beyond the arc; and Myer Myers's of c1765 from New York (fig.258) has a T-shaped set of struts connecting the sides with the rim of the bowl.

The most distinctively American in the Group, however, are those with simple scroll sides opening out to an arc that is very much wider than the rest of the handle, usually without – but occasionally with – a central knop on the arc. These date from the 1750s and 1760s by Boston makers such as William Burt, Samuel Burt and Paul Revere I. William, Samuel and Benjamin Burt, by the way, were brothers, all apprenticed to their silversmith father John; the first two died before the age of 30, but Benjamin had a long working life. The Yale University Art Gallery and the Boston Museum of Fine Arts each has a classic strainer of this type with almost identical handles and bowl motif but attributed to different makers: the first to Josiah Austin of Charlestown, Massachusetts (c1750-65; fig.255), and the second to John Allen of Boston (c1740). The renowned expert on American silver, Kathryn Buhler, in her catalogue of *American Silver 1655-1825 in the Museum of Fine Arts Boston* (1972), claimed that some pieces with the 'IA' mark pre-dated the end of Josiah Austin's apprenticeship and that one of them bears the arms of a family known to have commissioned silver from John Allen. Not only was John Allen in his late sixties (and 'weak in body') by 1740, however, but the bowl piercing style of these strainers, with their central panel of alternating crosslets and dots surrounded by scrolls, splashes and dashes, was used in Boston into the 1760s. The Yale example's maker's mark has Josiah Austin's full name on both handles and I'm inclined to believe that he made the Boston MFA's one as well, using an alternative 'IA' mark.

AMERICAN GROUP 5: OTHERS WITH TWO HANDLES

I know of nine two-handled American lemon strainers which for different reasons don't fit into any of the above categories. They include the earliest American strainer in my lists, from c1730 and by John Blowers of Boston, a seriously heavy (5oz 14dwt = 177g) piece whose auction photograph makes it look Irish until you read how large it is (27.5 cm long). It has solid, shaped, plain handles with the 'Irish snub nose', their uppersides bearing Blowers's mark; its bowl has a central small rosette of dots and diamonds surrounded by eight concentric rings of dot-holes. Another strainer with Irish-like handles came up for sale at a New York auction in 2001 with a complex geometric bowl motif and a more angular shape to its handles, consistent with a later, probably 1750s, date of production. No details of its maker were given. And a 26.5 cm-long 'punch strainer' was made with deeply-shaped, flat, snub-nosed handles – also very Irish-looking – and a typically American square panel of crosslets in the bowl; the American auction house that sold it in 2018 supplied a photograph of the maker's mark, which I have tentatively identified as Ezekiel Burr's from Providence, Rhode Island, who was working late in the 18th century.

Fig.259: Boston 1742-44, William Breed

The fourth in this Group of 'eccentric' strainers (fig.259) has a span of 30.5 cm thanks to its very long, solid, shaped, tongue-like handles, bearing the maker's mark of William Breed of Boston and engraved, top and bottom, with Latin inscriptions explaining why it was made "in memory of the departed, John Vryling, who died 25th November, 1744". The silver for the strainer came from the spoils of war during the siege of Cartagena in New Spain [now in Colombia] on "the day of our Lord April 12th 1741", in which Vryling participated. The Massachusetts Historical Society, which now owns the piece, has supplied extra information: Vryling (a Boston merchant) joined Admiral Vernon's fleet of ships in the Caribbean during the War of Jenkins's Ear (1739-1742) between Britain and Spain, which had victories against two ports in what is now Panamá. Its failure to take Cartagena, however, is euphemistically referred to in one of the engraved inscriptions on the strainer with a shortened version of the famous line from Virgil's *Aeneid*, often translated as "A joy it will be one day, perhaps, to remember even this". The fourth inscription gives the strainer's provenance after Vryling's death: "his heirs gave it to his relative and dear friend, Jonathan Tyng, at whose death it came to John Loring". The strainer is believed to have been produced between 1742 and 1744. Its bowl has the typical Bostonian square panel of dots and crosslets surrounded by short scrolls, rosettes and square grids of dots.

A smaller lemon strainer (22 cm across its handles), made much later – in about 1800 – by the New York maker, William Heyer, revisits the long, narrow-handled theme, solid in this case save for a small tear-drop hole near the tip and a short, three-strut basal section.

Fig.260: Boston 1724-58, Jacob Hurd

Fig.261: Charleston, S.Carolina, c1740-50, Alexander Petrie

Two of the remaining strainers in this Group have handles with single-scroll sides: one (from Boston probably in the 1740s or 50s; fig.260) has each handle's central area filled with latticework and the other (from Charleston, South Carolina, in the 1740s; fig.261) has exaggerated foliage and an end piece comprising two short leafy scrolls tied together.

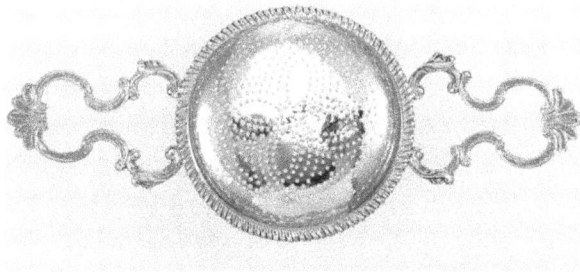

Fig.262: New York c1770, probably Thomas Hammersley Fig.263: Philadelphia c1800, Samuel Richards II

One believed to be the work of Thomas Hammersley of New York (c1770) mimics a classic London shell-ended strainer with double-scroll sides to the handles and a gadrooned rim around the bowl (fig.262). Another, from Philadelphia c1800, has a 12-petalled flower bowl design and short, flattened, minimalist 'loop' handles (fig.263).

AMERICAN GROUP 6: ONE HANDLE

This is the commonest Group of American lemon strainers, but also the most diverse in handle shape. It overlapped with all the other Groups, beginning in the 1740s, continuing until the end of the century and with late representatives from the 1840s. All of its strainers are small, with short handles, and were obviously designed to rest on much smaller containers than the super-long double-handled ones with which they co-existed. The variability in handle design in this Group highlights the isolation of the silver-making centres outside Boston: Boston itself has only one representative, while makers in New York, Albany (New York state), Philadelphia, Mobile (Alabama) and Baltimore (Maryland) produced the rest.

Fig.264: New York, c1739-63, Bartholomew Le Roux

The earliest one-handled strainers date from the 1740s, were made in New York and had ring-shaped handles so small that they clearly relied on their clip to support them on their container. John Brevoort and Bartholomew Le Roux were the makers, with Le Roux (fig.264) favouring more elaborate piercing patterns (a square panel of crosslets with scrolling patterns around it).

Fig.265: New York c1780, Benjamin Halsted

Also in New York appeared the first strainers with a single open, leafy-scroll and arc-ended handle like the simplest London Group-8 strainers (although the American ones are now valued much more highly because of their rarity). John Moulinar's has an unusual floral piercing design comprising 16 'petals'. Philip Syng Jr's (from Philadelphia) reverts to the old-fashioned concentric rings (and has its clip under the handle rather than opposite). As the first London examples date from the mid-1750s, the very early date attributions to the 1740s (Moulinar's) and c1750 (Syng's) are unlikely to be correct and both makers were still working at least until 1760. But they do suggest that the new London fashion quickly crossed the Atlantic.

The well-known New York maker, Thomas Hammersley, produced an example in c1760, as did Benjamin Halsted in the 1780s (possibly Philadelphia but more likely New York where he worked for much longer periods; fig.265). One of Halsted's has a beaded rim, like one probably by John David Jr and another by Joseph Richardson Jr (both of Philadelphia) at the turn of the 19th century. Two latecomers with a single-scroll, arc-ended handle are dated c1840 from Mobile, Alabama, and 1846 from Baltimore, Maryland (the only American centre which had – for a while – its own assay office and date letter punches).

Fig.266: Philadelphia, c1750, Philip Syng II

The solitary Boston strainer in this Group (c1750) has a handle like the truncated pierced triangles of the London Group 2 and Philip Syng's example from Philadelphia at the same time (fig.266) has a fully pierced triangle almost identical to some of John Albright's in London in the late 1710s. One would think that both of these should have clips but the available images don't show them. Both the handle shape and the bowl piercing design are very similar on a *two-handled* strainer, also by Philip Syng II, that was part of the Iris Schwartz collection of American silver, but the presence of a contemporary married couple's initials on the one-handled strainer, immediately below where a second handle would have been, suggests that it only ever had its one handle. Two more handles of this type, even more out of period, appear on strainers from the 1780s and 1790s by John David Jr and Samuel Richards Jr, both of Philadelphia; both of these have beaded rims (giving a stylistic mis-match of Baroque handle with Neoclassical bowl).

The highly-respected New York silversmith, Adrian Bancker, pierced his bowl in a similar way to the very Scottish unpierced six-petalled flower motif, surrounded by standard dot-holes, but pre-dating it by some 25 years (if the Hyman ascription of its age to c1750 is correct). This strainer's handle looks like little more than a flimsy teaspoon terminal.

Fig.267: New York, c1810, John Wesley Forbes

167

John Wesley Forbes of New York came up in the early 19th century with a variation on the single-scroll, arc-ended handle which had two cross-struts joined together centrally (fig.267). This is, to my knowledge, the only American lemon strainer that has been offered at auction in the UK in recent years, with its maker identified by Bamfords in Derby in 2009 but not by Woolley & Wallis in 2013, where it was described as "possibly Colonial". Bamfords, however, came up with the precise date of "1802", perhaps because Forbes had a predilection for pseudomarks that looked like Birmingham assay marks complete with date letter; but his career as a silversmith didn't begin until about 1808.

Fig.268: Albany, New York, c1760, Jacob Gerritse Lansing

Another American maker who was 'out on a limb' in terms of strainer design went by the name of Jacob Gerritse Lansing and worked in Albany, New York, between c1755 and 1774. His handle has single-scroll sides and an exaggerated arc end, relief-cast as a stylised sea shell attached to scrolls of its own (fig.268). The strainer was gifted to New York's Metropolitan Museum of Art by a Mrs Abraham Lansing, presumably a descendant of the maker. The same lady also donated another (unmarked) strainer with a handle stylistically related to the first one, but with a more Neoclassical look: its sides are engraved to simulate micromosaic and its arc-end has stylised leaves. It's tempting to suggest that it was a later work by Jacob Gerritse Lansing.

The final three 'oddities' in this section have unique handles. The first, by the highly respected New York silversmith Myer Myers in c1765, has his mark punched twice on the handle, attesting to its originality: it comprises sinuous side-scrolls, a terminal with a triple-ogee edging and a quatrefoil centrepiece connected by six struts. The Sotheby's auction listing in 2018 pointed out that the clip under the handle had been "torn out". The second, in the Philadelphia Museum of Art, has a long handle made of quite thin wire, in the form of extended figure-of-eight sides joined to a terminal ring; its bowl piercing is also unique, with six overlapping rings of concentric circles connected by twisting curves. The museum believes that its (unknown) maker worked either in Philadelphia or Reading, Pennsylvania, between 1780 and 1800. The handle of the third, by the New York maker John Vernon between 1789 and 1817, has double-arc sides, a standard arc end and a double-arc cross-strut. It seems that as the second half of the 18th century progressed, quirkiness in handle and bowl piercing designs became increasingly common in American lemon strainers.

BIBLIOGRAPHY

Ash, Douglas	*Dictionary of British Antique Silver* (1972)
Banister, Judith	*An Introduction to Old English Silver* (1965)
Barr, Elaine	*George Wickes 1698-1761 Royal Goldsmith* (1980)
Bennett, Douglas	*Irish Georgian Silver* (1972)
Bennett, Douglas	*Collecting Irish Silver* (1984)
Bohan, Peter & Philip Hammerslough	*Early Connecticut Silver 1700-1840* (1970, revised edition 2007)
Bowen, John R. & Conor O'Brien	*Cork Silver And Gold: Four Centuries of Craftsmanship* (2005)
Bowen, John R. & Conor O'Brien (Ed.)	*A Celebration of Limerick's Silver* (2007)
Buhler, Kathryn	*American Silver 1655-1825 in the Museum of Fine Arts, Boston, 2 Volumes* (1972)
Burke, Sir Bernard	*Genealogical and Heraldic Dictionary of the Landed Gentry of Great Britain and Ireland* (1862)
Butler, Robin	*The Albert Collection: Five Hundred Years of British and European Silver* (2004)
Clayton, Michael	*Christie's Pictorial History of English and American Silver* (1985)
Crewdson, Bernard	*Silver Strainers, a Little-Known Field for a Collector;* The Connoisseur (May 1950)
Crewdson, Bernard	*Maker of Early Georgian Strainers*; Country Life (November 23, 1951)
Cripps, Wilfred	*Old English Plate. Ecclesiastical, Decorative and Domestic: its Makers and Marks* (1886, 3rd Edition; 1894, 5th Edition)
Davis, John D.	*Silver punch strainers in the John A. Hyman Collection at Colonial Williamsburg*; Antiques (August 1991)
de Castres, Elizabeth	*A Guide to Collecting Silver* (1980)
Delamer, Ida & Conor O'Brien	*500 Years of Irish Silver: an Exhibition at the National Museum of Ireland* (2005)
Dietert, Janice M. & Rodney Dietert	*Compendium of Scottish Silver II* (2007)

Ensko, Stephen G.C.	*American Silversmiths and Their Marks III* (1948)
Fairbairn, James	*Fairbairn's book of crests of the families of Great Britain and Ireland, 4th Ed.* (1912)
Fairbairn, James	*Heraldic Crests: a Pictorial Archive of 4,424 Designs for Artists and Craftspeople* (1993)
Fales, Martha Gandy	*Early American Silver for the Cautious Collector* (1970)
FitzGerald, Alison	*Silver in Georgian Dublin. Making, selling, consuming* (2017)
Glanville, Philippa & Jennifer Goldsborough	*Women Silversmiths 1685-1845. Works from the Collection of the National Museum of Women in the Arts Washington, D.C.* (1990)
Grimwade, Arthur G.	*London Goldsmiths 1697-1837 Their Marks & Lives* (1976)
Harrison, Miles	*Exeter & West Country Silver 1700-1900* (2014)
Hartop, Christopher	*Geometry and the Silversmith: the Domcha Collection* (2008)
Harvey, Karen	*Barbarity in a Teacup? Punch, Domesticity and Gender in the Eighteenth Century*; Journal of Design History, Vol.21, Issue 3 (Autumn 2008)
Helliwell, Stephen	*Collecting Small Silverware* (1988)
Holland, Margaret	*Silver: an Illustrated Guide to Collecting Silver* (1973)
Hughes, G. Bernard	*Evolution of the Orange Strainer*; Country Life (9th May 1968)
Jackson, Sir Charles J	*English Goldsmiths and their Marks, 2nd Ed.* (1921)
Kaellgren, Peter	*Princess Amelia's strainer*; The Silver Society Journal 2002
Luddington, John	*Starting to Collect Silver* (1984 & later reprints)
Oman, Charles	*English Domestic Silver* (1934 and 1959)
Papworth, John W.	*An Alphabetical Dictionary of Coats of Arms belonging to Families in Great Britain & Ireland; forming an extensive Ordinary of British Armorials* (1874)
Pickford, Ian (Ed.)	*Jackson's Silver & Gold Marks of England, Scotland & Ireland* (2009)
Rudé, George	*Hanoverian London 1714-1808* (1971)
'Tardy' (published by Tardy of Paris)	*International Hallmarks on Silver Collected by Tardy* (1985 & later English editions)
Ticher, Kurt; Ida Delamer & William O'Sullivan	*Hall-marks on Dublin Silver 1730-72* (1968)
Turner, Richard W.	*Illustrated Directory of Scottish Provincial Silversmiths & Their Marks* (2014)
Wondrich, David	*Punch: the Delights (and Dangers) of the Flowing Bowl* (2010)
Young, W.A.	*The Silver and Sheffield Plate Collector* (undated, between 1911 & 1936)

IMAGE CREDITS

Auctioneers	Figure(s)
Aalders Auctions, Camperdown, New South Wales, Australia	125
Ahlers & Ogletree Inc., Atlanta, Georgia, USA	123
Anderson & Garland Auctioneers, Newcastle-upon-Tyne	118
Bamfords Auctioneers & Valuers, Derby	114, 267
Bonhams	75. 83, 91, 92, 124, 146, 181, 189, 202, 210, 212, 221, 222, 225, 235, 236
Brightwells Auctioneers & Valuers, Leominster	72
British Bespoke Auctions, Tewkesbury, Gloucs.	229
Bruce Kodner Galleries, Lake Worth, Florida, USA	119
©Christie's	19, 64, 150, 157, 158, 163, 204, 209, 227, 251, 258
Dreweatts, Newbury, Berks.	73, 121, 159
Fellows Auctioneers, Birmingham	164
Gorringe's, Lewes, E. Sussex	81, 107
Hansons Auctioneers, Etwall, Derbyshire	128
Lawrences Auctioneers, Crewkerne, Somerset	93, 142, 187
Lawsons, Leichhardt, New South Wales, Australia	113
Lyon & Turnbull, Edinburgh (Images courtesy of Lyon & Turnbull)	220, 223, 226
Mallams Ltd, Oxford	177
Matthew Barton Ltd, London (now part of Olympia Auctions)	69
Mellors & Kirk, Nottingham	115, 140, 160, 172
Northeast Auctions, Hampton, New Hampshire, USA	80
Nye & Company, Morris Plains, New Jersey, USA	162
Reeman Dansie Auctioneers, Colchester, Essex	74, 135
Richard Winterton Auctioneers Ltd, Lichfield, Staffs.	155
Skinner Auctioneers, Boston, Massachusetts, USA (Image courtesy of Skinner, Inc. www.skinnerinc.com)	168
Sotheby's Images	134, 190, 193, 195, 199, 206, 250, 256, 262, 265
Sworders Fine Art Auctioneers, Stansted Mountfitchet, Essex	78, 173

Tennants Fine Arts Auctioneers, Leyburn, N. Yorks.	82, 217
The Canterbury Auction Galleries, Canterbury, Kent	116
Thomson Roddick Auctioneers & Valuers, Carlisle, Cumbria	171
Toovey's Fine Art Auctioneers and Valuers, Washington, W. Sussex	31, 137
Whittons Auctioneers, Honiton, Devon	182
Woolley & Wallis Salisbury Salerooms Ltd, Salisbury, Wilts	16, 17, 71, 77, 85, 111, 120, 122, 144, 147, 148, 153, 170, 183, 191, 208, 230, 231

Online auction platforms

catawiki.com	234 (maledetto 16)
eBay UK	112 (unidentified Brussels dealer), 129, 138 (antique-silver), 167 (bubbleking), 174 (v6ogflowers), 178 (dreamcircus)
http://freepages.rootsweb.com/-silversmiths/genealogy/makers/silversmiths/57105.htm	246

Dealers

www.antiquesilverspoons.co.uk (Reign Beau Ltd, Mitcheldean, Gloucs)	51, 117
Britannia House Antiques, Wayne, Pennsylvania (Deborah J. Firth)	70
Cliff Nunn, Antique Silver & Decorative Arts, Dravosburg, Pennsylvania	53
J & W Duvallier, Dublin (William Crofton)	198
Eastdale Antiques, Buxton, Derbyshire	110, 130
The Fancy Fox, Bungay, Suffolk	33
Iain Marr Antiques, Beauly, Inverness	224
J.H. Bourdon-Smith, St James's, London (at BADA fairs)	154, 237
Langland Bay Antiques, Mumbles, Swansea (on ebay.co.uk)	99
Louis Wine Ltd, Toronto, Canada (online galleries)	88
M. Ford Creech Antiques, Memphis, Tennessee	62, 106, 109
M.S. Rau, New Orleans, Louisiana (Photos Courtesy of M.S. Rau, New Orleans)	93, 131
Mary Cooke Antiques Ltd, Mortlake, London	105, 139, 145
Mason Antiques, Canaan, Connecticut (eBay USA)	169
The Old Corkscrew, Franschhoek, South Africa	100
S.J. Shrubsole, New York	47, 67, 84, 156, 241, 263, 266
silfren.com	108
sterlingalize on ebay.co.uk	228
Wax Antiques, London Silver Vaults	58, 94, 166

Articles	
Bernard Crewdson, in *The Connoisseur*, May 1950: *Silver Strainers: a Little-known Field for a Collector*	32
Books	
English-Speaking Union London: *An Exhibition of American Silver & Art Treasures* (1960)	259
Ian Harris (1969): *The Price Guide to Antique Silver*, Antique Collectors' Club	194
John Bly, in *Discovering Hall Marks on English Silver. A pocket guide* (Shire Publications, 1968)	197
Judith Miller (2004): *Miller's Antiques Price Guide 2005*, Miller's/ Mitchell Beazley/Octopus Publishing Group Ltd	245
Michael Clayton (1971): *The Collector's Dictionary of the Silver & Gold of Great Britain & North America*, Hamlyn Publishing Group Ltd	68, 244
Miles Harrison (2014): *Exeter & West Country Silver 1700-1900*	184
Museums	
The Art Institute of Chicago	247, 254
From the Collections of the Charleston Museum, Charleston, South Carolina, USA	261
Photo by The Colonial Williamsburg Foundation. The John A. Hyman Study Collection. (Williamsburg, Virginia, USA)	18, 21, 23, 59, 65, 66
Photo by The Colonial Williamsburg Foundation. The John A. Hyman Collection.	100, 149, 211, 215, 216, 238, 243, 248, 253
The Colonial Williamsburg Foundation. Museum Purchase.	48, 98
Limerick Museum, Ireland	207
Metropolitan Museum of Art, New York, USA	252, 268
The National Museum of Women in the Arts, Washington DC	127
Image © National Museums Scotland	218
Norwich Castle Museum (author's own image; object reproduced with permission from Norfolk Museums Service)	180
Royal Collection Trust, UK © Her Majesty Queen Elizabeth II 2020	103, 161, 179
Courtesy of Royal Ontario Museum ©ROM (gift of Norman S. and Marian A. Robertson. Accession no. 993.53.127; photo by Brian Boyle)	143
Victoria and Albert Museum, London	5
Winterthur Museum, Delaware, USA (fig.260: Silver, 2001.0002.010, Gift of Denison and Louise Hatch; fig.264: Silver, 1976.0022, Gift of Mrs. Mary Stevens Baird)	260, 264
Yale University Art Gallery, Connecticut, USA	249, 255, 257

INDEX

Green, Henry, 98, 100
Gurney, Richard & Thomas Cooke, 45, 62, 66, 67, 73
Halsted, Benjamin (New York), 166
Hamilton, John (Dublin), 126-128, 132, 133
Hammersley, Thomas (New York), 165, 166
Harvey, John I, 70
Havers, Thomas (Norwich), 116
Hayens, Henry, 107
Heming, Thomas, 4, 105, 114, 115
Henchman, Daniel (Boston, MA), 158, 159, 161
Hennell, David I, 72, 77, 85, 91
Hennell, David I & Robert I, 90
Hennell, Robert I, 98, 100, 101, 103, 104
Herbert, Samuel, & Co., 30, 53, 71, 72, 80, 84, 87, 89, 92, 94, 97
Heyer, William (New York), 164
Holt, Jason (Plymouth), 120, 121
Hunter, George I, 87, 88
Hurd, Jacob (Boston, MA), 157, 160, 161, 164
IC, pellet below, in heart-shaped shield (?Cooke or Cawardine, John), 55, 56, 58
IG (?Graham, James) (Dublin), 134
Innes, Robert, 80
Isaac, Thomas (Dublin), 127, 129
IT (John Touliet), 98, 99
IW over TB, 27, 111
Jamieson, George (Aberdeen), 138
Johns, Joseph (Limerick), 39, 130-131
Johns, Samuel (Limerick), 133
Jones, George Greenhill, 43, 53, 61, 66, 67, 69, 77, 112
Justis, William, 37, 57, 105
Keay, Robert (Perth), 143
Kedden, Thomas, 53, 55, 56, 58-60
Ker, James (Edinburgh), 139
King, David (Dublin), 125, 127
Kinnersly, Philip (Dublin), 126, 127
Kirkby, Samuel & Co (Sheffield), 118
Lansing, Jacob Gerritse (Albany, NY), 168
Le Roux, Bartholomew (New York), 166
Letablere, John (Dublin), 131
Looker, William, 59, 63
Luff, John, 53, 77, 80
Maidman, Ralph, 32
Meach, Richard, 53, 85, 89, 96
Meriton, Samuel I, 100
Meriton, Samuel II, 89, 100, 108
Meriton, Thomas, 101

Minott, Samuel (Boston, MA), 161
Mitchell & Russell (Glasgow), 150
Mitchell & Son (Glasgow), 147, 150
Moulinar, John (New York), 166
Manjoy, George, 56
Myers, Myer (New York), 39, 162, 163, 168
Newenham, William (Cork), 39, 127
Newlands, James & Philip Grierson (Glasgow), 138
Nicolson, John (Cork), 133
Nutting, Henry, 104
Parker, Daniel (Boston, MA), 157, 160, 161
Petrie, Alexander (Charleston, SC), 164
Plummer, William, 30, 32, 35, 43, 53, 75, 80, 83-84, 89, 92, 94-97, 114
Rait, David Crichton (Glasgow), 29, 150, 151
Ramsey, John (Newcastle), 117
RB (?Butterfield, Robert), 57, 58
Reily, John, 72
Revere, Paul I (Boston, MA), 157, 159, 163
Revere, Paul II (Boston, MA), 160, 162
Richards, Samuel II (Philadelphia, PA), 165, 167
Richardson, Joseph II (Philadelphia, PA), 23, 166
RN (?Norman, Richard), 85
Robertson, Patrick (Edinburgh), 43, 141, 142, 146, 147
Rush, Thomas, 17, 87
Saunders, Alexander, 93, 95
Scott, William I (Aberdeen), 151-152
Shepherd, Thomas, 95, 96
Slater, James, 67-68
Smith, Michael (Dublin), 129
Solomon, William, 32, 40, 43, 65, 71, 88, 89, 90
Steven, James (Dundee), 152, 153
Steven, John (Dundee), 144
Steward, Joseph I, 31, 62, 63
Stone, James, 78
Symons, Pentecost (Plymouth), 118-120
Symons, Roger Berryman (Plymouth), 120
Syng, Philip II (Philadelphia, PA), 157, 162, 166, 167
Tanqueray, Anne, 28, 67, 68
Taylor, Peter, 80
Terry, Carden (Cork), 134
Thompson, Alexander (Aberdeen), 138
Touliet, John, 98, 99
TT, 36, 91, 117
Turner, Francis, 26, 53, 62, 66
Vernon, John (New York), 168
Walker, Joseph/John (Dublin), 129

www.ingramcontent.com/pod-product-compliance
Lightning Source LLC
Chambersburg PA
CBHW050643150426
42813CB00054B/1164